HEADHUNTER HIRING SECRETS 2.0

HOW TO FIRE UP YOUR CAREER AND LAND YOUR IDEAL JOB!

BY

SKIP FREEMAN

with

Michael Garee

© Copyright 2016 by **Skip Freeman** and **Michael Garee**. All rights reserved.

Except in the case of brief quotations embodied in critical articles and reviews, no part of this book may be reproduced or transmitted in any form or by any means, graphic, electronic, or mechanical, including photocopying, recording, taping, or by any information retrieval system, without the express, written permission of the copyright owners.

FIRST EDITION

Also available in Kindle® format on www.amazon.com

ISBN-13: 978-1519631046
ISBN-10: 1519631049

Printed and published in the United States of America by **HHS Team, Inc., LLC**.

Edited, designed and co-written by **Michael Garee**

Cover Design: **Pixel Studios**

All photographs and illustrations used in this book are legally licensed for use by the copyright owners.

All product and service trade names and websites cited in this book are owned by their respective companies and/or organizations. Site interfaces were accurate at time of publication, but are always subject to change.

LEGAL DISLAIMERS

The views, opinions, comments and suggestions featured in this book are solely those of the authors and not of any company or individual who may recommend or endorse this book. Also, no portion of this book is intended to be construed as legal advice. The information presented is based on years of experience and observations of how the hiring game is actually played and is intended only to provide the reader with additional options for consideration in any current or future job search. If the reader needs legal advice on any topic, or needs to discuss the legality of anything he or she may say or do during the job search, or anything a potential hiring company or its representative may say or do, he or she should consult qualified legal counsel.

Nothing in this book should be construed as any type of "guarantee" that the reader will get a job, or even an interview, by following the advice and recommendations contained herein. There are no "guarantees" in the current, or for that matter, any job market. Too much simply depends on the individual himself/herself to make, or even to imply, such a "guarantee." What *can* be *guaranteed*, however, is that those job seekers who diligently and consistently apply the principles, tactics and strategies outlined in this book during their job search will be significantly better prepared to compete for available jobs than the overwhelming majority of those job seekers who do not take this approach.

To the very best of our knowledge, all stories, anecdotes and examples featured in this book are true and accurate. In virtually all cases, however, individual names and sometimes geographic locales, have been changed or disguised, in order to protect individual privacy. Any resemblance between persons and/or situations cited in this book and persons and/or situations the reader may know or recognize, is purely coincidental.

A Modest (*Surprising!*) Testimonial

Although the principal target audience for *Headhunter Hiring Secrets* consists of professionals who have been in their jobs for a few years, it turns out that the tactics and strategies featured in the book can also significantly benefit another (and somewhat surprising!) group of job seekers: recent college graduates.

Here is what **Michael Little** of the **University of Alabama** and creator and designer of the original book cover had to say about *Headhunter Hiring Secrets*:

> "A few years ago, **Skip Freeman** approached me about working on the cover for the first edition of this book. I was pretty busy at the time and thought very seriously about declining. Then I read the manuscript. If there is a better job-hunting book, I haven't seen it. It so impressed me I had to see it come to the marketplace if only for the selfish reason of sharing it with my own students.
>
> "In my position, I've worked with thousands of college students on the internship and job hunt. I've used the first edition as recommended reading for several years now with spectacular results. Many of the book's principles and tactics are as sound for college students looking for jobs and internships as they are for the job hunter with years of experience.
>
> "I have so many stories from my students sharing the success they've had from using *Headhunter Hiring Secrets*. The young man who so excelled in a job interview that he was offered the position an hour later. The young woman who *tripled* her email response rate. The graduate student who, after one month with the book, got THREE job offers, not just for random positions but for jobs she really wanted!
>
> "With this book AND the will to put its teaching into practice, you will *dramatically* improve your chances of winning the hiring game!"

OTHER BOOKS IN THE HEADHUNTER HIRING SECRETS SERIES

By

SKIP FREEMAN

Headhunter Hiring Secrets: The Rules of the Hiring Game Have Changed . . . Forever! is the inaugural book in the series. This ground-breaking bestseller details how very, very much the job market has changed in recent years, as well as outlines the NEW "rules" of the "hiring game." Then, it shows a job hunter how in essence to become his or her own headhunter and WIN in today's still competitive job market!

First published in 2010, the information featured in this international bestseller is as applicable and relevant to today's job market as it was when it was first written.

KINDLE EDITION

Kindle editions of both *Headhunter Hiring Secrets: The Rules of the Hiring Game Have Changed . . . Forever!* and *Headhunter Hiring Secrets 2.0* are also available on Amazon.com.

The *Application Workbook for Headhunter Hiring Secrets: The Rules of the Hiring Game Have Changed . . . Forever!* is a *step-by-step guide* designed to allow the job hunter to "flesh out" the tactics and strategies for finding a new job that are featured in the paperback and Kindle editions of *Headhunter Hiring Secrets: The Rules of the Hiring Game Have Changed . . . Forever!*

An invaluable guide that can help a job seeker quickly and easily organize his or her job search!

NOTE: All publications in the series are available on Amazon.com

OTHER KINDLE PUBLICATIONS IN THE HEADHUNTER HIRING SECRETS SERIES IT CAN PAY YOU TO CHECK OUT

How to be 'Headhunted' by TOP Recruiters Want to learn how *you* can get on—and *stay* on!—the radar of the TOP recruiters and be among the first to learn about the "sweetest" career positions in the job market? Skip, a TOP recruiter himself, tells you *precisely* how to do that in this Kindle publication.

How to ACE the Job Interview! is a step-by-step guide that shows you how to interview the way **Super Stars** do!

The tactics and strategies featured in this publication are used by all candidates The HTW Group (Hire to Win) presents to its hiring company clients. The results? When these candidates go up against other candidates competing for the same career positions, the HTW candidates walk away with the job offer **seven out of ten** times!

Contents

Introduction	12
9 FATAL Career Mistakes Most *Employed* People Make	18
PART I – Getting Ready to "Play" in the *New* Hiring Game!	**23**
Chapter One – Defining *Your* Ideal Job	24
Chapter Two – The Job Market	36
Oh, How Far We've Come in Recent Years!	38
Number Employed Steadily Increasing	39
Job Sources: The Broader View	40
Monthly Jobs Report	40
"Hidden" Job Market	41
JOLTS report	42
Bright Spots in Today's Job Market	44
Bottom Line on the Job Market	45
Chapter Three – Start with the "Paperwork" (Your Résumé)	48
11 Résumé "Truths"	52
Other Important Résumé Considerations	59
Important Next Steps	63
Sample *Before* and *After* Résumés	64
Remember, You are in the "Sales" Business	69
Chapter Four – Your Cover Letter	71
Cover Letter the Preamble, the Entrée, to Your Candidacy	73
9 Secrets That Make a Cover Letter Work	76
Additional Tips/Comments About *Effective* Cover Letters	80
Chapter Five – Your LinkedIn Profile	81
Getting Started with LinkedIn	83
Complete Your LinkedIn Profile – 100%!	84
Vital Importance of Key Words	85
Change LinkedIn-Assigned Profile URL to User-Friendly One	85

Contents

Chapter Five – LinkedIn *Continued*

Create Strong, Specific Masthead for Your Profile	85
Your LinkedIn Profile Picture	87
Your LinkedIn "Professional Summary"	89
Next Steps in Completing Your LinkedIn Profile	89
Link to or Create a Company Profile	90
Immediately Start Making, Soliciting Connections	91
Enhancing Your LinkedIn Presence	92
Stay Active, Continually Involved on LinkedIn	92
What Effective Networking is—and is NOT!	92
Other Professional Networking Sites to Consider	94

PART II – Let the (Hiring) "Games" Begin! — 96

Chapter Six – The "Loyalty" Issue — 97

Where Your True Loyalty Should Lie	98
On Any Given Day . . .	99
What You Actually Owe Your Current Employer	100

Chapter Seven – Beginning Your New Job Search — 102

Schedule Job-Hunting Times Each Day	103
Every Aspect of New Job Search on Your Time, Your Dime	103
How Should You Network?	104

Chapter Eight – Role of the Internet — 109

The Internet is NOT the Problem	111
See the People!	111

Chapter Nine – Headhunters — 112

Misconceptions About Headhunters	113
Getting on, Staying on a Headhunter's Radar	115
Be Findable	116
Be Desirable	118
Be Contactable	118

Contents

Chapter Nine – Headhunters *Continued*

Be Selectable	119
Becoming Part of a Headhunter's Inner Circle	120
"Due Diligence": A Final Consideration	123

Chapter Ten – Finding Jobs, People Who Hire — 125

Unleash the POWER! of Google Search to Find Most Jobs	126
TURBO-CHARGE! Your Job Hunt with SimplyHired, Indeed	128
Integrate SimplyHired with LinkedIn	129
How to Learn Who is Actually Doing the Hiring	131
The LinkedIn "Hack"	131

Chapter Eleven – The Stealth Job Search — 134

Keeping Your Stealth Job Search Stealthy	135
Should You Tell Your Current Boss You're Looking?	137

Chapter Twelve – "Prospecting" for "GOLD"! — 139

Key Contact Methods/Approaches	140
Online Job Applications	141
Don't Play the "Online Lottery"!	142
The Internet Job Boards—with a Twist	142
Back to Basics: Pick Up The Telephone (PUTT)!	146
Typical Voice Mail Message Left	150
Voice Mail Message Left by True Professionals!	151
Getting Around the Gatekeeper	152
The Resistant Hiring Manager, Headhunter, et al.	155
Incorporating Email into Your Prospecting Activities	160
How to Find Email Addresses	160
Testing Email Addresses	161
How to Get Your Emails Opened—and READ!	162
Make Your Emails Part of an Overall "Touch" Plan	166
Make Sure Emails Just Part of Overall Marketing Package	166
Some Other Things to Keep in Mind About Business Email	167
The Old Stand By—"Snail Mail," (aka The U.S. Postal Service)	168

Contents

Chapter Twelve – "Prospecting'" for "GOLD"! *Continued*

How to Use the U.S. Mail to Reach Today's Hiring Managers	170
Reaching the Point of Diminishing Returns	180
No Magic Approach	180

Chapter Thirteen - The Inbound Marketing Plan — 181

Sites That Can Get Jobs, Career Opportunity News Coming to You	183
Take Control of Your Career, Your Destiny	184

PART III – Starting to Reap the Rewards of Your Efforts — 186

Chapter Fourteen – The Telephone Interview — 187

Initial Telephone Screen: First Step in the Exclusion Process	192
Primary Purpose of the Initial Telephone Screen	194
How the Typical, Initial Telephone Screen is Conducted	195
Screener Call from a Headhunter, Corporate Recruiter	204
Important Considerations During the Interview Process	206
Questions You Should Anticipate—and How to Answer Them	210
NEXT STEPS After Telephone Interview	218
How Many Times to Follow Up After Telephone Interview	219

Chapter Fifteen – The Face-to-Face Interview — 220

Pre-Planning for the Face-to-Face Interview	221
Do Your Homework Well in Advance of the Interview	223
Your 90-Second Elevator Speech	225
At Last! The Day of the Interview	227
How Well Did You Do in the Interview?	245
What are Your NEXT STEPS Now?	246
Questions to Anticipate in Subsequent FTF Interviews	251
While You're Waiting. . .Waiting to Hear How You Did	251
A Review – 8 Basic Rules for ACING the FTF Interview	252

Contents

PART IV – When Everything Comes Together!	259
Chapter Sixteen – The Job Offer	**261**
Initial Job Offer Likely to be a Telephone Call	262
The Written Job Offer	263
Salary Offered . . . Surprise?! Disappointment?!	263
Now Comes the Low Ball Salary Offer	264
Consider TOTAL "Compensation" Package, Not Just Salary	267
Other Elements of the Job Offer	269
Don't Tarry in Responding to Job Offer!	270
Chapter Seventeen – Negotiating a Job Offer	**273**
Negotiation Tips from an Expert	274
Role of Professional Brand, Employment Status	277
Not Everything Negotiable in Job Offer	278
Chapter Eighteen – Resigning Your Current Job	**283**
The Best, *Professional* Way to Resign	285
Chapter Nineteen – The Counter-offer	**288**
A TRUE Story About the Perils of Accepting Counter-offer	293
Chapter Twenty – The Winner's Circle	**294**
Important NEXT STEPS for you at This Point	296
Appendix A – The Top Ten Rules of the "Hiring Game"	**298**
Appendix B – Recommended Additional References	**301**
Index	304

About This Book...

This book is the revised and updated sequel to the ground-breaking, international bestselling job-hunting book first published in 2010, ***Headhunter Hiring Secrets: The Rules of the Hiring Game Have Changed... Forever!***

Everything in this book is based on fact and informed by years of experience as a professional headhunter, someone who is in the job market each and every business day of the year. As a result of my professional experience, I know what works, and equally important, I know what does *not* work in today's job market.

Absolutely nothing you will read in the book is based on theory—what I *think* might work (or not work) during the job hunt, or what I *hope* might work. All suggested tactics and recommended strategies featured in this book actually *work*! Not every single time, of course, because no approach works *all* the time or with *all* people and in *all* situations. But these tactics and strategies work often enough to use them—if you're really serious about landing your new, *ideal* job.

All of the candidates our executive recruiting firm, The HTW Group, grooms and presents to our client hiring companies use the job search tactics and strategies featured in this book. The result? When the candidates we present go up against other candidates vying for the same positions, our candidates walk away with the job offer **SEVEN** out of **TEN** times! A pretty good endorsement, I believe (and so should you!).

Moreover, the stories and anecdotes featured in this book are real, and they actually happened as reported. Only certain facts, such as specific names and sometimes locations and time frames, have in some cases been altered to protect the privacy of persons involved.

INTRODUCTION

The career development advice and the tactics and strategies featured in this book can be used by any professional who desires to enhance and enrich his or her career. It can also prove especially helpful, and of significant value to *true* survivors of our age, the millions of men and women worldwide who somehow found a way to survive during the Great Recession, when the job market literally turned upside down and washed out tens of millions of jobs, many of which simply aren't likely ever to return.

Being able to remain employed during these tumultuous times, however, proved to be a mixed blessing for many of the survivors. More often than not they ended up doing not only their own jobs but also the jobs of their fellow employees who lost theirs. Raises and/or promotions became out of the question for many if not most. Their employers rarely missed an opportunity to remind them, either implicitly or explicitly, of how "lucky" they were to still have a job, while so many of their fellow employees had lost theirs.

As a result of this highly stressed and stressful situation and environment, most of these survivors hunkered down, kept their nose to the grindstone and looked forward to better, more prosperous times, when the economy and the job market were able to rebound. Then, they reasoned, their employers would (finally?) show them the appropriate gratitude (and respect) for their sacrifices during rough economic times. Unfortunately, that wasn't necessarily the case in many companies.

Once the recovery set in and production and profits began increasing, the only bottom lines that were fattened up were those of the employing companies. The careers of many of the survivors continued to languish. Many have come face to face with this old—and not so slightly *insulting*—attitude from their employers: "What have you done for me lately?"

Maybe *you* are among this group of survivors, most of whom are dedicated, highly talented and exceptionally skilled men and women. If so, maybe you've become embittered by the way you were treated during the rough years—and maybe you're still being treated in that fashion! The problem may be, though, you're not exactly sure how to turn your situation around and get your career back on track. If so, then you've made a wise choice by investing in **Headhunter Hiring Secrets 2.0**.

In this book you'll learn how to successfully compete in the current job market, as well as how to get *your* career out of the "stall" mode, if in fact that is the mode it's in at this point. I show you how to stand out from the crowd, land an exciting, new job and move your career to the next level!

So, let's begin by first answering an all-important, key question: What factors/situations, precisely, are primarily driving *your* quest to find a new (different? better?) job that can move your career to the next level? Quite probably it is one (or more) of the following:

- You are **CURRENTLY EMPLOYED** and may still be essentially *satisfied* with your job but are *always open to the right opportunity* to move your career to the next level.

- You are **CURRENTLY EMPLOYED** and at least **somewhat dissatisfied** with your job—perhaps even a **LOT dissatisfied**. Why?

    - Because of layoffs and/or downsizings at your current employer during the relatively recent turbulent years in the job market, as a "survivor," you ended up *doing the work of two (or more!) people*, and you remain somewhat embittered toward your employer because of that experience.

    - Despite having gone "the extra mile" for your employer when times were rough, you still have *received few, if any, pay raises* in recent years. And, even if you've been fortunate enough to have received raises, they may have been miniscule at best and perhaps even somewhat insulting, considering the contributions you feel you made to the company.

    - You're *feeling under-appreciated* or *not appreciated at all* by your current employer. In fact, a word I have been hearing with increasing frequency in recent years is "*dis*-respected."

    - Even if you are satisfied overall with your current job, you are not as happy as you could be (or should be) with the apparent direction your career is heading (or not heading!) these days.

- ➢ You're just simply burned out on your current job, for a whole variety of reasons.

- ➢ Regardless of the reason(s) for wanting to seek new career opportunities, you know you're ready to take the plunge and seek them out. And, being the true professional that you are, you want to know the very best and most powerfully effective ways to pursue new opportunities.

- You are **CURRENTLY *UNDER*-EMPLOYED** and, while you are "grateful" to at least have *some* type of job, you also feel like the proverbial racehorse tied to a plow, and yearn to get back in the game and get your career back on track and out of the "stall" mode.

- You are **CURRENTLY UNEMPLOYED** as the result of a downsizing, layoff or similar unfortunate event at your former employer. You *know*, instinctively, that you have a great deal to offer a potential employer but have become so discouraged and beaten down recently that you're no longer sure at all how to go about getting your career back on track.

Since most of us spend at least a full one-third (or more!) of our lives working, I'm sure you will agree, then, that one's job should certainly be engaging, interesting and fulfilling. If yours isn't (or you find yourself completely out of the game at this point), then you've come to the right place and you've chosen the right job-hunting book. In **Headhunter Hiring Secrets 2.0** I'll show you *precisely* what you need to do to **recharge your career** and get it back on the right track and headed in the right direction. I'll also show you how to *effectively* compete in today's job market, and ultimately, how to land a new, exciting, enriching job.

Just for the record, you have a *lot* of company if you're currently employed and ready to seriously consider a job change—for *any* reason. While overall job satisfaction has been edging up recently, literally **TENS OF MILLIONS** of *currently employed* people nonetheless remain at least *somewhat dissatisfied* with their jobs and employers. Some have become so bitter about the way they (and their fellow employees) were treated by their employers in recent years that any sense of loyalty they may have once felt toward their current employer disappeared long ago.

In the inaugural edition of the **Headhunter Hiring Secrets** series, the international bestselling job-hunting book *Headhunter Hiring Secrets: The Rules of the Hiring Game Have Changed . . . Forever!*,[1] I introduced the concept of hiring as a "game," a very serious game, to be sure, but nonetheless a game. And it's a game with all *new* rules! Job-hunting strategies and tactics that once worked no longer work, and quite probably won't work again for the foreseeable future.

No longer, for example, can you simply go online, locate a few jobs that look "promising" or "interesting," send in the same, generic résumé to those postings, then merely sit back and wait to be contacted. Job seekers who continue to play by these old rules of the hiring game—and their numbers are legion—are destined to lose today. Believe that with all your heart and soul! On the other hand, those who learn how to play by the *new* rules of the game dramatically improve their chances for success.

It's important to keep in mind, however, that the job-hunting game is *not* a game of *perfection.* Just as in any game, you can't (and won't!) "score"/"win" each and every time. But, if you dedicate yourself to learning, and then diligently and vigilantly *playing* by the *new* rules of the hiring game, you certainly will score and win more times than you will lose, and definitely many, many more times than those job seekers who insist on continuing to play by the old rules of the hiring game, waiting for "the good old days" to return. (**ALERT!** They're not going to return!)

Many currently employed professionals today are virtually paralyzed by the mere thought of leaving their current position—no matter how distasteful/trying it may be—to venture into today's still challenging job market. Why? For far too many people, the fear of loss is far greater than the desire for gain.

In **Headhunter Hiring Secrets 2.0** I show you how to develop a *solid*, *workable* plan to land your new job—regardless of your current employment situation. I show you how to wisely invest in your career to reap the substantial rewards, both professional *and* personal, that can await you. But in order for you to ultimately reap these benefits, you must first sow the seeds, beginning today! Scary? Yes. Achievable? Again, a definite "yes"!

---

[1]Available on Amazon.com in both paperback and Kindle editions. The **Headhunter Hiring Secrets Application Workbook** is also available, in paperback, on Amazon.com. If you need to review the "basics" of a job search in today's job market, both of these books can still serve as great reference sources.

So sit back, relax, dig in and begin absorbing the wealth of information in *Headhunter Hiring Secrets 2.0.* Among other things, I will show you that you have significantly more to offer a new employer than you may think you do.

I'll also show you the tactics and strategies you can employ to *successfully* compete in today's job market and land an exciting new job! I'll show you that *your* future can be far brighter than you may have had reason to believe it could be. The future *can* be yours, believe that. But you must be willing to take a fresh, new look at your career, step completely out of your comfort zone and embrace substantive change and the genuine prospect of ultimate career success.

A LIGHT, THOUGH STILL SERIOUS TONE DELIBERATELY TAKEN IN BOOK

I'm quite aware that, to the average person, plowing through page after page of sometimes highly detailed, quasi-complex job-hunting facts and other pertinent information is probably about as exciting as getting a root canal.

To take some of the sting out of the information featured in *Headhunter Hiring Secrets 2.0*, wherever possible, I have deliberately infused the copy with a lighter, more conversational tone than you are perhaps used to in books of this type. That is not to say that I mean to be flippant, however. Be assured that I still take the subject matter—and how it can affect your career *and* life—very, very seriously.

Also, to the extent that it made sense, the information featured in this book is arranged in chronological order by task, i.e., what you should do first, do next, etc., when you get ready to get your career headed toward the stratosphere!

An Underlying Theme in This Book

The Boy Scouts of America Took the BEST Slogan Ever Created!

That's right! The Boy Scouts of America took (and kept!) the BEST slogan ever created:

BE PREPARED!

This slogan aptly applies to virtually any situation we're likely to encounter in life, and it is particularly applicable to a new job search. Almost always, the difference between being successful at landing a new job and *not* being successful in this endeavor can be directly related back to the degree (and quality) of *preparation* on the part of the job seeker. Those who are the BEST prepared usually succeed in finding a GREAT new job. Those who aren't so well prepared? Not so much. It's really just that simple.

Throughout **Headhunter Hiring Secrets 2.0** you will notice that **Be Prepared** is an underlying, constant theme for succeeding in landing your new job.

Sadly, the overwhelming majority of job seekers today, whether employed, under-employed or unemployed are *not* prepared. Not even close. So, as you begin your journey toward your new job, make sure that *you* are prepared, by following the advice, tactics and strategies outlined in this book. If you do, you will *automatically* enjoy a HUGE advantage over your competition, i.e., other job seekers contending for the same positions as you!

9 FATAL CAREER MISTAKES MOST *EMPLOYED* PEOPLE MAKE

If you are currently employed, before you begin your new job search in earnest, you are strongly encouraged to first read over the **nine fatal career mistakes** featured on the following pages. Ask yourself, How many of these mistakes am *I* now making? If you discover you are making even *one* of these mistakes, then take *immediate* corrective action! If you are currently making *two* or *more* of these mistakes, stop everything you are doing now and remedy the situation!

Based on my experience as a professional headhunter, it has become abundantly clear to me over the years that most professionals make at least **nine FATAL**[2] (and, of course, numerous other, *near* fatal) **mistakes** throughout their careers. And these otherwise intelligent, highly skilled men and women continue to make these same mistakes year after year after year, until one day, they may suddenly find that it's too late to correct or recover from these career mistakes.

FATAL CAREER MISTAKE 1

Forgetting (or not realizing) that the *best* time to find your next career opportunity is while you still *have* a job.

Stop and think about this for a moment. When a college decides to go looking for a new sports coach, whom do they include in the search pool? Isn't it usually the coach who is at the pinnacle of his/her career—the coach who is *consistently* winning games TODAY!?

So, whether you are happy in your current job or not, if you are performing well, consistently hitting the performance goals and objectives and doing the job, NOW is the best time ever to consider new career opportunities.

In today's still highly competitive economic environment and job market, you oftentimes have to make a job change in order to:

- Receive more competitive pay;
- Achieve appropriate, *deserved* recognition;
- Obtain your next, *deserved* promotion;
- Get back on an *upwardly mobile* career path.

---

[2]To your *career*, of course, not to you personally!

Fatal Career Mistake 2

Believing that your company will be as loyal to *you* as you are to it.

Company loyalty to employees has long been a thing of the past, if it every truly existed at all. Make no mistake about it, companies today don't really care if you end up in the unemployment line. They don't care if you and your family have no health insurance. They don't care if you are unable to adequately feed, clothe and house your family.

Bottom line: Your keeping an eye open for better career opportunities is really no different from the company keeping an eye on its bottom line and determining each and every month whether or not *you* are worth keeping on the payroll.

Don't be lulled into a false sense of security on your present job. Don't believe, even for one second, that your current position is secure—*know*, with absolute certainty and clarity, just how secure it is NOT!

Fatal Career Mistake 3

Thinking that there still are not enough jobs available today for you to even *consider* "risking" the one you have to look for a new one.

As you will see in **Chapter Two** (The Job Market), the job market today is much improved and improving. Great new jobs are continually being added by great companies as they strive to stay competitive in a fiercely competitive global marketplace. If you have positioned (or can position) yourself as a top candidate, you certainly can take maximum advantage of new, significant career opportunities in today's job market.

Fatal Career Mistake 4

Not effectively branding yourself as someone who can *make* a company money and/or *save* a company money, or ideally, as someone who can accomplish *both* of these goals.

Today, you will *not* be hired *exclusively* because you have the correct technical skills, experience and/or know-how. You must also brand—and position—yourself as someone who can a.) solve a hiring manager's (or hiring company's) problem(s); and/or, b.) deliver a solution (or solutions) to his/her business needs. In other words, today, it all boils down to this simple question: **Can you *make* a company money or *save* a company money or BOTH?!**

If you aren't already in the mindset of recognizing the vital importance of being able to make a company money or to save a company money, **start today**. Regardless of the position you currently occupy, learn to *translate* (in dollars, numbers and/or percentages) how *everything* you do has a definite impact on your current company's bottom line. (You'll particularly need this type of quantitative information when you start putting together your brand-new, *job-winning* résumé, covered in **Chapter Three**.)

FATAL CAREER MISTAKE 5

Thinking that the *only* way to find a new job (or to be able to capitalize on a *genuine,* new career opportunity) is to actually go *looking* for one.

I know (or at least surmise) that you are now thinking:

- Yes, I am good at what I do—actually, *really, really* good at what I do.

- You're probably correct, when it comes right down to it, I don't honestly believe that the company will be as loyal to me as I have been to it.

- I *do* **make** *and* **save** my company money, but no one seems to either be aware of it, or if they are, they certainly don't seem to appreciate it!

- So why shouldn't I be rewarded and go after one of those *millions* of jobs that go unfilled each and every month? Why shouldn't I take the opportunity to enhance my professional career so that I can get a much-deserved promotion, and yes, even a much-deserved pay raise?

Unfortunately, if you are like the majority of currently employed men and women, you probably already have a built-in answer to these quite logical questions: **Because I simply don't have time!** And certainly, if you are a currently employed person, you obviously can't make your fulltime job finding another one—unless, that is, you want to risk losing your current job.

So, how about this: Would you feel more comfortable, more committed to landing a new job if the jobs could actually find *you*?! If you position yourself correctly, and if you can realistically be considered to be among the *crème de la crème* of all job candidates today, you can actually accomplish that goal! (See **Chapter Thirteen** for more details!)

FATAL CAREER MISTAKE 6

Not building a meaningful, ongoing business relationship with a headhunter in your professional niche NOW!

As you will learn in **Chapter Nine**, while only **three percent** of all jobs are actually filled by headhunters, it's significant to note that a good headhunter nonetheless knows about the sweetest opportunities in the marketplace. The *first* people they will call about these opportunities will be the people they know and with whom they have established a meaningful, ongoing business relationship. Fact of life.

The odds of you calling a headhunter and he or she having that perfect opportunity available when you call are low, extremely low. Start building an ongoing relationship NOW with three to four recruiters who specialize in your professional niche, so that they know about you and will then *proactively* call you about appropriate, often *hidden* career opportunities.

FATAL CAREER MISTAKE 7

Failing to become *visibly* and *meaningfully* involved in your industry and/or your professional specialty.

Now is *not* the time for staying hunkered down, if there ever is a good time for *winners* to do that. It is critical—no, make that *imperative!*—today that a true professional achieves *maximum* visibility!

Become a hub, an industry expert, the go-to person in your professional circle. Join organizations in your professional specialty. Become an *active* participant in appropriate LinkedIn groups.

If companies are looking to replace a vice president, are they going to advertise? NO! If you are branding yourself as a highly visible, impactful, contributing member of your profession, YOU may very well be among the select few professionals contacted by the hiring manager, the corporate recruiter or the headhunter for that *once in a lifetime* career opportunity.

Fatal Career Mistake 8

If offered a new, better position with another company, you even *think* about entertaining a *counter-offer* from your current employer.

To do so, usually, is virtual "career suicide"! Why? From the moment you submit your resignation you will forever be considered to be "disloyal" to your current employer, a "traitor." (It doesn't matter that they wouldn't hesitate to be disloyal to you.)

When made a counter-offer, you will be led to believe that the company values you. That they simply can't do without you. Nothing could be further from the truth! All the company really is doing is buying time until it ultimately can replace you with someone who is more "loyal" to the company.

Fatal Career Mistake 9

Failure even to *entertain* an exploratory conversation about your career, your future.

I wish I could honesty say that most professionals I contact about exciting career opportunities are at least *somewhat* open to considering them. Unfortunately, that's not the case at all. Usually, out of some misplaced sense of loyalty to their current employer or because of unreasonable feelings of guilt and/or betrayal to their employer, many professionals will not even *consider* exploring such a conversation. That is certainly their right, of course, but it could also spell the demise of their career! (See **Fatal Mistake 2**.)

If and when you receive a call from a hiring professional, i.e., a headhunter, hiring manager or Human Resources professional, about a potential career opportunity, unless it is *totally* off the mark, don't you genuinely owe it to yourself to at least have a non-committal, exploratory conversation? Think about it, you really have nothing to lose and, potentially, a tremendous amount to gain!

PART I

GETTING READY TO 'PLAY' IN THE *ALL-NEW* HIRING 'GAME'

If you haven't ventured into the job market in recent years, you are definitely in for quite a shock when you enter today's job market! What often—maybe even *usually*—worked in landing a job in the recent past no longer works at all today.

In the first book in the **Headhunter Hiring Secrets** series of Career Development/Management publications, the international bestselling **Headhunter Hiring Secrets: The Rules of the Hiring Game Have Changed . . . Forever!**, I compared the entire hiring process in the job market then to a "game," a *very* serious game, but a game nonetheless. Like *all* games, there are certain *rules* that must first be learned and then strictly adhered to, if the "players" (in this case, job hunters) ever hope to have a chance of winning. And finally, I clearly outlined the *new* rules in the job market.[3]

I wish I could tell you that, today, everything (or even *almost* everything) is back to "normal" in the job market. Unfortunately, that is not the case at all. The job market as we once knew it no longer exists, and it hasn't existed for a number of years now. Nothing I'm seeing today even remotely suggests that "the good old days" are ever coming back, either.

Part I of **Headhunter Hiring Secrets 2.0** begins by strongly suggesting that, before you even get started on your journey toward your new job, you first *define* what your *ideal* new job would look like. After all, in order to accurately measure progress toward any goal/destination, you must first and foremost define that goal/destination, right?

Next, we look at an overview of the job market, where it's been in recent years, where it seems to be today, and where it appears it's likely headed for the foreseeable future.

Part I concludes by showing you how to create a *job-winning* résumé and cover letter, as well as how you can *substantially* enhance your online presence at sites such as LinkedIn, to have a steady stream of career opportunities coming to *you*!

---

[3]For a general overview of the Top 10 *new* rules of the hiring game see Appendix A.

CHAPTER ONE

FIRST THINGS FIRST:
DEFINING YOUR *IDEAL* NEW JOB

Regardless of the reason(s) you've finally decided to search for a new job, one of the first things you'll want to do is to define, as precisely as possible, what your *ideal* new job would look like. Most people have at least a pretty good *general* idea of what it might take to make them happier at work, e.g., a promotion, more money, a less hectic schedule, etc. But there is more—actually, much, much more—you should consider as you begin your new job search.

> ### A Cautionary Note
>
> As you are defining your ideal new job, keep in mind that prospective new employers will be looking for *current* and *relevant* job experience *only*. So, while your ideal/dream job may be to become a graphic artist, even though you have been employed as a chemist for the last five years, your chances of actually being seriously considered for a graphic artist position are largely unrealistic.
>
> Common sense, right? Maybe, but we still see something like this at least once a week at The HTW Group.

Of course many factors go into determining the overall level of job satisfaction. In this chapter we'll examine some, though certainly not all, of the key factors. Consider each of these factors, as well as any others that may be pertinent to your specific job/career situation, as you begin to design *your* ideal new job. Using these factors, compare and contrast where you feel you are now in your current job, if currently employed, with where you would *like* to be in your ideal new job.

Here are some key factors I strongly advise you to consider as you begin defining your ideal new job:

- **The *size* of the company.** Are you most comfortable being a big fish in a little pond, or would you prefer to be a little fish in a big pond? Or, would you actually prefer something in between, i.e., a *medium-sized* company? If currently employed, how would you describe your current situation, and how comfortable are you with it?

    As a general rule, the larger the company the greater the overall career opportunities, the higher the salaries and the greater the choice and range of employee benefits. But there usually is a price to be paid for these factors, too:

More (and tighter) employee rules and regulations, a far greater risk that you will get lost in the shuffle and find yourself laboring for years in anonymity, or being downsized the moment the company has a soft quarter.

- **The *culture* of the company**. Every company, no matter the size, has its own distinct culture, and if for some reason you don't fit in to that culture, well, suffice it to say, your work days can indeed become long and tedious.

   If employed, how would you describe the culture of your current employer? Friendly? Caring? Easy going? Or, is it cutthroat? Back-stabbing? Or nurturing, creative, cutting edge?

   Who are the people (or the job types) who most often seem to get rewarded and promoted in your current company? Which employees seem to be the most valued? Salespeople? Accountants? Engineers? Are *you* among any of these groups? Or, do you find yourself continually on the outside looking in?

   Is your company a FUN, rewarding place to work, or do you absolutely dread getting up each and every business day to go to the office or to the work site? Is the predominant atmosphere one of courtesy and respect, or rather, one of rudeness and disrespect? Are the people, especially the officers of the company, honest and ethical?

- **The *pace* and *tempo* of the company**. Are you essentially comfortable with the *pace* and *tempo* at your current job, if employed? Or, do you quite often feel like a race horse tied to a plow? Or, conversely, does the pace at your current employer often leave you feeling anxious, overwhelmed and sometimes depressed because of your inability to keep up? Are you working 12- to 15-hour days with no end in sight?

- **The company's competitive position within its industry**. Everyone likes to be associated with a winner, and usually the winner in any industry and/or business segment is the one that has the most market share, or at least is among, say, the Top Ten. And typically, though certainly not always, market leaders tend to be more innovative, more creative than the also-ran companies within the industry. (Hey, there is a reason these companies are at, and remain at, the TOP of the heap!) Obviously, this can have a very definite effect on employee morale, initiative and innovativeness.

If currently employed, are you now associated with a winner, or are you working for one of the also-rans? How is this affecting *your* morale, *your* desire to be innovative and/or creative in your current job? Maybe not at all; Maybe quite a bit. Only you can make that determination.

- **The company's overall financial stability**. Even some of the market leaders were negatively affected by deteriorating economic conditions in recent years, but most nonetheless remain financially stable.

If currently employed, how is your employer's overall financial position these days? How can you tell? How many times has your company downsized recently? How many layoffs have occurred and how frequently have they occurred? Has there been a recent (or even a *current*) hiring freeze implemented? If your company is a public one, what has been the recent performance of its stock? The long-term stock performance?

Are you willing to risk riding out any current financial downturns your company may be experiencing, in the hope that everything will ultimately be fine? Are you even willing to go down with the ship, if that should become necessary? Will any loyalty you may now have toward your current employer be reciprocated if things go south, or are you merely fooling yourself into believing that the company will be as loyal to you as you are to it?

- **The company's salaries and benefits**. Rare indeed would it be for an employee—virtually *any* employee!—to say something like this: "I am paid a fair and competitive salary." Why? Because most of us *think* we are *not* paid a fair and competitive salary, that's why! Most of us believe we are "worth" far more than any company seems willing to pay us.

The fact is, though, salaries, like virtually *all* products and services offered for sale, are essentially determined by one factor and one factor only: Supply and demand. Some companies will pay salaries approaching the astronomical in order to attract (and hire) certain candidates with unique, hard-to-find skill sets because the demand is so far greater than the supply of such candidates. Most companies, however, will *not* take this same approach to attract the typical candidate because the candidate supply is either in sync with the demand or there is a greater supply of candidates than there is a current demand for them. That means that companies will pay a salary that is *competitive* within the industry, and usually, not one penny more!

So, with this caveat in mind, how do you rate your salary at your current job, if employed? Is it at least adequate? Do you honestly believe that it is *competitive*? (Rather than guess at the answer to this question, or go strictly on gut feel, go to www.salary.com and do a little research.)

Many, though certainly not all, of the new jobs that have been created in recent years offer few, if any, employee benefits, e.g., health insurance, dental insurance, 401(k), company retirement plan, etc. The whole issue of employee benefits, then, can take on far greater importance and significance than was the case several years ago. How do you feel the employee benefits you currently enjoy with your employer stack up against competing companies within your industry? Better? Worse? About the same?

This is certainly more than an idle question. Many candidates consider *compensation* to be largely limited to *salary* alone and can easily overlook the significant amount of *hidden* compensation that can be contributed, oftentimes *tax-free* to the employee, by employee benefits.

- **The company's management (including the person you work for directly at the company, i.e., your boss).** You could be working for the best company in the world, and be making a very good salary and have superior employee benefits, but if the person you actually report to, the person you actually work for, your boss or supervisor, leaves a great deal to be desired in the human relations category . . . well, you quite likely are miserable in your current job, if employed.

How is *your* current boss or supervisor? Fair? Honest? Reliable? Quick to offer praise when it's due and appropriate? Quite willing to share the spotlight with those he/she supervises? Or, is he or she simply a jerk of the first order? Someone who offers nothing but negative criticism and feedback, someone who is virtually impossible to please? Someone who would make Attila the Hun look like a diplomat?

Remember, unless supervisory personnel are routinely moved onward and upward in your company—or, unless you anticipate being promoted out of your current position soon—you can expect to be stuck with your current boss or supervisor for the foreseeable future! Can you live with that? Do you *want* to live with that? *Will* you live with that?

And keep in mind that, if you are now working for the boss from hell, he or she can only continue his or her evil, very counter-productive ways by having, either implicitly or explicitly, "permission" from those occupying more senior positions within the company hierarchy, i.e., those men and women in top management. (Coincidentally, the Number One or Number Two reason people give for leaving their current job is "the boss"!)

- **Geographic locale of company**. Where one lives and works can, of course, have a dramatic impact on the overall quality of life, as well as overall job satisfaction. Every geographic locale has both its appeal and drawbacks. Not surprisingly, and as a general rule, the more populous an area the greater the number and variety of jobs, the higher the salaries, etc. The drawback, however, can mean a higher crime rate, more traffic (and greater travel times to and from work), a higher cost of living, etc.

If you have a spouse and small children these factors can become even more pressing and important when it comes to selecting the geographic locale of your next job, your ideal job. What is the median cost of housing? What is the quality of the schools? What is the traffic situation? Will you have to spend several hours a day simply traveling to and from your job?

Your background, your individual temperament, will also play a vital role in what you are likely to be able to accept, and successfully adapt to, insofar as the geographic locale of your next job is concerned. If, for example, you grew up in a medium-sized city in the Midwest, you probably will experience significant culture shock if you choose to relocate to New York City for your new job. Likewise, if you are a NYC gal or guy, you, too, would have quite an adjustment to make if your next job happened to be in, say, Bloomington, IL, a medium-sized Midwestern city.

- **Work-life balance.** Very few people, when they are approaching the end of their life, are likely to regret not having spent more time at the office. To be sure, in order to survive in today's job market, one usually has to put in more than the "normal" eight-hour day, but there still should be a reasonable limit. After all, every hour (or weekend, holiday, etc.) spent at the job is an hour you cannot spend with your family, enjoying your favorite hobbies, or doing other things that are important to you.

  If currently employed, how is *your* current work-life balance? Are you required to spend an inordinate amount of time at your job—at the tremendous expense of spending valuable time with your family and friends? Would your ideal job afford you far less time at the office and far *more* free time to spend as you wish?

- **Career growth potential.** Almost no job offers virtually unlimited career opportunities. Eventually, nearly everyone will reach his or her career ceiling, as the result of reaching the top of a pay grade, for example, or by there simply being no place else to move within the organization, in order to have the opportunity to advance to the next level.

If employed, is this where you find yourself in your current job? Is this at least part of the reason you may feel, rightfully so, that *your* career has plateaued?

You don't have to accept your fate, you know, and you certainly should *not* accept it, either. If you are among the top professionals in your particular area of specialty, there can be tremendous opportunities to *significantly* advance your career. Now. Today!

As business continues to pick up across the board—and it *is* picking up—if you properly position yourself to attract the attention of major employers that are currently desperate for top-tier talent, I think you will be pleasantly surprised at just how much more growth potential you may actually have in your career!

As you are designing *your* ideal job, then, take all of these factors into consideration, as well as any other factors that you may consider relevant and important to you. Use them to paint a picture of what your ideal job looks like. You might even strongly consider writing your own job description for your next job. That way, you can keep referring back to this description as your new job search advances, making changes and alterations as circumstances and opportunities dictate.

Why reduce your ideal job description to writing? If you're like most of us, the mere act of writing something down, such as a daily/monthly agenda, appointments, goals and obligations, etc., makes it *real*, which usually also means that we are far more likely to actually accomplish (or a least *attempt* to accomplish) these things! Otherwise, we oftentimes just end up talking about what we are going to do, what we would *like* to do, and never seem to actually get around to doing it.

YOU'RE IN A VERY UNIQUE POSITION IN TODAY'S JOB MARKET IF . . .

Regardless of your employment status—currently employed, currently *under*-employed, or yes, even *unemployed*—if you have taken (or will take) the time and made (or will make) the effort to position yourself, to *brand* yourself, professionally, as clearly and unmistakably being among the Top 20% of *all* job candidates, the *crème de la crème,* you have a meaningful advantage over most other job hunters, who clearly are *not* among this select group of men and women. The reason that is true is due to the so-called **"80-20"** rule. It is a truism, for example, that, in sales, 20% of the salespeople generate 80% of the business. Just coincidentally, the same maxim applies to job hunters: 20% of the candidates typically land 80% of the really good jobs!

A key point made again and again in **Headhunter Hiring Secrets 2.0** is that the job market still remains somewhat of a "buyer's market" for many professional segments. That dictates, therefore, that the hiring process remains one of *exclusion*, not inclusion. That is—and quite contrary to what most job seekers actually think and believe—a hiring company today continues to look for ways to *eliminate* applicants for most open positions—not for ways to *include* them in the general hiring pool.

Hiring companies take this approach for one primary, very simple reason: Because of the significant number of applications hiring companies continue to receive for many open positions, they want to *reduce* the size of the hiring pool as quickly and as efficiently as possible. As a result, they look for practically *any* reason to eliminate a candidate, and the earlier in the process that they can accomplish that goal the better.

These same companies, however, are *not* taking this same rather brutal, insensitive approach to candidates whom they *want* to attract and hire! And that's where *you* can come in. That's where *you* can capitalize on the situation. But in order to do that, at a minimum, you must . . .

- **Be currently employed** (or relatively *recently* employed) **in a position that is at least *similar* to the position a hiring company is attempting to fill**, plus have **relevant experience** in your current (or relatively recent) position.

- **Be able to produce** (and *quantify*, by using *numbers, dollars* and *percentages*) a **record of continuous, *significant* career achievements** and **accomplishments**.

- **Position yourself** (and be widely perceived) as definitely being **among the top ten to 20 percent** of *all* other men and women in your profession.

- **Be able to be *found* and to be *contacted*** by hiring companies, hiring managers, Human Resources professionals and headhunters in your professional market niche, i.e., through your LinkedIn profile and other online job-hunting sites.

You'll Still Have to EARN a Job in Today's Job Market!

Even if you have managed to position yourself, and be perceived as being, among the TOP candidates in the job market today, there still are no "gimmes." (For you non-golfers, a "gimme" is a *conceded* shot, i.e., one the player isn't required even to attempt, such as when the ball is just inches from the cup.) That is, you still will have to EARN a job in today's job market!

In the remainder of **Headhunter Hiring Secrets 2.0** you will see, precisely, how to accomplish that goal.

What My Ideal New Job Would Look Like[4]

Satisfaction Factor	Current Job[5]	Ideal Job
Company size	Medium-sized, about right	Medium-sized, but would consider larger company.
Company culture	Too much "back-stabbing." Salespeople get all the glory.	A company where *my* professional specialty would be valued.
Pace and tempo of company	Too fast-paced, too "rah-rah" for my liking.	I would have more time to do better work, and that work would have greater value to the company.
Company's competitive position, overall financial stability	We're number five and probably always will be because top management is too timid, unimaginative.	Doesn't have to be THE leader, but should encourage creativity, initiative, etc.
Salary & benefits	Livable salary, about average benefits.	Would like at least 5% more salary and more liberal benefits.
Company management (including boss, direct supervisor)	Too timid, unimaginative. "Pennywise, pound foolish." Supervisor primarily concerned about himself. Employees "on their own."	Top management should set the pace and strongly encourage *constructive* input from employees. Would like a supervisor who is much more supportive.
Geographic locale	I love where we live, but the traffic here is brutal! I spend two hours a day commuting to and from the job!	My ideal locale would be an area that offers nice schools, low crime—and a far less strenuous commuting schedule!
Work-life balance	Not really a problem. I go in, do my job and go home. No incentive to do much else.	I wouldn't mind spending more time working, as long as I still had adequate time for my family and other personal/family interests.

---

[4]Consider designing and completing a table like this to better define *your* ideal job.

[5]If currently employed.

What My Ideal New Job Would Look Like

SATISFACTION FACTOR	CURRENT JOB	IDEAL JOB
Career growth opportunities	If you keep your head down and your mouth shut, you will inch along for most of your career.	Everyone feels (or should feel) that he or she can advance as far as his or her talents allow. I want to be promoted and given more responsibility, if I can prove I am worthy of such consideration!
ADD ANY OTHER FACTORS THAT ARE IMPORTANT TO YOU		

Overall Assessment – Current Job Versus *Ideal* Job
I am at least somewhat dissatisfied with my current job. I feel as if I am essentially "marking time," waiting for opportunities and challenges that simply may never come. If I don't take control of my own career, my destiny, somebody else will!

MAKE SURE YOU'RE 'IN IT' FOR THE 'LONG HAUL'!

As is the case with anything worthwhile, you should not expect (or anticipate) that landing a new job, your *ideal* job, is going to be either *easy* or necessarily *fast*. Depending on your skill set, as well as the demand for top-notch people in your professional niche, that may indeed prove to be the case, but you would be wise not to *plan* on that happening in today's job market.

You should therefore commit to the long haul. You should exercise patience and carefully plan each and every vital step toward your ultimate destination, that of steadily advancing your TOTAL career.

As your career advances (and changes) over the years ahead, the definition of your *ideal* job will likely also change. So, rather than to view your *ideal* job as a specific *destination*, view it as an ongoing, *career-long* journey.

CHAPTER TWO

THE JOB MARKET
APPEARS SET TO . . .

If you've been waiting for just the right time to venture into the job market to find your ideal job, judging from a number of very significant indicators, NOW would appear to be that time! In stark contrast to recent years, as these words are being written,[6] the job market appears set to literally SIZZLE!

Here are just a few of the key indicators from 2015 that clearly point to the job market's tremendous future potential:

- **June** — The number of Americans working finally surpassed the previous peak of 138.4 million, set in January 2008. At yearend 2015 that number was nearly 143 million.

- **July** — Marked the highest number of open jobs recorded in 15 years.

- **July** — The unemployment rate for the professional category (25 years of age and older, with a bachelor's degree or higher) dropped below 3%, the lowest since July 2008.

- **September** — "Time to fill" positions reached the longest time in recorded history, due to there not being enough qualified people to fill open jobs.

- **November** — Bank of America released its annual "CFO Outlook." Of 500 chief financial officers of companies with revenues ranging from $25 million to $2 billion, 54% said that their companies plan to hire additional full-time employees in 2016, the best hiring outlook since 2007.

- **December** — U.S. jobless claims registered a 42-year low.

Despite such very positive indicators, could the job market still fizzle instead of sizzle? Of course it could, but the prospect of that looks unlikely in the extreme at this point. For example, at yearend 2015, Chairman of the Federal Reserve Janet Yellen put the chance of a U.S. recession in 2016 at just 10%. Plus, as just indicated above, the companies that will be doing the actual hiring as we enter a new year apparently have a very high degree of confidence in the foreseeable future economy and job growth outlook.

---

[6]Yearend 2015

Recent conversations I have had with CEOs and presidents of our recruiting firm's client hiring companies also reflect the following trends and thinking:

- Beginning in 2016 more cash will start flowing into the hiring process simply because it must. People and the companies they now work for have been spread far too thin for far too long and retention of top talent is a growing concern for many companies.

- Forward-thinking companies are looking to increase investment in hiring to gain a competitive edge in their market niche(s). The post-recessionary approaches of cutting costs and staff, while still attempting to increase productivity and develop differentiating products and services, have already begun to produce diminishing returns.

- Evolutionary thinking on workforce diversity continues to expand and is proving to be a key driver of future, sustained growth. The new thinking goes well beyond the traditional Equal Opportunity Employment (EEO) concepts and principles. In a truly global economy more intricately connected than ever before, the embrace of genuine diversity is accelerating people's ability to learn and adopt new ideas, understand and accept a wider range of perspectives, broadening virtually everyone's thinking about situations leading to more effective solutions, and exponentially increasing creativity as well as production.

OH, HOW FAR WE'VE COME IN RECENT YEARS!

Not so very long ago at all, and as indicated in the graph on the next page, the job market looked bleak, very bleak indeed. If you were among the millions of men and women who were forced to hunker down at jobs they may have grown to detest, for a whole variety of reasons, then you certainly can relate to just how bleak the job market became in recent years. Or worse, you may have been among the millions of people who ended up *losing* their jobs and were forced to spend years trying to get their careers back on track!

As illustrated in the graph below, just six years ago, in 2010, the "official" unemployment rate hovered dangerously close to the double-digit rate, at 9.6%. And, while admittedly, and as shown on subsequent pages in this chapter, this "official" rate of unemployment represents only a *subset* of the overall employment picture at any point in time, it nonetheless is illustrative of general employment trends. Just coincidentally, it is also the rate most often referred to and/or cited by both politicians and the media as a measure of progress (or the lack thereof) in overall employment.

Traditionally, "full employment" has been considered to be at or near a six% unemployment rate, a point that was finally reached in 2014. At yearend 2015 the rate had further declined to a very respectable five percent. To be sure, this should prove to be a solid harbinger for positive future job growth projections.

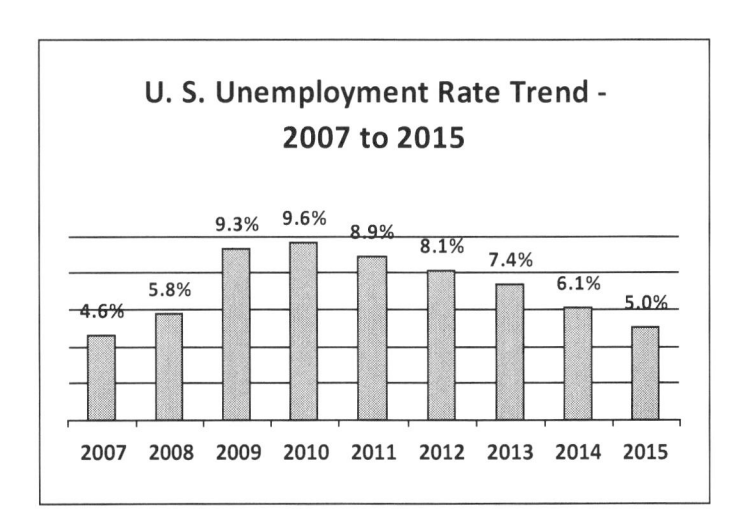

U. S. Unemployment Rate Trend - 2007 to 2015

Year	Rate
2007	4.6%
2008	5.8%
2009	9.3%
2010	9.6%
2011	8.9%
2012	8.1%
2013	7.4%
2014	6.1%
2015	5.0%

NUMBER EMPLOYED STEADILY INCREASING

The Bureau of Labor Statistics graph featured on the next page clearly demonstrates the solidly upward employment growth trend that began in 2010 and continues apace. So, despite what some politicians and/or the news media may say, employment very definitely is on the rise and is quite healthy. The debate on the "quality" of these jobs, however, rages on, and one often encounters claims and arguments that these numbers are either unrealistic, fudged, or both. Quite often, those having such opinions and attitudes are people who either can't find a job or at least can't effectively compete for one.

Whatever your own opinion may be in this regard, a number that you can be assured is real is the number of jobs posted on the Internet each and every month, particularly from aggregators such as www.indeed.com.

Numbers of Employed Americans

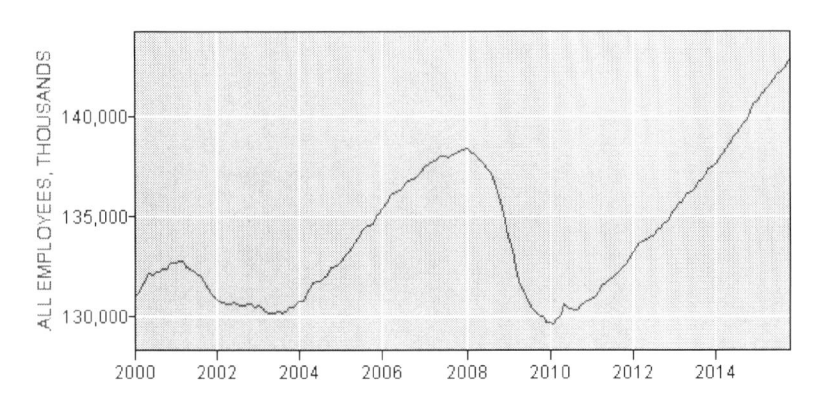

JOB SOURCES – THE BROADER VIEW

MONTHLY JOBS REPORT

Each month economists, politicians and employment professionals eagerly await the **Monthly Jobs Report**. This report is based on the number of *new* jobs created in the private sector for the previous month and is generally perceived as being indicative of *potential* future trends in the overall labor market.

While the addition of *any* new jobs is always good news, like many economic and job market data, to genuinely understand their true significance one has to take more than a cursory, surface look at the data.

Let's say, for example, that 250,000 new jobs were added in the previous month. Great news! Wall Street reacts with an upward spike in the markets, politicians pat themselves on the back. Everybody celebrates, and of course there certainly is genuine cause for celebration, notwithstanding of course the aforementioned and somewhat specious argument that many if not most of these new jobs are lacking in "quality." But the *complete* jobs picture can be even better than what is suggested by the monthly jobs report! The truth is, these new jobs still represent only the tip of the iceberg when it comes to the TOTAL jobs available today! Read on!

The 'Hidden' Job Market

I'm confident that you have at least some familiarity with what is known as the "hidden" job market. You may be surprised to learn, though, that **fully *one-half* (or more!)[7] of *all* jobs available today are in this job market segment**! What's more, many if not most of these jobs are *not* advertised—anywhere! Nonetheless, these are real jobs, and ones companies fully intend to fill.

Why aren't these jobs made generally known to the average job seeker? Good question! (And I have a few good answers too.)

Because virtually any position that is advertised today can still generate a significant number of applications, many companies remain selective about the open positions they advertise. Otherwise, they know that they may be inundated with applications, and that it will not only take considerable time and effort to process them all, it will also significantly increase their employee acquisition costs. Add to this the fact that, statistically, at least one-half of the applicants for these jobs can be expected to possess few (oftentimes, none) of the skill sets and/or experience required to be seriously considered for the positions.

> **Jobs in the "hidden" job market are *real* jobs, and having access to them—or even being sought out for them!—can pay you *significant* dividends, if you have positioned yourself as a TOP candidate!**

---

[7] Some estimates go as high as 75% to 80%.

Another possible reason for not advertising these types of jobs is because the company may be intending to replace an existing incumbent in a key position and does not want to forewarn the incumbent.

Yet another reason for not advertising certain jobs has to do with the *level* of the position. Let me give you an example. I recently attended an industry conference for one of the market sectors our firm recruits in. I was approached by a Fortune 500 company representative who needed to fill a key vice president position. She told me that, while the position ultimately would be advertised, she wanted to have several viable candidates waiting in the wings before the position actually was advertised.

By the way, this type of scenario occurs all the time to recruiters, and it can be a boon both to the recruiter *and* to those job seekers who have established and maintained an ongoing professional relationship with a recruiter. Why? Because these job seekers may be among the first—and perhaps only!—ones to learn of such choice job openings *before* they are ultimately advertised, if in fact they ever *are* actually advertised.

THE JOLTS REPORT

Here is another fact that I am sure will surprise most people: At any given point in the job market, there can be as many as **ten million jobs available each and every month**! Now, before you start to think I have completely lost my mind at this point, let me amplify and clarify this (apparently outrageous) statement.

When it comes to available jobs, for the most part, the news media focus only on *one* set of employment figures each month—the number of *new* jobs added to the workforce. From time to time you may see a more informed, more detailed and comprehensive analysis of the *true* picture (and scope) of the job market, usually deep within the business news sections, but even that is rare. Almost without exception it is the report released each month by the Bureau of Labor Statistics, the aforementioned "jobs report," that captures all the headlines and gets all the "buzz." That's unfortunate because, actually, the job numbers represented by the BLS report represent only a small *subset* of the *actual* number of TOTAL jobs available during any given month.

It is the **Job Openings and Labor Turnover Survey (JOLTS)** report that gives us the best, most *comprehensive* picture and scope of the current (and potentially, the future) labor market. The JOLTS report

THE JOB MARKET

encompasses all positions open on the last day of the month where there is actually work available for that position, the job could start within 30 days and there is an active process in place for filling that position.

The openings include both the "new" jobs reported by the news media, as well as the openings created by separations, such as retirement, resignations and discharges. (Temporary and contract staffing openings are not counted in the report.)

This is what the **JOLTS** report was showing as of August 2015:[8]

  4.7 Million people hired in August 2015

 +5.4 Million positions remaining open/unfilled.

=**10.1 Million TOTAL positions available in August 2015**

Now, here is a very telling statistic: **2.7 million of these total open positions were due to people quitting their current jobs**. Further underscoring the fact that the overall job market is finally picking up some genuine steam is that, recently, more people have *quit* their jobs (usually to take *new* jobs) than at any other time since late 2008!

THE BIG PICTURE

At the beginning of 2016, here was the BIG picture in the job market:

  142.9 Million *full-time employees* in the U. S.

  +7.9 Million *unemployed* people in the U. S.

=**150.8 Million people available for full time jobs (TOTAL POOL)**

- As early as 2012, 5% of the labor pool was considered "active" and 15% semi-active, for a total of 20% "routinely looking for jobs online, networking, and/or open to hearing about opportunities from a recruiter."

- As these words are being written that number is 31%, which means that, at any given time, nearly **47 million people** are interested in new jobs.

---

[8] The JOLTS report trails the employment report by one month.

These facts, of course, contribute, at least in part, to some people claiming that the jobs numbers are inflated, not real or fudged. More precisely, because an ever-increasing number of men and women are now seeking one of the finite number of new jobs, competition for these new jobs is also ever increasing. And that's especially true where the really GREAT jobs are concerned.

SOME PARTICULARLY BRIGHT SPOTS IN TODAY'S JOB MARKET

In virtually any job market there are always bright spots. The current job market, of course, certainly is no exception. For example, as you can see in the chart below, if you are 25-years-of-age or older, have at least a bachelor's degree, you are in a job market segment that, at a 3.2 percent unemployment rate, is considered to have virtually "full employment." Wait a minute you might be saying! How can 3.2 percent be considered virtually "full employment"? Let me explain.

**'Full Employment' Reached in 2014
For Those 25-years-of-age and older
With Bachelor's Degree or Higher**

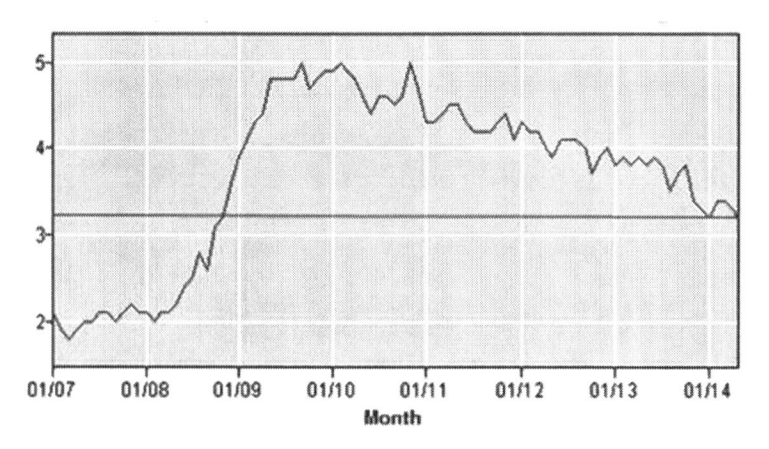

The true definition of **full employment** is the balance between the demand for labor and the supply of fully qualified workers to meet that demand. For men and women who meet the criteria outlined in the chart, we are on the verge (if we are in fact not already there!) of demand actually *exceeding* the available supply of fully qualified candidates. As this is being written, for example, our executive recruiting firm has more client companies looking for mechanical engineers than we can find potential candidates to fill those positions.

STEM Disciplines/Professions

Another particularly bright job segment in today's job market are the **STEM professions/disciplines**. (STEM is an acronym that stands for Science, Technology, Engineering and Math, and refers to candidates who have education, training and/or experience and expertise in these professional disciplines.) The time is already fast approaching when the number of positions open for fully qualified STEM candidates will *far exceed* the number of candidates available to fill them.[9] That's GREAT news for the candidates, of course. Conversely, though, it has the significant potential to prove disastrous for those companies *already* having a *critical* need to fill STEM positions, but which nonetheless continue to subject ALL candidates—including the STEM candidates—to an unnecessarily lengthy interview process before making a hiring decision.

Other 'Hot' Job Segments

Some significant job gains are also being registered in key professional and business services sectors. Employment in **computer systems** and **technical consulting** is trending upward. Jobs in the **healthcare professions** continue to expand at near-record levels, with ambulatory services such as doctors' offices and outpatient clinics accounting for much of the action. As the overall population continues to age, further increases in the demand for healthcare workers is also expected.

The Bottom Line on The Job Market

It is my intention in this chapter to demonstrate to you that a more in-depth look at the make up of the *total* available talent pool and career opportunities can go a long way toward gaining a better, more thorough understanding of the true make-up and total dimensions of the job market.

---

[9]The U.S. Department of Labor estimates there will be 1.2 million STEM job openings by 2018, but not nearly enough qualified candidates to fill these positions.

Clearly, the job market is showing significant and growing improvement. The number of people open to considering new career opportunities has dramatically increased—and continues to increase. However, in order for *you* to be in a position to take full and complete advantage of these great career opportunities, at a minimum, you must ensure that you . . .

- Can clearly **differentiate yourself from the competition,** i.e., others seeking the same jobs as you;

- Have **professionally positioned** yourself as clearly being among the top job candidates in your professional discipline; and

- Learn and then strictly implement the **best, most workable approaches**, i.e., tactics and strategies, when you enter the job market.

If you are merely someone who is just "looking for a job, any job," the current (and prospective) job market isn't likely to hold much promise for you. Similarly, if you are one of those people waiting for the job market to return to "normal," i.e., "the way things used to be," you're also going to be sadly disappointed.

On the other hand, if you have positioned (or can position) yourself as being among the *crème de la crème* (essentially, the top 20% of all candidates in your professional niche), then clearly, for you, the time to step out of your comfort zone and move your career ahead is NOW!

So, if for any reason you have been hesitating to venture into the job market in search of an exciting, much more rewarding, new job because you assumed there were few if any jobs that even remotely fit into that category—or if you have felt "lucky" in recent years just to have your current job, no matter how bad it may have become—you really do need to re-think your position.

Now, don't misunderstand me here. I am *not* saying (or even implying) that it is *easy* to get a new job in today's job market. That's not true by any stretch of the imagination. What I *am* saying is that it certainly is much easier to get a new job today than it was just a few years ago. And that's particularly true if you have positioned yourself (or are willing to *begin* positioning yourself) as being among the TOP candidates in today's job market!

As a professional headhunter who is in the job market each and every business day of the year, I can truthfully and categorically say this:

At no time in recent years have the opportunities for career advancement been better for TOP job candidates than is the case today.

Make no mistake about it, as production among hiring companies in key industries continues to expand, these companies have been pursuing and will continue to aggressively pursue such top candidates to meet rising demand for the companies' products and services. That trend is expected to continue. Real companies today have real jobs that they are *seriously* trying to fill.

HOW TO FIND THE REALLY GREAT JOBS TODAY!

The key to finding jobs—really GREAT jobs!—in today's job market is to search out companies that want *and* need top-notch men and women to help them more effectively compete in what's clearly (and irreversibly) become a global marketplace.

Do NOT spend all your time monitoring the "news" about how BAD the economy and job market are. That's essentially just a waste of valuable time and energy!

Chapter Three

START WITH THE 'PAPERWORK'

Dust off Your Old Résumé, Read it Very Carefully, Then Throw It in the Waste Basket and Create a **NEW**, *Job-Winning* One!

What type of comment do we most often hear from currently employed people when they start thinking about looking for a new, better job? Usually it goes something like this, doesn't it?

"I'm going to get out my résumé, dust it off, and start sending it to a few headhunters and to some online positions and see what happens."

If you are currently employed and are even *considering* such an approach . . . **STOP**! You're definitely headed down the wrong road! You're going in the wrong direction! Forget everything you *think* you know about getting a new job because virtually everything has changed if you landed your current position quite a few years ago! And that includes how to design and craft an *effective* résumé, the topic focused on and discussed in this chapter. (In later chapters we will take a look at how a headhunter *may* be able to help you with your quest for a new job, as well as how to incorporate your online job-searching activities into your overall job-search plan.)

Now you may indeed be an exception to the rule and already have an *exceptional*, well-designed résumé, and feel that you can merely skip over this chapter. I strongly advise against that! At Hire to Win we receive from 300 to 500 résumés each and every week, and many are from truly well-qualified professionals. Unfortunately, the overwhelming majority of these résumés are neither well designed nor exceptional in any way whatsoever. In fact, most are weak, while some are really, really bad. So pay attention!

Before the tsunami of change hit the job market, about the time the Great Recession set in, when jobs were so plentiful that virtually anyone and everyone who wanted a job could probably find one, employers tended, at least somewhat, to overlook a résumé that was oftentimes little more than a listing of previous (and current) job descriptions. Those days are over! Today's hiring managers and the companies they represent take an entirely different approach. They are much more demanding and far less tolerant of sloppy résumés.

In broad general terms, here is what the typical hiring manager today is looking for in a résumé (and if they don't find it, *immediately*, the résumé is almost certainly destined to be hit with the big DELETE key or end up in the nearest waste basket):

- ***Specific* evidence** that **you have continued to grow** with your current (or most recent) company, by heading up (or being intricately involved in) key projects/programs, etc.

- ***Specific* evidence** that **you have made an ongoing, *substantial, measurable* contribution** to your existing or most recent employer, expressed in **dollars** (saved and/or earned) and/or **percentage**s (of sales *increases*, cost *decreases*, etc.). In other words, you need to show how you have either ***made* your current** (or most recent) **company money** or ***saved* the company money**, and ideally, how you have managed to accomplish *both* of these goals.

So, if you don't already have the information at your fingertips, start putting together *quantitative* evidence of how you have contributed—and continue to contribute, if still employed—to the success of your current (or most recent) employer. Make a list of your achievements and accomplishments, e.g., "Led a manufacturing initiative that resulted in first-year cost savings of 15%, or $2 million; was an integral member of an ad hoc team that successfully introduced a new chemical manufacturing process that netted the company $10 million in new annual revenue," etc.

Why do hiring managers look for such things in a résumé? Why do they even care what you've done or are now doing for your current (or most recent) company or what contributions you may have made to its bottom line? Simple. They want to have at least *some* comfort level that you can also be expected to do these very same kinds of things for *their* companies, if you are the candidate ultimately selected for a position they are trying to fill.

How Important is a Well-Crafted Résumé in Winning a Job? Very Important!

The key role a well-designed, well-thought-out and well-crafted résumé plays in landing the really good jobs today simply cannot be overstated. Let me briefly relate a story to illustrate this point.

As this book was being written in its final form, The HTW Group was presenting three candidates for an Industrial Business Development position with one of our Fortune 500 client companies. Two of the three candidates won interviews. The third candidate was rejected outright by the Vice President of Sales.

Here is what the VP told me after interviewing—and ultimately also rejecting!—the two remaining candidates:

> **"Skip, it looked to me like these two candidates simply didn't invest enough quality time and care in the crafting of their résumés. The résumés just weren't focused enough for me to clearly see how they could be a valuable addition to our team."**

Game over! For all THREE candidates!

The greatest irony here was that one of the candidates we presented was very highly qualified, yet he still was summarily dismissed—primarily because of his résumé!

So there you have it!

11 Résumé 'Truths'

There are some excellent books currently on the market that can provide you very valuable, in-depth information about how to prepare job-winning résumés, and it isn't my intention here to cover all that is covered in those books. Plus, I am *not* in the résumé writing business, nor do I intend to get in that business. However, some top-quality, very affordable résumé writing resources are recommended at the end of this book.

In this chapter you will be provided with the basics, the nuts and bolts, if you will, of résumé preparation. If you commit to mastering just what is presented here, you will be far, far ahead of most of your competitors for a new job, i.e., other people seeking new jobs. Then, while it is entirely up to you, it is strongly recommend that you seek professional assistance with the final product that becomes your new résumé—*before* you begin using it in your new job search.

That said, then, through extensive professional experience and considerable research over the years, I have identified **11 essential "truths"** about what goes into creating a *job-winning* résumé.

RÉSUMÉ TRUTH 1

It ***must*** be ***visually appealing,*** i.e., it must adhere to the generally accepted principles of good layout and design for *any* printed or digital publication:

- Good, effective use of "white space."
- Use of appropriate and variable type *sizes*, e.g. 10-point, 11-point, etc. (not type *faces,* however, because the *same* typeface, e.g., Arial, Times New Roman, etc., should be used *throughout* the document) and fonts (e.g., **bold face** and *Italics*).
- Appropriate and effective use of "bullets" or other typographic symbols to highlight key accomplishments, duties, etc., and to break up large bodies of text. (All of these elements are also explored in considerable detail in **Headhunter Hiring Secrets: The Rules of the Hiring Game Have Changed . . . Forever!**)

If a résumé doesn't *immediately* give me "cause for pause," it instantly screams "amateur" to me, and my finger moves rapidly toward the big DELETE key! No second chances, unfortunately, because neither I nor a hiring manager nor a Human Resources professional at a hiring company have the luxury of time these days to dig into a résumé if it's not initially inviting. With so many, many applicants for many jobs available today, there simply aren't enough hours in the day to allow for that.

RÉSUMÉ TRUTH 2
Bear in mind, a résumé is a **"movie trailer"**; It is *not* the entire movie!

Today's companies (and staffs) remain somewhat lean, and no one has much time to waste over *anything* these days, particularly lengthy, rambling, poorly organized and largely unreadable résumés. Remember, we're living in a Twitter and text messaging world today, and that means your résumé must get right to the point, be very, very focused and not rival the length of *War and Peace*. In other words, it must POP!, and do so as quickly as possible and in as few words as possible.

Here is how you need to view the crafting of your résumé: Assume every single person who *may* read it has a serious case of Attention Deficit Disorder. The principal goal, then, is to project yourself as someone the person reading your résumé will want to get to know better, to arrange an interview with. That's it!

Another way to look at this aspect of résumé preparation is to think of your résumé as your Marketing Brochure because that's precisely what it is, or at least that's what it *should* be, and how you should look at it.

And now, for the perennial, much debated résumé question: How *long* should a résumé be? My answer (not everyone agrees with it, of course): In all but the most rare situations and circumstances, a résumé should *not* exceed TWO pages. Period. End of discussion. (Well, not really, but as far as I'm concerned it is!)

> **RÉSUMÉ TRUTH 3**
> A résumé **should *not* include a "Career Objective"** section.

What?! you're probably saying to yourself at this point. How will a potential employer know what kind of a job I am seeking if I don't include a "Career Objective" section in my résumé?! (You're probably not going to like the answer.)

> **News FLASH!**
> While at the end stage of the new job search the career opportunity indeed must meet *your* objectives, guess what? Until that stage is in fact reached, today's hiring companies are not interested whatsoever in what *you* want, or what will make *you* happy. At this stage they are only interested in what *they* want, what will make *them* happy!

> **RÉSUMÉ TRUTH 4**
> A résumé should feature a ***Reverse* Chronological** approach.

Today, most hiring managers and companies prefer a résumé which presents work history (and accomplishments, etc.) in *reverse* chronological order. That is, the most recent job history is featured first and all other history is featured, by dates, in the order they occurred, beginning with the next most recent and so on, as indicated in the example below:

ABC COMPANY – 2010 to present

XYZ COMPANY – 2008 to 2010

In an attempt to perhaps mask one's age (or length of time in the workforce), some job-seekers adopt the so-called "functional" approach in their résumé, which presents job titles/positions by presumed order of importance. The fact is, though, today the functional résumé is more likely to get deleted than it is to have any time spent on it by hiring managers or

YOUR RÉSUMÉ

the companies they represent. Occasionally, a "hybrid" résumé, which involves using a *mixture* of résumé approaches, is acceptable. Still, I strongly suggest you use the *reverse* chronological approach because I *know* it's acceptable.

RÉSUMÉ TRUTH 5

A job-winning résumé includes a **brief description of what each employing company** actually does.

Keep in mind that the readers of your résumé don't have the time (or the patience) to learn what the companies you have worked for (or are now working for) actually do, if they don't already know. If, for example, the hiring company is looking for a sales manager with experience in *industrial filtration*, they want to know—*immediately*, without having to search through your résumé—that you actually have that experience.

Typical Example:

National Filtration Systems, Inc.
Vice President of Sales and Marketing

What does this company do? Provide water filters for the home? Make filters for cigarettes? Neither! It is "A $60 million design build engineering firm of industrial filtration units for natural gas and oil." By including that one sentence, you will have just positioned yourself as a potential candidate and have made it easier for the person reviewing your résumé to say "yes" to your candidacy, instead of hitting the big DELETE key and sending your résumé off to the résumé black hole.

Remember, if it is read at all, the ***average résumé gets less than a minute of "face time"*** with a headhunter, hiring manager or Human Resources professional. Don't expect them to guess about *anything* on your résumé! They simply won't take the time to do that.

RÉSUMÉ TRUTH 6

A résumé should include **numbers, numbers, numbers**—and a few **percentages** thrown in for good measure!

A *job-winning* résumé will tell the reader, i.e., a hiring manager, headhunter or Human Resources professional, as quickly and as efficiently as possible, using *quantitative* measurements, about past (and current) job functions and performance, as well as *significant,* notable accomplishments. That means you *must* use **numbers, numbers** and then **more numbers**! And then you must also throw in few **percentages** for good measure!

Below is a real life, recent example of how a Quality Manager for a manufacturer addressed this issue in his résumé. (Hey, I are NOT making these things up!):

> **"Responsible for improving processes and reducing defects. . . ."**

The only thing this candidate managed to accomplish with his résumé was to brand himself as being someone in the bottom 80% of all potential candidates. But, what if he had taken this approach?

> **"Reduced equipment failure rate by 89% in first year as Quality Manager, while increasing annual production by 15%, resulting in an overall revenue increase of $12.5 million."**

See the difference? Which candidate would *you* be interested in learning more about? Which candidate would give *you* "cause for pause"?

RÉSUMÉ TRUTH 7

Never, never, never include any **family** or other **personal information** in your résumé.

Oftentimes this résumé admonition confuses and confounds job candidates. Why wouldn't it be OK, they ask, to include relevant personal information that makes me sound like a real live human being, not a robot? Here is an example of the kind of personal statement being referred to:

> **"Excellent health, happily married with two children."**

At first glance, this kind of statement on a résumé sounds pretty tame and innocent, rather innocuous. In fact, however, it is anything but, at least from the standpoint of Equal Employment Opportunities (EEO) considerations.

As crazy as it may sound (and seem!), let's say that the candidate who is ultimately selected for the position you sought is *single*. Human Resources could then potentially face an unlawful discrimination suit from *you*!

"I was unfairly discriminated against because I am married and have a family," you might allege. "The only reason the company hired a single person was to avoid the increased cost of adding a family to the group health insurance plan."

Don't believe this type of thing happens? Think again! Best advice: Simply leave *any* and *all* personal or family information off your résumé.

RÉSUMÉ TRUTH 8

Never resort to a **"liar, liar, pants on fire!"** résumé.

There may have been a time when you might possibly squeak by with, shall we say, an "inflated" résumé. Those times are now over and have been for quite some time. *Always* tell the truth in your résumé. The *absolute* truth. If you don't, it can cause you to be eliminated at some critical point in the hiring process, or worse, even after you may actually have been hired!

Résumé "fact checks" may have been rather slipshod and half-hearted (or even non-existent) in relatively recent years. Today that certainly is no longer the case—particularly for the really good jobs.

RÉSUMÉ TRUTH 9

Leave the **"pyrotechnics"** and other **"razzle-dazzle"** elements out of your résumé.

The array of "pyrotechnic," "razzle-dazzle" graphic elements that computers have made available today can work GREAT in the hands of professional graphic designers and artists and can be very effective in enhancing communications. But, in the hands of amateurs, they can turn disastrous, and when it comes to a résumé, bordering on the deadly (as in, it will live a *very* short life in the hands of a hiring authority). Therefore, it's usually best to avoid using such things as yellow (or some other dynamic color) highlighting, HUGE type sizes or type faces, colored paper, etc., etc., in your résumé. The only thing this approach will do is make you look like an amateur!

RÉSUMÉ TRUTH 10
Don't include a **"References Available on Request"** section in your résumé.

The "References Available on Request" section has been considered a mainstay in résumés probably ever since there have been résumés. But you know what? In today's job market this section has become largely unnecessary, as well as somewhat irrelevant, at least insofar as most people in the hiring business are concerned. Of course you have references! What professional doesn't?!

That is not to say, however, that you won't at some point in time during the hiring process be asked to produce your references. You will be, but that will come during the final innings of the hiring game, provided you make it that far in the process.

If you are currently employed it will of course be very difficult (not to mention, highly risky!) to ask the right people to serve as references for a possible new job. It's therefore far, far better simply to ask for "recommendations" to your LinkedIn profile. Then, if and when you reach the point in the hiring process where you have to produce current references, the task will be far easier. Or, you might simply see if you can use your LinkedIn recommendations as your *de facto* references.

RÉSUMÉ TRUTH 11
To include **dates of graduation** or not to include dates of graduation in a résumé—that is the question!

This is another one of those perennial "résumé questions" that has been (and continues to be) endlessly debated. One camp *strongly* believes you should indeed include dates of graduation in your résumé, while another camp just as strongly believes you should *not* include them. I don't have "the" definitive answer, but I do know this: The more quantifiable, relevant and important your accomplishments and achievements are, the less of an issue it becomes.

OTHER IMPORTANT RÉSUMÉ CONSIDERATIONS

Naming your résumé. Since virtually all résumés today are categorized in some way in a database, how you *name* your résumé is of utmost importance. Here is an example of why this is true.

Suppose this is the header copy at the top of your résumé:

**The Résumé of
Julie Jones**

As a result of using this naming approach, you will then be categorized in the company's (or headhunter's) database as having a first name of "The" and a last name of "of." Might pose somewhat of a problem locating your résumé for future reference, wouldn't you agree?

How does this happen? Because almost all résumés these days are computer read and electronically parsed. The computer algorithm causes the first and last words of the first line to be read as one's first and last *names*.

You should therefore ensure that you use the standard résumé heading (shown below):

**Julie Jones
123 Main St.
Your Town, USA 12345-6789
123-456-7890 / jjones@myisp.net**

Telephone contact information. Make sure your contact telephone number is current and has a *professional* greeting (not one featuring your cute little children!) and is constantly monitored for incoming calls using voice mail. (You should, however, never, never, never actually answer the phone. Rather, be sure to screen all incoming calls using voice mail. That way, you will be able to respond thoroughly and intelligently, at your own convenience, if a call is about a career opportunity.)

Email address. You should also make certain that the email address you use for any and all job-hunting endeavors and activities is a *professional* one. Don't use, for example, a "cutesy" email address like one of these:

partygirl@myisp.net

golfguy@myisp.net

beerman@myisp.net

YOUR RÉSUMÉ

Oh, come on!, you may be saying to yourself at this point. Who in the world would use an email address like these during a job search? Unfortunately, I've seen email addresses precisely like these (and worse!) used quite frequently by job seekers. The result? DELETE! Happens all the time.

Best advice? While it usually is OK to use an email address such as:

<u>bestsalesgal@myisp.net</u>

or

<u>topsalesguy@myisp.net</u>

It's usually *better* to simply use a standard, professional email address such as this one:

<u>skip.freeman@hiretowin.com</u>

That way, you can be *guaranteed* to come across as a true professional!

Phrases to avoid using. In *Headhunter Hiring Secrets: The Rules of the Hiring Game Have Changed . . . Forever!*, I quoted Zig Ziglar, the world-renowned motivational speaker and author:

"Be a meaningful specific," he said, "not a wandering generality."

Although Ziglar's quote was used in another context in my first book in the *Headhunter Hiring Secrets* series, it also is equally applicable when it comes to how you position yourself in your résumé. If, for example, you use tired, worn-out phrases such as the following to describe your past positions, as well as your level of performance in them, then you become, as Ziglar said, merely "a wondering generality":

"Performed all marketing and PR duties for a large PR firm in a major market."

"Responsible for (fill in the blank)**, while staying within budget."**

"Conducted ongoing research activities to ensure that the company was meeting its overall customer satisfaction target."

Men and women in the sales professions—and remember, if you are looking for a new job you, too, are in the *sales* profession, or at least you would be wise to look at it that way!—learn early on that, in order to be successful, they must continually stress to customers (and potential customers) the *features* of the products and/or services they are selling. *Top* sales men and women also learn to stress the *benefits* provided by the features! Let me give you an example of what I'm talking about here.

Remember the last time you went shopping for a new vehicle? Chances are, if you were dealing with a new salesperson, he or she told you such things as, "The trunk space in our vehicle is x percent larger than our competitor's comparable vehicle." You may have thought to yourself, hmm, that's interesting, but so what? The *seasoned* salesperson would have also cited the *benefit* of this feature, by saying something like this: "That means you'll be able to put ALL of your groceries in the trunk, and not end up having to put some of them in the back seat!"

To put this "feature-benefit" issue in perspective for you, a job-seeker, consider the significant difference between the following two statements that might be featured in a résumé:

"Led a team that is widely recognized for its ability to reduce production costs while, at the same time, increase revenue."

All a potential hiring manager will be able to glean out of a statement like this is the *feature* aspect of it. Now, let's add the *benefit* to this feature, as illustrated in the example below:

"Led a team that, during the last five consecutive years, has reduced production costs by an average of 15%, a savings of $10 million, while increasing annual revenue by 10%, going from $100 million a year to an average of $110 million."

The difference? In the first statement it is indeed quite clear that one of the "features" of the candidate is that he or she is recognized for having the ability to reduce production costs, while also increasing revenue. Great, but so what? What benefit, specifically, might this feature have for the potential hiring company? In the second example it is quite clear what the potential benefit could be for the hiring company because the candidate *quantified* those benefits with numbers and percentages. That's something hiring managers (and the companies they represent) can easily wrap their minds around.

Including "professional designations" (and other abbreviations) **in your résumé.** Have you noticed that, today, it seems that there is a professional designation for virtually *every* profession and related organization, as well as for virtually every little *niche* within those professions? (I have too and I'm about as confused by most of them as you probably are.)

Once upon a time (long, long ago, it seems), *most* professional designations were generally understood by most people, such as, **CPA** (Certified Public Accountant), **PhD** (Philosophical Doctorate), **MBA** (Master of Business Administration), **PE** (Professional Engineer), **MD** (Medical Doctor), **RN** (Registered Nurse), et al. But today? Not so much.

For example, do *you* have any idea what the following examples of professional designations refer to: **CFE, CPP** and **CPL**? I'll answer the question for you. Here's what they mean:

- **CFE** (Certified Fraud Examiner)
- **CPP** (Certified Protection Professional)
- **CPL** (Certified Professional Logistician)

The point is this: If you *do* include a professional designation (or any other abbreviations that aren't common knowledge) in your résumé, and if you have *any* reason at all to suspect that it will not be *readily* identified by *and* meaningful to the person (or persons) who may read your résumé, then be sure to spell out *precisely* what those letters after your name mean, as I have done above. Don't make the reader guess!

Also, use some good common sense if you have a multitude of professional designations and use only a few of them, or the most prestigious of them. Avoid taking the approach I happened to run across recently in a LinkedIn profile:

Pete Jones[10], CFE, CISA, CISSP, CPA, CRISC, PMP

I mean, come on now! When the length of space taken up by one's professional designations exceeds the length of his or her name, isn't it time to seriously reconsider such usage?!

Bottom line: **If there is a risk of doubt** (that your abbreviation(s) will not be readily recognized and understood by your intended audience) . . . **then spell it out—or LEAVE it out!**

---

[10] A pseudonym, but *all* of these designations were indeed listed.

IMPORTANT NEXT STEPS

I realize that quite a bit of information has been presented in this chapter on how to go about crafting a *job-winning* résumé. Standing alone, this information can sometimes seem disjointed and slightly confusing, and perhaps even a little too theoretical. That's why I have chosen not only to *tell* you how to go about putting together *your* own *job-winning* résumé, but also to *show* you how all of this information fits together in one nice, neat package that can become *your job-winning* résumé.

On the next five pages two résumé samples are featured. The first—the *before* example—is the résumé a sales professional had been using in his fruitless search for a new job. He was getting no traction at all from it, or at least not enough to get him where he wanted—and needed!—to go, in order to land a new job—an initial interview. The second résumé—the *after* example—is the résumé he created using the coaching we provided. (He landed not only several interviews, but also a new job with this one!)

Examine each of these résumé examples in some detail and you will see the vast differences between the *before* example and the *after* example. You should also see why one was essentially a "loser" and the other a "winner." Can you spot why this is true?

(***Feel free to examine the sample résumés and return to this page.***)

Note that the same general information was used in both résumé examples. It was the **redesign** and the **overall graphic presentation** of this information that created the "winner" résumé out of the "loser" one. Notice, for example, how your eye is far better drawn to the key elements in the résumé, e.g., "Executive Summary," "Education," etc., in the *after* example than is the case with the *before* example.

And, of course, in the *after* résumé example, you should notice how the candidate's achievements and accomplishments have been far better *quantified* by the appropriate use of **dollars earned/saved** and the **percentages of increases/decreases** these earnings/savings have represented to his current (and previous) employers.

Let's face it, none of this is exactly rocket science or strictly the purview of a select few people. If you will simply study the tips, suggestions and recommendations featured in this chapter, and then put them into action for yourself, you, too, will soon be able to design your own *job-winning* résumé and be well on your way to landing your next job!

SAMPLE RÉSUMÉ - **BEFORE**

Confidential Sales Professional

1234 East West Drive, Any Town, MO 12536 | Cell: 129-985-9855 | confidential@gmail.com

OBJECTIVE   To pursue a sales position by utilizing current and previous business skills and experiences.

EXPERIENCE   **2004 – Present – Confidential Company, Kansas City, MO**

Advanced Wound Care Product Specialist

- Sold advanced would care products in acute care and long-term healthcare accounts.
- Sold silver anti-microbial dressings for OR applications.
- Sold mesh product for hernia repair in OR setting.
- Successful launch of new products including: collagen, silver anti-microbial dressings, and post-op surgical dressings.
- Attained quote achievement six out of seven years.
- Achieved President's Club four out of seven years.

2001 – 2004 – Huntleigh Healthcare, Inc., Kansas City, MO

Sales Consultant

- Sold pressure-relieving and pressure-reducing support surfaces in acute care and long-term care facilities.
- Sold DVT prophylaxis systems in acute care facilities.
- Quota achievement three out of four years.
- Achieved President's Club three years.
- Increased market share by 129%.

1995 – 2001 – Novartis/Sandoz/Innovex Pharmaceuticals, Kansas City, MO

Sales Consultant

- Sold cardiovascular prescription drugs Diovan and Lotrel to Family Practice Physicians, Internal Medicine Physicians, General Practitioners, and Cardiologists in Kansas City sales territory. Also selling Starlix, a prescription drug for treatment of Type II diabetes.
- Worked closely with managed care specialists to gain favorable formulary status of Lescol, Starlix, Diovan, Lotrel, and Lamisil Tablets.
- Worked with the CME Department of University Health Sciences and Dr. James LaSalle, the head of the CME Department, to secure nationally renowned speakers for conferences and conventions.
- Coordinated major entertainment events & programs for physicians.
- Successful launch of new drugs, Starlix, Lamisil Tables and Diovan.

- Increased Diovan market share sales by 71% in 2000.
- Performed 48% better than the national average for share change in 2000.
- Consistently rank in the top 10 percent of market share sales over my career.
- Served as regional computer trainer. Trained 12 representatives on new computer system and software.
- Successfully completed management training course.

1998 – 1995 – Emery/PECC/Roadway Services, Peoria, IL

Territory Manager

- Sold small package transportation services to small and large companies.
- Ranked in top 5% of representatives for year 1993.
- Served as regional computer trainer for shipping systems.

EDUCATION

1998 – 2000 – Confidential University, Overland Park, KS

Masters of Business Administration

- GPA 4.00.

1985 – 1989 – Confidential University, Urbana, OH

Bachelor of Science Degree

- Secondary Education with emphasis in Math and Business
- Minor: Business Administration with an emphasis in Economics
- GPA 3.63.

COLLEGIATE ATHLETICS

1985 – 1988 – Confidential University, Urbana, OH

Football

- Four-year varsity letter-winner.
- All-Conference Lineman – 1987.
- Academic All-American – 1987.

REFERENCES Available upon request

SAMPLE RÉSUMÉ - **AFTER**

Confidential

1234 East West Drive Cell 129-985-9855
Any Town, MO 12536 confidential@gmail.com

EXECUTIVE SUMMARY

Medical Sales Specialist with 15+ years of consistent, progressive experience. Proven track record in account management and implementation of cost-benefit solutions to acute care and long-term care facilities.

- Wound Care Education
- Protocol Design
- Skin Care Education
- Formulary/Contract Creation
- Infection Control Education
- In-service/Implementation

EDUCATION

Confidential UNIVERSITY – MASTER OF BUSINESS ADMINISTRATION May 2000 – GPA 4.00

Confidential UNIVERSITY – BACHELOR OF SCIENCE June 1989 – Education/Business – GPA 3.63

CAREER EXPERIENCE

CONFIDENTIAL COMPANY – March 2004 – Present

Specializing in selling advanced wound care and skin care products in acute care and long-term healthcare accounts. Selling silver antimicrobial dressings for infection prevention in OR applications.

Advanced Wound Care Product Specialist

- Achieved President's Club five out of seven years.
- Designed and implemented customized silver antimicrobial dressing protocols for applications of infection control in key hospitals (Shawnee Mission, Research, Wesley, and Freeman hospitals) and nursing homes (Tutera Group). This process resulted in an increase of silver dressing sales of 453% ($450,000+) and reduced facility acquired infections by 90% and an average cost-savings of $300,000 per facility.
- Converted key GPO accounts (HPG, Premier and Novation) for skin care products by taking consultative approach and selling on value and reduction in hospital acquired pressure ulcers. These conversions resulted in a 557% ($750,000) increase of skin care products in the acute care accounts and reduced hospital acquired pressure ulcers by 85%, saving facilities, on average, $43,000 per incident.
- In just four years, grew territory from sales of $250,000 to $1.6 million, resulting in the necessity to split the territory into two separate territories.
- Ranked #3 in total sales growth for 2009, with sales of $750,000.

HUNTLEIGH HEALTHCARE – April 2001 – February 2004

Specialized in selling pressure-relieving and pressure-reducing support surfaces in acute care and long-term care facilities, as well as DVT prophylaxis systems in acute care facilities.

Sales consultant

- Achieved President's Club three years.
- Quota achievement three out of four years (average quota attainment 115%).
- Increased market share by 129%.
- Reduced facility acquired pressure ulcers in Beverly Healthcare accounts by 85% ($190,000) by selling alternating air pressure-relieving DFS3.
- Converted Heartland Hospital from Kendall DVT system to Huntliegh DVT by selling value of increased patient satisfaction and cost-savings associated with reprocessing of re-usable garments. This conversion resulted in $125,000 in new business per year, while at the same time, saving the hospital $80,000 per year.

SANDOZ/NOVARTIS PHARMACEUTICALS – January 1995 – February 2001

Specialized in selling cardiovascular prescription drugs Diovan and Lotrel to Family Practice Physicians, Internal Medicine Physicians, General Practitioners, and Cardiologists in the Kansas City, MO, sales territory. Also sold Starlix, a prescription drug indicated for the treatment of Type II diabetes.

- Increased Diovan market share sales by 71% in 2000.
- Performed 48% better than the national average for share change in 2000.
- Consistently ranked in the top 10% of market share sales over my career.
- Served as regional computer trainer. Trained 12 representatives on new computer system and software.
- Successfully completed management training courses.

EMERY/PECC/ROADWAY SERVICES – October 1990 – January 1995

Specialized in selling logistics solutions and services to small and large businesses.

- Converted Caterpillar Parts Distribution Center small package shipments which resulted in $160,000 in new business per year, while saving Caterpillar $90,000 in labor costs associated with shipping packages.
- Converted L R Nelson Corporation to ground and air services, by integrating customer service, accounting and shipping departments, resulting new sales of $145,000, while saving L R Nelson Corporation $50,000 and dramatically improving customer service.
- Ranked in top 5% of sales representatives in 1993.
- Quota attainment 1991 – 1995 (average quota attainment 120%).
- Served as regional computer trainer for shipping systems.

SAMPLE RÉSUMÉ – **AFTER** Continued

ADDITIONAL INFORMATION

COLLEGIATE ATHLETICS - 1985 – 1988

Played four years of college football at the NAIA level.

- Four-year varsity letter winner.
- All-Conference Lineman – 1987.
- Academic All-American – 1987.

REMEMBER, YOU ARE IN THE *SALES* BUSINESS!

Once our recruiting firm decides to present a candidate to one of our client companies to fill one of their open positions, we stress to the candidate that, from that point forward, he or she should consider himself/herself in the *sales* business. As you can perhaps imagine, we quite often get some stammering and stuttering from some candidates, who usually say something like this: "No, I am a chemist (or whatever). I don't know anything about sales!" Our usual response? "*Au contraire.* You're definitely in the sales business, whether you know it or not, or whether you *like* it or not. And the 'product' you are selling is YOU!"

If you intend to be successful in landing your new job, you have to adopt this same type of thinking, this same attitude. Your marketing/sales brochure is your résumé, and it better be a good one to succeed in today's still challenging job market. Just as you wouldn't be likely to make a major purchase from a person (or his/her company) who handed you a sloppily designed, unfocused and largely unprofessional, rambling sales/marketing brochure, you can be absolutely assured that a hiring manager, headhunter or Human Resources professional will eye your résumé in the same light!

Once you have crafted your brand-new, *job-winning* résumé, though, you are hardly done. Next comes the crafting of another, equally important job-hunting document, the all-important **cover letter**. This very important, though oftentimes largely ignored, document is addressed in the next chapter.

Thinking of 'BLASTING' Your Résumé? Think Again!

A number of companies offer a résumé "blasting" service, and they promise that they can get your résumé in front of "thousands" of headhunters and other appropriate hiring professionals. And for the most part they can! The only problem is, taking this approach reduces you to a mere "commodity," not a unique professional with marketable skills and a specific professional *brand*! You become nothing more than just another member of the job-hunting "herd"!

Is a Visual Résumé for You? Maybe.

While the number of hiring companies today that will consider (or are actually set up to consider) visual résumés is still rather limited, as technology advances, it's likely that we will undoubtedly see a greater shift toward visual résumés and away from the traditional paper résumé. But we're probably still years away from that situation.

Today, a still rather limited number of job seekers are employing a visual résumé in their job search, usually by integrating it with professional networking sites such as LinkedIn, but growing numbers are using a visual *supplement* to their paper résumé. This visual supplement, for example, might illustrate your career history and significant accomplishments during your career through use of a timeline or infographic.

To locate sites that offer visual résumé services, simply go online using your favorite search engine and enter something such as this search string: "visual résumé services." Many sites offer FREE services which may be of value to you during your new job search.

Chapter Four

YOUR COVER LETTER

Craft a Lazy, One-Size-Fits-All Cover Letter and It (*and* Your Brand-New, *Job-Winning* Résumé) Can Easily End Up in a Place You Never Quite Intended!

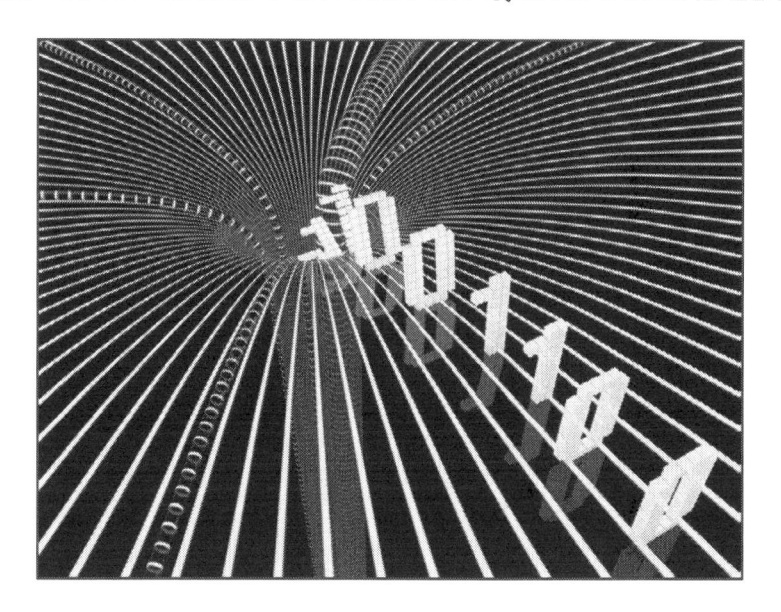

Once you have created your new, sparkling, *job-winning* résumé, it's then time to create the accompanying cover letter. Don't *you* make the mistake that so many, many job seekers make today, by creating a lazy, one-size-fits-all cover letter, one that's obviously merely thrown together almost as an afterthought! Here is an example of the type of cover letter I'm talking about:

DATE

ABC Technology Company
123 Main Street
Anywhere, USA 12345

To Whom It May Concern:

Please find enclosed my résumé, which I am submitting in reference to the (**name of position**) you have advertised in (**anywhere**).

I am very interested in this position and would appreciate the opportunity to visit with you about it at your very earliest convenience.

Feel free to call me at 123-456-7890.

Thank you for your consideration and I look forward to discussing this position with you in the very near future.

Sincerely,

Your Name and Signature

Well, you may be thinking to yourself, actually, this cover letter looks (and sounds) pretty good to me. It's professional in tone, direct and to the point, specific as to the position being sought, etc., etc., etc. While you may indeed think all of these things about this cover letter example, you would nonetheless be wrong—very wrong! Why is that so? Oh, let me count the reasons:

First, I've never met a hiring manager, headhunter or Human Resources professional named "To Whom It May Concern," have you? I didn't think so. The point is, if you can't (or won't) take the time and make the effort to learn the *name* of the person doing the hiring for a position you're seeking, why would you expect that person to take the time and make the effort to read *your* cover letter and résumé?!

Second, what is the primary focus of this cover letter? Is it on the company? The person doing the actual hiring? No, it's pretty much focused on the job seeker! "*I* am very interested in this position . . ." "Please feel free to call *me* . . ." You know what, at this very early stage in the hiring game, neither the company nor the hiring professional, who *may* read this cover letter (and, it is hoped, *may* actually read your résumé), couldn't care less about what *you* want! All the hiring professional and the company he or she represents care about at this stage of the game is what *they* want, nothing more.

And third, there is nothing—absolutely nothing!—in this cover letter that would give the recipient any "cause for pause." What does the writer include that might make the hiring professional have any desire whatsoever to read on, to investigate further, let alone to actually give this candidate a call?! What past (or current) qualifications/accomplishments are cited or highlighted in the cover letter that might grab the reader's attention?

COVER LETTER THE PREAMBLE, THE ENTRÉE, TO YOUR CANDIDACY

Think of your cover letter as the preamble, the entrée not only to your résumé, but also to your entire candidacy as well. It must therefore *immediately* grab the reader's attention and make him or her actually *want* to read on, actually want to further investigate what you may have to offer him or her and the hiring company. Otherwise, your cover letter *and* your résumé, which may in fact be a sparkling, *job-winning* one, likely will end up in the cover letter and résumé black hole!

Your Cover Letter

On the following page is a cover letter that I *know* meets the criteria outlined in the previous paragraph. How do I know that? Because this cover letter is from a candidate whom we coached and presented—successfully!—to one of our Fortune 500 client companies.

DATE

Mr. Tom Jones
Vice President of Engineering
XYZ Corporation
412 Industrial Parkway
Atlanta, GA 30045

Dear Mr. Jones:

How I can reduce your utility system's energy costs
and ensure that your utility system doesn't keep you awake at night!

I have a **proven track record** of . . .

- Reducing utility system energy costs
- Effectively implementing preventative maintenance programs to avoid unexpected downtime

The utility system of a plant is its "heartbeat." As an experienced utility engineer, **I understand the criticality** of . . .

- Preventative maintenance
- No unexpected downtime
- Reduced energy costs
- Reduced emissions
- And no lost time due to health and safety issues

Mr. Jones, my mission is to ensure that you don't get a phone call at midnight because something went down due to utilities.

I will call you on Thursday, March 8, 2015, at 8:00 a.m. ET to discuss how I can be of value to you at any of your facilities in the Midwest. If this is not a convenient time, **please ask Ms. Roberts to call me and suggest another time.**

Sincerely,

Skip Freeman
678-123-4567
Skip.Freeman@HireToWin.com
www.linkedin.com/in/skipfreeman

P.S. – Please call me today to learn how I **reduced energy costs 12%** and **effluent discharge by 15%** over the past year at my current manufacturing facility.

9 'Secrets' That Made This Cover Letter Work

Why did this particular cover letter work? There are essentially NINE primary reasons, or "secrets," that went into making this cover letter, along with the candidate's résumé, a *job-winning* one:

SECRET 1

This cover letter is **addressed to a *specific person***, i.e., the person doing the actually hiring, the person who is "feeling the pain" of not having a critical position filled. It is therefore *vital* that your cover letter also be addressed to a specific person.

SECRET 2

Actually, this particular cover letter was **sent to the decision-maker via U.S. Certified Mail**. (And that is a tactic *you* might *strongly* consider using for your own cover letter because, as this is being written, at least, it is a tactic that is working very well for reaching a decision-maker in today's job market.) That meant that it was absolutely *guaranteed* to be delivered! It also *substantially* improved the chances that it would get opened *and* read. (After all, how many people today could resist opening a piece of mail like this?!) (NOTE: No "return receipt" was asked for and, if you use this method of delivery for your cover letter, you shouldn't ask for one, either.)

SECRET 3

Notice the **"newspaper" headline** that was featured at the top of the cover letter:

How I can reduce your utility system's energy costs and ensure that your utility system doesn't keep you awake at night!

I think you will have to agree that this device quickly and effectively draws the reader's attention to the body of the cover letter and certainly would tweak his or her interest in reading further.

Your COVER LETTER

Here are some other effective newspaper-style headlines:

**Is your open Sales Manager position
in the Southwest keeping you awake at night?**
(Include a packet of instant Starbucks® coffee.)

**I can alleviate your headache
caused by your vacant Controller position!**
(Include a packet of Aleve® in the letter.)

SECRET 4

Notice how effectively both the **"lead-in" sentence** and the following **bullet points** were used in this cover letter example:

The utility system of a plant is its "heartbeat." As an experienced utility engineer, I understand the criticality of . . .

- Preventative maintenance
- No unexpected downtime
- Reduced energy costs
- Reduced emissions
- And no lost time due to health and safety issues

This candidate not only positioned himself as someone who clearly knows what the job consists of, but also as someone who can offer substantive *solutions* to the problems inherent in the position. Unlike so many candidates, this candidate clearly defined himself and what he can bring to the table. He didn't make the hiring manager *guess* what he could do, what he had to offer.

SECRET 5

This candidate included information in his cover letter that was designed to get the hiring manager EXCITED! To make the hiring manager actually *want* to speak to the candidate. Why? Because the candidate clearly branded himself as someone who understands and empathizes with the hiring manager's "pain":

> Mr. Jones, my mission is to ensure that you don't get a phone call at midnight because something went down due to utilities.

SECRET 6

In his cover letter, this candidate clearly **underscored his commitment to seeking the position** by telling the hiring manager that *he*, the candidate, would be **calling him** (not presuming to ask the hiring manager to call him!) **at a *specific* time** and **date**:

> **I will call you** on **Thursday, March 8, 2015, at 8:00 a.m. ET** to discuss how I can be of value to you at any of your facilities in the Midwest.

SECRET 7

One very workable—and very rarely thought of—"secret" that contributed to the success of this candidate's cover letter is that he **included the name of the hiring manager's administrative assistant:**

> If this is not a convenient time, **please ask Ms. Roberts to call me and suggest another time.**

Not only does this add a personal touch to your letter, it also positions you as a professional who is courteous and detailed in his/her approach to business matters. Plus, if you are successful in getting an interview, "Ms. Roberts" may indeed be able—and willing!—to assist you in some way.

This secret only works, of course, if the letter is going to someone high enough in the organization to have an assistant. (Oftentimes, these higher-level people, by the way, **actively** look for talent!)

How can you learn the names of administrative assistants? Easy! Call up the company and simply ask!

SECRET 8

Note that this candidate also featured the following information in the signature block:

- Phone number
- Email address
- LinkedIn profile link

Make sure you do too! Why? Because you want to make it as easy and as convenient as possible for the hiring manager to contact you!

SECRET 9

A key element of a good, effective cover letter is the addition of a postscript (P.S.), and of course this candidate included one in his cover letter:

> P.S. – Please call me today to learn how I **reduced energy costs 12%** and **effluent discharge by 15%** over the past year at my current manufacturing facility.

Actually, this is nothing more than Marketing 101 logic and practice. Study after study has shown that **eight out of ten** people who open a letter (and remember, if you send your cover letter via U.S. Certified Mail, it *will* be opened!) and read it will *first* read the P.S.

Here are some other sample P.S.'s that have proven quite effective:

> **P.S.** By the way, Jim Treadwell of Cannon Engineering suggested that we speak. (*Yes! drop a name, if indeed you have been able to get a reference or a referral.*)

> **P.S.** Your article in the February 2015 edition of ***Engineering News*** was excellent! I have a question I would love to ask you.

Additional Tips/Comments About Effective Cover Letters

This chapter is by no means intended to serve as an exhaustive study of cover letters. Rather, the intention here is to provide you with a useful, usable primer on the subject. Indeed there are many fine books on the market today that solely address this specific topic. (To locate such resources, go to Amazon.com, and in "books," type in this search phrase: "cover letter books." Yes, you'll see ***Headhunter Hiring Secrets: The Rules of the Hiring Game Have Changed . . . Forever!*** and ***Headhunter Hiring Secrets 2.0*** included in the books that will be returned by your search, but my books are hardly the only really good ones featuring information about writing effective, interview-getting, job-getting cover letters!)

Here are a few more tips to keep in mind when crafting *your job-winning* cover letter:

- **Keep it simple and focused**, while retaining the necessary specifics, and avoid using BIG words, i.e., use everyday, simple language and sentence constructions.

- **Make sure that you "ask for the order"!** If the goal of your cover letter is to a.) get the hiring authority to become interested enough to at least scan your résumé at this point; and b.) to get an interview (and certainly both of these things *better* be among your cover letter goals!), then make sure you indicate that in your cover letter.

- **Keep your cover letter to *one* page** and *one* page only!

Now that you have a well-crafted, *targeted* cover letter to include with your *job-winning* résumé, the next step is to get them both in the hands of hiring professionals, in order to make them aware of your qualifications—and your availability! One of your very first stops to accomplish this task should be www.linkedin.com, and that's the topic addressed in the next chapter.

CHAPTER FIVE

YOUR LINKEDIN PROFILE

POSTING YOUR PROFILE & PICTURE ON LINKEDIN IS NOT THE SAME THING AS REALLY BEING *ON* LINKEDIN!

As this is being written, about 400+ million professionals worldwide have joined LinkedIn, by far the most popular, most effective professional networking site on the Web. Today, it is the first-stop shop for most headhunters, hiring managers and Human Resources professionals when they go searching for new, top professional talent to fill their open career positions.[11]

You probably have already posted your profile and picture on LinkedIn, but that certainly isn't the same thing as actually being *on* LinkedIn in any meaningful way. Chances are, if you are like many (if not *most*) professionals, you may have let your profile languish. That is, you haven't kept it updated and current since you first posted it. You haven't ensured that your profile includes the key words and phrases that you know (or at least *should* know) headhunters, hiring managers and Human Resources professionals will include in a talent search. The picture you posted probably does you more harm than good, or at least it does *not* project the professional image you need to project, if you do indeed want to land a great new job.

No single chapter in *any* book, including this one, could possibly do justice to the many facets of LindedIn and its wide array of networking opportunities for professionals. In this chapter, you will be provided with a general overview of this dynamic site and be made aware of some of the basic professional networking services it can offer you. If you want to delve much, much deeper into all that LinkedIn offers you, then check out some of the current Amazon.com bestsellers on the subject. (Suggestion: Pay particular attention to books that have at least a couple of hundred four-star and above reviews. That way, you can be assured that the material has been pretty thoroughly vetted by readers seeking to learn *useful* information about LinkedIn.)

That said, however, I caution you *not* to try to do everything at once on LinkedIn. Take your time and proceed at a measured pace, carefully building your professional image, your professional *brand*, block by block.

If, perchance, you happen to be one of the ten or so professionals in the world who are *not* yet on LinkedIn, following is a brief summary on how to accomplish that very necessary professional task. (If you already have an account, then merely pick up on the appropriate steps outlined in this chapter to repair or expand your presence.)

---

[11]The information featured in this chapter was accurate when these words were written (yearend 2015). However, because LinkedIn is such a dynamic site, interface information and site features are always subject to change. The basic information featured, as well as the overall approaches recommended, nonetheless remain unchanged.

Getting Started with LinkedIn

It's easy and FREE to sign up for a basic LinkedIn account. Merely go to this link to get started: www.linkedin.com. Simply follow the on-screen, step-by-step instructions to begin building your professional presence on LinkedIn.

Before you actually begin the process of building your in-depth LinkedIn profile, you will be asked to select the type of account you want on the site, i.e., free basic account or the premium account. For most of you, the free account will more than adequately serve your purposes at this point.

The FREE basic account allows you to do the following:

- Create a professional profile and build your network.
- Join industry or alumni groups.
- Search and apply for jobs.

Essentially, the information that you will have to provide to begin building your complete profile consists of the following:

- Job experience and employers
- Education
- Skill sets and expertise

Although, theoretically, you can expedite the building of your professional profile by uploading a copy of your current (and new and sparkling!) résumé, the information contained in your résumé sometimes doesn't always translate well into your LinkedIn profile. You can certainly test it out for yourself, though, by uploading your résumé to your profile.

(**Suggestion:** Try converting your résumé to an Adobe .pdf file. That seems to work best for uploading to your LinkedIn profile, particularly if your résumé was created in Microsoft Word and you used the Table function to create it.)

If you do in fact upload your résumé and are satisfied with the way the information was translated, great! If not, well, you can simply manually enter the information, which really isn't all that tedious. Be sure to keep your résumé handy as a reference, though, as you're completing your profile because you will want to be sure to pick up (and incorporate) the various key words and phrases, as well as sentence structure, featured in your résumé. Remember: Headhunters, hiring managers and Human

Resources professionals all employ **key words** and **key phrases** in their LinkedIn searches for top talent. Make sure you have these elements in *your* LinkedIn profile!

COMPLETE YOUR LINKEDIN PROFILE—100%!

Although you certainly don't have to complete *everything* at once on LinkedIn, you would be well advised to make sure your profile is **100% complete** as soon as possible.[12] Why? Research clearly shows that users with completed profiles are ***40 times more likely*** to receive opportunities through LinkedIn than those who have *not* completed theirs. So, don't even *think* about joining groups, making comments on discussions, etc., until you have completed your profile—100%!

What is the definition of a *completed* LinkedIn profile? At a minimum, your profile should feature the following information:

- Your **industry** and **location**.
- An **up-to-date current position** (with description), as well as *two* **past positions**.
- Your **education credentials** (both formal and professional).
- A specific **description of your unique skill sets** (minimum of three).
- A **profile photo**.
- At least **50 connections**.

Also, make sure your *public* profile is indeed "public," i.e., that it is visible to any and all visitors to the LinkedIn site. Keep in mind: Your public profile is the one that is visible on search engines, and that means hiring professionals can then find you through online searches. Therefore, ensure your public profile is set to be visible to everyone and it will appear in search engine listings.

---

[12] It's easy to see whether your profile needs more work because LinkedIn displays a "percentage score," indicating level of completeness.

VITAL IMPORTANCE OF KEY WORDS

The importance of incorporating key words throughout your LinkedIn presence, particularly in your profile and professional summary, simply cannot be overstated. Whenever a hiring professional conducts a search for top talent on LinkedIn, he or she designs that search using key words, e.g., "vice president – marketing," "technical sales," etc. In order for you to be included in such searches, obviously, you are going to have to incorporate the key words used by these hiring professionals in their searches in *your* LinkedIn presence. But how do you know which key words to use? There is help out there.

There are a number of key word generator sites on the Web, and some are free and others charge fees, the amount of which depends largely on level of usage. Simply type in "key word generation sites" to your search engine to locate such sites.

CHANGE LINKEDIN-ASSIGNED PROFILE URL TO A MORE USER-FRIENDLY ONE

Your public profile is the version (and the page) of your LinkedIn profile which appears in search engines, such as Google. However, the standard Uniform Resource Locator (URL) which LinkedIn assigns you is *not* at all user-friendly, or for that matter, Search Engine Optimization (SEO)-friendly, either (both equally important considerations when it comes to being able to be contacted by a hiring professional). To address this issue, reconfigure your public profile URL in the following (or similar) fashion:

www.linkedin.com/in/firstnamelastname

CREATE STRONG, *SPECIFIC* MASTHEAD FOR YOUR PROFILE

In the event your profile surfaces during a search conducted by a hiring professional, because it included at least *some* of the keywords included in his or her search, you need to give very serious consideration to the professional headline you feature in the masthead of your LinkedIn profile. (It is displayed at the top of your profile, just below your name, as shown in my LinkedIn profile at the top of the next page.) The quality, or lack thereof, of the headline you use largely determines whether or not a hiring professional will actually take the time to learn more about you and

YOUR LINKEDIN PROFILE

Skip Freeman
CEO, HTW (Hire to Win) Executive Search || Author - Headhunter Hiring Secrets - Amazon bestseller || www.hiretowin.com
Greater Atlanta Area | Staffing and Recruiting

Current   The HTW Group (Hire to Win) Executive Search
           www.hiretowin.com

Previous   National Filtration Systems, Berendsen Fluid Power, BetzDearborn

Education United States Military Academy at West Point

Send Skip InMail   500+ connections

your potential qualifications for any position(s) he or she is attempting to fill.

How likely, for example, is it that a profile that features a headline saying "Open to New Opportunities" will entice someone to click on that profile to learn more about the person? Many people are open to new opportunities, aren't they? Since you only have **120 characters maximum** for your professional headline, don't waste valuable real estate by featuring a meaningless, ho-hum headline.

My suggestion: Consider using this type of headline at the top of your LinkedIn profile (total character count = 119):

JANE SMITH

Salesperson – Chemical (Surfactants) Sales – Driving Results Through Solution Selling!

Current – XYZ Chemical Co.

Previous – ABC Chemical Co.

A hiring professional looking to fill a position such as this will undoubtedly include terms such as **"Sales"** or **"Salesperson," "Chemical Sales,"** and quite probably, (if he or she is looking for a *surfactant* salesperson) **"Surfactants"** in his or her keyword search. All of that information will be in this masthead, while the remainder of the copy has been used to creatively *differentiate* this candidate from other candidates, i.e., "Driving Results Through Solution Selling!"

YOUR LINKEDIN PROFILE PICTURE

You will also be able to upload your picture to your LinkedIn profile, and it is *strongly* recommend that you do so![13] Studies have shown that **posting a *professional* picture with your profile *significantly* increases the number of "views" on LinkedIn**. And also, remember, in virtually all instances, the first time a headhunter, hiring manager or Human Resources professional gets the chance to actually "see" you is when they look at the picture you posted of yourself on LinkedIn.

What kind of a photograph should you upload? In short, a *professional* picture! What is meant by a *professional* picture? Well, maybe the best way to answer that question is to first tell you what is *not* considered to be a professional picture (and yes, I have seen every single one of these picture types—and much, much more on LinkedIn!):

- **Any "group" or "couple" picture** (unless you mean to imply that any potential employer must consider hiring *everyone* in the group if they want to consider hiring *you*!)

- **"Glamour" shots** (Keep these types of photos for your boyfriend/girlfriend or husband/wife or significant other.)

- **Pictures taken from 1,000 yards** (or more) **away**.

- **A photo of you and "Rover" (or "Fluffy")**. Unless you are a veterinarian or animal trainer, keep these types of pictures on your mantle at home or in your wallet/purse.

- **Your wedding photo** or **a picture of you and baby**. (GREAT for Facebook; not so great for LinkedIn.)

    A "pixelated" (blurred) or "warped" photo. These types of photos result from trying to make an existing, *very small* photograph, which lacks adequate definition, into a larger photograph, or by improper "sizing."[14]

---

[13] You should *never* put a picture on your résumé, however.

[14] **Tip:** After "selecting" (with your cursor) a digital photo, which is *suitable* for enlarging, you must "grab" a *corner* and stretch the entire photo to enlarge it. If you grab, say, either the horizontal *or* vertical lines/borders to enlarge the photo, it will appear to be "warped" because you will have lost the original proportions of the photo.

- **A ten-year (or 15 or more!) old photo.** Yes, I know you want to appear as "young" and as attractive as you possibly can, but LinkedIn is not the place to do this. Posting a photo that doesn't even come close to reflecting the current "you" smacks of "bait and switch," so don't do it!
- **Black and white pictures.** Remember, *color sells*, so never use any photo that is *not* in color.
- **"Avatar"**[15] **pictures**. While indeed the hiring process is a "game," as a general rule, you still shouldn't use avatars (or logos, products, etc.) to represent yourself on LinkedIn.
- **A *clearly un*professional picture,** i.e., one taken in a bar (or one of you holding what looks to be an alcoholic beverage in *any* location!), on the beach, at a party, etc.

Here are some additional tips on photo considerations provided by the experts at LinkedIn:

- **Make sure you are dressed to reflect the atmosphere of the profession that you're in or hope to join.** For example, an open-neck shirt or blouse might be appropriate for a sales position, but if the position is a top sales *management* position, you would be far safer wearing a business suit (and for men, a tie) for your photo.
- **Choose a picture that conveys your energy and personality.** Example: If you want to project the image of being a people person, make sure you have a *genuine* smile on your face and a twinkle in your eyes!
- **Be aware of your posture. Sit up straight. Good posture signifies confidence and competence.** (As it turns out, your mother was offering you good, sound advice when she may have continually told you to "sit up straight!")
- **Make sure your eyes are relaxed and you have a smile on your face.** You've undoubtedly heard the saying about "the eyes have it"? Well, they do. Squinty eyes or a dagger-like stare will absolutely, positively *not* communicate anything positive about you!

---

[15] A graphic image used to represent a person.

- **Posting a photo is a must, especially for women who have married and changed their names.** Or, if you have a common name such as "Nicole Williams," since there can easily be several (or more!) women with this same name on the site.

Your LinkedIn 'Professional Summary'

Arguably, today, your LinkedIn "professional summary" is at least as important as the one you should include in your résumé. Also, your LinkedIn professional summary may be as much as two to three times longer that the one included in your résumé. Usually, a professional summary featured in a résumé is just one paragraph or two very short paragraphs, but your LinkedIn professional summary could easily be two or three sizable paragraphs.

There is of course no one way to design your professional summary in your LinkedIn profile. (See how I have designed mine at the top of the next page.) It is crucial, however, to keep in mind that, like all elements in your profile, you must make maximum use of the rather limited space you have *and* it must *immediately* give a hiring professional "cause for pause."

The use of bullet points, arrows and other graphic elements (such as I've used in my professional summary) can serve to focus a hiring professional's eyes on the key elements of the summary.

Next Steps in Completing Your LinkedIn Profile

Once you've completed the masthead, the professional summary and selected an appropriate, *professional* picture to run with your LinkedIn profile, the next steps are to complete additional vital information that a hiring professional will want to know, including, but certainly not limited to the following:

- Work experience (in reverse chronological order).
- Honors and awards you may have received.
- Any publications (or blogs) you have been/are associated with.
- Education (formal *and* professional).
- Any appropriate groups and/or associations.

> Skip Freeman's Summary
>
> Skip.Freeman@HireToWin.com
> 678-377-4706
>
> *Notice that my **contact information** is the first thing you see in my "Professional Summary." If you want to be found by hiring professionals, yours should be as prominent!*
>
> We are currently recruiting for over 100 openings.
> View them at: http://www.hiretowin.com/index.asp?id=164
>
> ▶ CEO: The HTW Group (Hire to Win) Executive Search
>
> ▶ Author of:
> • Headhunter Hiring Secrets (Amazon.com bestseller - Job Hunting Category - http://bit.ly/HeadhunterSecrets)
> • How to be Headhunted by Top Recruiters (Amazon.com)
> • Resume Writing Made Easy (Includes 6 downloadable easy to use templates)
>
> ▶ Contributing Author to: Guerrilla Marketing for Job Hunters 3.0

If you are new to LinkedIn, or uncertain about how you should proceed in providing this additional information, please feel free to visit me on LinkedIn and see how I've designed my profile. Go to this link:

http://www.linkedin.com/in/skipfreeman

LINK TO OR CREATE A COMPANY PROFILE

Many headhunters, hiring managers and Human Resources professional look for a completed profile on previous and/or current employers you've included in your LinkedIn profile. (If a *company* has completed a LinkedIn profile, the company icon automatically appears next to the company name.) Knowing something about previous and/or current employers, i.e., what products and/or services the company markets, competitive market position, etc., helps better position *your* professional brand, as well as strongly influences a potential hiring company's perception of your overall professional qualifications and credentials.

If, for some reason, any of your previous employers have *not* completed a LinkedIn profile, consider contacting them and asking them to do so. You might even offer to assist them in that endeavor.

IMMEDIATELY START MAKING CONNECTIONS, SOLICITING RECOMMENDATIONS!

Once you have completed (or nearly completed) your LinkedIn profile, you'll *immediately* want to start making **connections**. Until you do that, you will *not* begin to fully employ and utilize the amazing, tremendous professional networking power the site offers you.

A good place to start is by *immediately* making **connections** with other professionals (and groups) on the site, and once connected with them, to begin soliciting **recommendations** from individual professionals. But use caution here and ask for recommendations *only* from those professionals with whom you've had a *meaningful* and *logical* previous connection, e.g., a colleague, a current or former boss, an associate, et al.[16]

To the extent possible, ask those writing recommendations for you to be *specific,* by mentioning *specific* achievements/accomplishments, citing *specific* professional characteristics they feel you exemplify, etc.

How many recommendations should you feature in your profile? My recommendation is **three** to **four**, maximum. Any more than that will make your recommendations look "fishy" and/or contrived, any fewer than that, though, will make you look as though you're not even in the game.

The real power of LinkedIn is in the richness and depth, i.e., number and types of **connections**, you have in your network. Why? Because it is only through these connections that you will be able to be found by hiring professionals searching for top talent. If you are not in *their* network, you simply may not appear in their searches.

> Most LinkedIn job search experts contend that **it takes at least 300 *views* before you become a serious job contender**. The *average* number of views, however, is about 1 to 2 a day!

---

[16]Obviously, if you ask a *current* boss (or other superior) to write a recommendation for you, caution is definitely called for. That is, it can't even be *suspected* that you are searching for a new career opportunity! Rather, the request should be positioned as merely your quest to become more involved in your particular professional specialty by networking with other professionals in your specialty.

The way to tell how frequently your profile is surfacing during searches is to click on the "profile" tab on your LinkedIn page and select **"Who's Viewed Your Profile"** from the drop-down menu. You are also provided valuable tips on how to actually *increase* the number of views your profile is getting.

ENHANCING YOUR LINKEDIN PRESENCE

Got a work sample, presentation, image or video that you're especially proud of and would like to highlight in your LinkedIn profile? It's relatively easy to accomplish that goal, and it can definitely enhance your overall image and profile on LinkedIn.

Simply select "Edit Profile" on the "home" page of your profile, scroll down to the appropriate section (for example, "Work Experience") where you want to add a video, image, presentation, etc., click on the dropdown menu in the symbol that is a box with a "+" sign (next to "Edit") and follow directions.

STAY *ACTIVELY* AND *CONTINUALLY* INVOLVED ON LINKEDIN

No matter how well-built and professionally prepared your LinkedIn profile may be, or how many connections and recommendations you have managed to accumulate, unless you stay *actively* and *regularly* engaged on LinkedIn, it will all be meaningless and come to naught. Check your messages *daily*, and then *respond* to those messages while you have them on the screen of your computer (or other device)! Don't wait until "tomorrow," which sometimes never seems to come for some people.

If you don't stay *continually* and *actively* engaged, you will be perceived as a.) lazy; b.) virtually non-responsive; or (worse) c.) not really all that interested in new career opportunities. Then, your professional image, your professional *brand*, will be irrevocably tarnished and any realistic hopes of landing your *ideal* job will essentially be extinguished!

WHAT *EFFECTIVE* 'NETWORKING' IS—AND IS **NOT!**

Notwithstanding the tremendous power and versatility of networking on LinkedIn, you should keep in mind that it is still *networking*. And that means that, in order to be effective, you must adhere to the proper protocol, practices and approaches inherent in good, *effective* networking.

To many, if not most, job-seekers, "networking" means going to various meetings, parties, industry events, etc., and seeking out other people there who may be able to "get you a job." Wrong! **Truly *effective* networking does *not* involve *asking* for a job!** Rather, it's seeking advice and assistance from other professionals with a challenge you (or even they!) are facing: Attempting to advance your career by seeking out, and then landing, your *ideal* job.

As I point out in ***Headhunter Hiring Secrets: The Rules of the Hiring Game Have Changed . . . Forever!***, THE **key phrase** to use while networking is this:

> **"Whom do you know. . . ?"** As in, **"Whom do you know that I should be talking to, if I want to move my sales career to the next level?"**

This question literally takes the person you're networking with off the hook, while still perhaps getting you information and valuable leads.

Another vital point to keep in mind about *effective* networking is that it is *reciprocal*, i.e., after asking another professional's advice and/or assistance, you should end the contact with a statement such as this:

> **"Now, Susan, what can I do to help you advance in *your* career, if that's what you would like to do?"**

That way, you and the other person ("Susan," in this case) have at least tentatively formed a professional bond, which may produce amazing results, if not now, then perhaps not too far down the line.

The point is, while it's extremely unlikely that you will ever meet any of your LinkedIn contacts personally, you should still strictly adhere to the same rules of decorum and good practices that would apply to those whom you actually do meet—and network with—personally. Those job-seekers who buy in to this concept, and then put it into regular and routine practice and use while interacting with LinkedIn contacts, can expect good results. Those who don't? You don't even want to know.

OTHER PROFESSIONAL NETWORKING SITES TO CONSIDER

While LinkedIn is without question the "800-pound gorilla" in the professional networking room, there are also some "400-pound gorillas" in the room, and it can pay you to also check them out.

I strongly advise you to develop, and then tightly control and *maintain*, your professional image and information, as well as your presence, at these FOUR other sites:

- **ZoomInfo** (www.zoominfo.com)
- **Google+** (https://plus.google.com)
- **Data.com** (formerly Jigsaw.com) (FREE edition: https://connect.data.com/registration/signup?signUpLinkType=buttonLink)
- **Slideshare** (www.slideshare.net) (Upload your résumé on Slideshare. Google algorithms will ensure that it will surface in a search.)

Make Sure You Can Be Contacted!

As pointed out in considerably more detail in the later chapter on headhunters, if you want to be in a position to take *maximum* advantage of the very best jobs available today through headhunters, hiring managers and Human Resources professionals, then make absolutely certain that you can be *easily* and *readily* contacted through LinkedIn and/or other professional networking sites.

In LinkedIn, you accomplish this task by making sure that you have checked the appropriate boxes on your contact settings, which can be accessed by clicking on the link entitled, "Change your contact settings," located at the bottom of your profile page.

Social Media Screening of Job Candidates on Rise!

With all of the clamor (outrage?) in recent years about employers using social media (particularly Facebook and Twitter), or more precisely, *posts* on these media, to screen job candidates, you might expect that a lot of hiring companies have wised up and have started backing off the practice. You would, however, be wrong, very wrong!

According to a 2014 joint CareerBuilder and Harris Poll survey of 2,138 hiring managers and Human Resources professionals, as well as 3,022 adults employed in the private sector across a variety of industries and companies . . .

- **Forty-three percent of employers** surveyed said they **now use social networking sites to research job candidates**—up 39 percent over 2013 and up 36 percent over 2012.

- Although **12 percent of employers** surveyed said they **don't now research candidates on social media**, they said they plan to start the practice.

How can this possibly be? you might be asking. Why are companies continuing, and even *escalating*, this practice, which is so "unfair," so unnecessarily "invasive" of a candidate's *personal* life? Simple answer: Because they can!

As long as the job market remains at least somewhat of a "buyer's market" from the standpoint of the hiring companies, employers will continue to do pretty much as they please. And, quite obviously, they are doing precisely that by continuing not only to use social media screening but even to *increase* its use when evaluating job candidates.

Be therefore forewarned: Take great care about what you post to any and all social sites. Plus, carefully monitor what *others* may post about you! Make absolutely certain that *your* image on social sites is always one of professionalism.

PART II
LET THE (HIRING) 'GAMES' BEGIN!

Now you have a good, clear mental picture of what your ideal job would look like. You have created a *job-winning* résumé and a hard-hitting, *laser-focused* cover letter. You have polished to near perfection your LinkedIn profile and other online presence. You also have a much clearer, more informed understanding of the job market. Guess what? You are now ready to begin playing in today's "hiring game"!

As you begin your journey toward your new, *ideal* job, you'll still have several more key decisions to make, including, but certainly not necessarily limited to, the following:

- What kind of a job hunter are you going to be, i.e., active? *somewhat* passive?[17] Or, a little of each approach?
- What role should the Internet play in your job search?
- Does it make sense for you to consider working with a headhunter during your new job search (the answer to this question may surprise you!)?
- What are the *best* ways to find—and then *target*—potential employers? How do you find the names of important contacts within these companies? And then, what are the best ways to actually make contact with them?
- How can you set up and maintain a steady, largely *passive* stream of contacts from potential employers and/or headhunters?

All of these considerations are covered in detail, along with the answers to the questions inherent in them, in the chapters featured in Part II.

Part II begins by first briefly addressing a phenomenon that most *currently* employed experience: Feelings of "guilt" and/or "betrayal" when they start seriously considering leaving their current employer to seek new, better career opportunities.

---

[17] Absolutely *no one*, including the currently employed, can be *completely* passive in today's job market and expect to land a GREAT new job!

Chapter Six

THE 'LOYALTY' ISSUE

IF CURRENTLY EMPLOYED . . .
FEELING A LITTLE 'GUILTY,'
A LITTLE 'DISLOYAL'
ABOUT LOOKING FOR A NEW JOB?
DON'T BE!

Let's get this out of the way right up front: I know that some of you who are currently employed are probably feeling a little "guilty" about searching for a new job, a bit "disloyal" to your current employer, right? Well, get over it!

Loyalty is indeed an admirable and highly valued trait—in *personal* relationships, i.e., our friends, families and spouses (or significant others). And oh, did I mention how very important it is to also be loyal to *ourselves*?! When it comes to business situations, however—and in particular the *business* relationship we have with a current employer—the waters can rather quickly become quite murky regarding the whole issue of loyalty.

For a surprising number of men and women, looking for a new job while currently employed is tantamount to being grossly disloyal and "unfaithful" to their current employer. Some people even compare the feelings they experience in this situation to those they might experience if they were "cheating" on their spouse or other love interest!

All of the recruiters at The HTW Group have had candidates approach them for assistance in finding a new job *after* they had already quit their existing jobs because they said they simply felt "too guilty," "too disloyal," to look for a new job while they were still employed! (Once they became unemployed we couldn't help them, of course, because no hiring company is going to pay a headhunter a fee for finding candidates they can easily find themselves.) Reality check!

In virtually any job market, and particularly in today's job market, it is always, always, always easier to get a new job if you already have one. No matter what you may *say* is the reason for quitting an existing job to search for a new one, potential employers will almost always perceive your leaving primarily in *negative* terms, e.g., "He/she probably quit because he/she was about to be fired, anyway." Or, "This person appears to be somewhat 'unstable' and lacking in good judgment. We'll pass."

WHERE YOUR *TRUE* LOYALTY SHOULD LIE

When it comes to loyalty in business, your *primary* focus should always be on *yourself* and on your overall, *entire* professional career. In other words, *you* should determine what's best for you and your family, not let the company you happen to be working for at the present make that decision for you. If you don't take FULL and COMPLETE control of your own career, your own destiny, by default, you'll end up leaving it to the capricious whims and ever-present uncertainties inherent in *any* business organization—including your current employer, if employed.

Being all too human, most of us tend to endow the company we work for, no matter the size or specific business focus, with certain, *positive*, *human* characteristics, such as warmth, caring, and reliability. All well and good perhaps, but this perception tends to overlook one very important fact about *any* business entity: Businesses are *not* social organizations, at least not in the traditional sense and general understanding of that term. The company is *not* the employee's "family," and fellow employees generally are *not* necessarily one's "best friends." A company—*any* company!—is in business for one *primary* reason and one reason only: To make money! Or at least it better be, because if it isn't in business to make money, it won't be in business long.

ON ANY GIVEN DAY . . .

Make no mistake about it, when (notice I didn't say "if"), on any given day at some point in the future, *your* job becomes redundant and/or counterproductive to *your* current company's ability to *make* money, you and your job will be history, usually without so much as even a moment's notice or a fare thee well.

It won't matter how long you've been with the company or how much of a personal/professional contribution you may have made (or are currently making) to the company's overall success—or even, the *intensity* of the loyalty you have consistently shown the company. You might even be told something like, "Hey, it's not personal, it's just business." And you know what? That is *precisely* what it is—*business*. It doesn't necessarily mean that the company and/or the people running it are "bad," or "evil," or "uncaring," it *is* just business. Happens every single business day. Let me give you an example of what I'm talking about here.

I recently received an email comment from one of my LinkedIn connections regarding a posting I had made about how tenuous one's position can be in today's job market. Here is what the man had to say:

> **"My 'wake-up call' was after talking with my District Sales Manager. I was telling him about all I felt I had done for the company. He looked at me and said, 'When you get that check every other week you and the company are even!'"**

'Nuff said?

WHAT YOU *ACTUALLY* OWE YOUR CURRENT EMPLOYER

Without question, as long as you are receiving a wage or salary (and provided benefits?) from a company, *any* company, you do *owe* that company, but what you owe is *not* undying, irrevocable loyalty! You owe the company your very best efforts and the honest exercise of your talents and skills while you are physically *on the job* or officially representing the employer elsewhere. You also of course owe the company honesty and integrity. That's about it! Anything you do while you are not on the job is your *personal* business! And that includes looking for a new job—for whatever reason(s)—**on your own time** and **using your own facilities and resources**.

The substance of the last sentence in the preceding paragraph is of course a key consideration, if you are currently employed and decide now is the time to start looking for a new, better career opportunity. Never, never, never conduct your new job search on company time. Don't use your current company email address as your contact email, and certainly don't use your company phone number as your contact number. Make sure that every single aspect of your new job search is done *on your dime* and *on your time*. (Remember, I said that you *do* owe your current employer both honesty and integrity!)

One other thing: If you're currently employed, don't be concerned that you may lose out on career opportunities if you have to tell potential employers (or those hiring professionals representing them) that you can only be contacted, or contact them, after business hours. Any headhunters, hiring managers or Human Resources professionals worth their salt will certainly understand—and respect!—the necessity for your taking this approach while you are currently employed. Believe me, if you have branded yourself as a candidate worthy of additional consideration, you definitely will get it.

Have I convinced you of where your *first*, your *true* loyalty should lie when it comes to your career, your *life*? I hope so! Now, if you are currently employed and do indeed have a genuine desire—or need!—to seek a new job, your *ideal* job, go for it—absolutely guilt-free!

How Misplaced 'Loyalty' to Your Employer Can Come Back to BITE You! BIG Time!

I was recently recruiting to fill a regional sales manager position with one of my Fortune 500 client companies in the chemical industry. As I routinely do when searching for top performing candidates, I began calling in to companies that are key competitors of my client company, talking to men and women who were performing in the role of a regional sales manager and who, by all appearances, were indeed top performers.

After explaining the career opportunity to one man, although quite polite and attentive, he ended up telling me . . .

> "Oh, I would feel like such a 'traitor' if I even *considered* (emphasis mine) **going to work for our biggest competitor**," the man said. "**I have worked here for going on 16 years now and the company has always treated me right and fairly. I'll have to pass, I'm afraid.**"

Fair enough, I thought, and simply moved on to calling the next prospective candidate. About three weeks later, though, I received a call from the above referenced individual. To say the least, during this call the man was much more animated and his tone significantly more desperate:

> "**Is that regional sales manager position still open?**" he asked hopefully. "**I just got let go in a reorganization! I can't believe they did this to me!**"

(Unfortunately, the position *had* been filled.)

Think this kind of thing couldn't happen to *you*? Think *your* company would never be so crass and unfeeling toward *you* and/or any other employees? Think again. Happens each and every business day of the year!

Chapter Seven

Beginning Your New Job Search

What Kind of Job Hunter Will *You* Be?
A *Passive* One? An *Active* One?
(Better be a Little of Each!)

One of the most crucial decisions you will need to make as you begin your search for a new job is what type of job hunter you will be. Do you plan to be a very active[18] one, taking the initiative and driving the process from day one? If you are employed and extremely dissatisfied with your current job, or if you have *any* reason whatsoever to believe (or even suspect) that your current job is in jeopardy, that's precisely the type of job hunter you *should* be!

On the other hand, if you are currently employed and essentially satisfied, or at least not *extremely* dissatisfied, and you *honestly* believe that your current job is secure enough to proceed at a more leisurely pace, then perhaps you can take a *somewhat* slower, more leisurely pace, a somewhat more *passive* approach. That does not mean, however, that you can simply sit back and wait for the jobs, or at least the really good jobs, to come to you with little or no effort on your part.

SCHEDULE JOB-HUNTING TIMES EACH DAY

A recommended method for conducting a new job search while you are still employed is to set aside certain times each day (including the weekends, of course) to conduct your job search activities.[19] For example, just by getting up an hour earlier during the work week, and spending that hour on your job search activities, e.g., sending emails, doing prospecting research on the Internet, etc., you will have five hours job searching time under your belt each week. Then, on the weekends, schedule, say, two to four hours both Saturdays and Sundays, and you could easily register a total of 13 hours each and every week, or over 50 hours each month.

REMEMBER: *EVERY* ASPECT OF NEW JOB SEARCH SHOULD BE ON YOUR OWN TIME, YOUR OWN DIME!

Regardless of *when* you actually decide to conduct your new job search, as pointed out in the previous chapter, if you are currently employed, make sure you do it *on your own time* and *on your own dime*! That is, don't send or receive emails relating to your new job search using your current employer's email address or computer system. Don't take or make telephone calls related to your job search while on company time, and certainly do NOT use your phone number at your current employer as your contact number! Don't "surf the Web" on company time or on its computers. Don't work on your new résumé and cover letter, or

---

[18]Or at least as active as you *can* be, if you're currently employed.

[19]Obviously, if you are not currently employed, your *fulltime* job is finding a new job.

make photocopies of new job search documents on company time or using company equipment.

Failure to observe such common sense rules, if you are currently employed, can quite suddenly change your current employment status, and you could easily find yourself on the outside looking in, which would certainly infuse your new job search with a GREAT deal more urgency!

How Should You Network?

Because you must make sure that you remain under your boss's and your company's radar during your new job search, if you are currently employed, you can still network effectively, but you will have to take some precautions here as well—and use some good common sense.

When you posted—and, it is hoped, *perfected!*—your professional profile on LinkedIn, ZoomInfo and other professional networking sites, you took the first, very important step toward effective networking. But what about networking locally or regionally? You can still do that, if you're currently employed, but you have to be cautious.

Let's suppose that, while attending the monthly meeting of one of your professional organizations, you have occasion to interact with someone you know is employed by a competitor of your current company. It just so happens that the company this person works for is included in your consideration set as a potential employer, or at least an employer that you would like to investigate further. How would you be able to explore possible career opportunities at the company with this man or woman? Here is one suggested approach:

(YOU)

"Hi, John, how is everything going these days at ABC Company?"

(JOHN)

"Great, how about XYZ company? You guys still knockin' em dead?"

(YOU)

"Well, we still got our line in the water, that's for sure.

"Say, John, while I am certainly very happy with my current job, in your opinion, is there anyone I should

be visiting with here to learn about any new career opportunities?"

(JOHN)

"What, you looking?"

(YOU)

"Oh, not necessarily. It's just that I am dedicated to my profession for the long haul and I always try to keep abreast of opportunities that may present themselves from time to time."

(JOHN)

"Well, that certainly makes sense. Right off the top of my head I don't have anybody in mind that you might want to be talking to, but let me think about it a few days and get back to you, OK?"

Under absolutely no circumstances should you ever say something like this, however:

(YOU)

"Hey, John, you got any openings at ABC Company? Man, I am so sick of my job I'll take just about anything at this point."

There are at least a couple of reasons why such an approach can be—and usually *will* be—totally self destructive:

- You will have **just announced to the world** (or at least the little corner of it represented by the members attending your professional meeting) **that you are *actively* looking for a new job**! How long do you suppose it will take for this information to find its way back to your boss, your company?

- You have **put "John" on the spot and likely made him feel very uncomfortable**. His only desire will not be to help you, it will be to get away from you as quickly as he can. Remember: **The *proper* way to *effectively* network for a new job is NOT to blatantly ASK for a job**!

The first approach mentioned is far more likely to produce positive results for you. You asked "John" for his help, his advice, and few people can resist at least *considering* helping others—if they are approached in the proper manner.

If you have positioned yourself as one of the TOP performers in your particular professional niche among the other members of your professional associations, the chances are really quite good that one (or more) of those members will one day soon after being approached by you call you up and say something like this:

> **"I've been thinking about our discussion at the last XYZ meeting, and I can recommend some people it might be wise for you to visit with. I don't know if anything will come of it, but I think it might be worth a chat. . . ."**

Think this kind of thing doesn't happen? Actually, it happens all the time—IF you use the correct, *non-threatening* networking approach just outlined.

How to Enhance Your Image, Enrich Your Network Through Your Professional Associations

One of the simplest, most logical ways both to enhance your professional image and increase and enrich your professional network is to become *actively* involved in your professional associations, both locally and regionally. Here are some things to consider doing:

- Volunteer to **chair** (or even just serve on) **important, high-profile committees**.

- Serve as a **guest speaker** on an important, timely professional topic or issue at association meetings.

- If you have the skill and talent, **write an article (or blog)** on a **key issue in your profession** and have it published either online or in an association publication. (Professional websites and publications are constantly in search of and in need of well-written articles and blogs that will have broad appeal/application to their audiences.)

- Get actively involved in fund raisers, new membership drives, etc.

In other words, establish, and then diligently and consistently maintain, an *active, obvious* involvement in your *profession*, not just in your current job, if employed. Odds are, many if not most of the key players in your local and regional profession or industry are themselves actively involved in these organizations and associations. A little "face time" with the right people could end up playing a significant role in your future career!

How 'Safe,' Really, is *Your* Current Job?

If you already have a job and have concluded that you can afford to be essentially a *passive* job seeker, just make sure that you do indeed have that luxury. How do you make that determination? By asking yourself, *honestly*, how safe your current job is, really.

In a perfect world, each of us would have perfect information and be able to perfectly anticipate—and then avoid—those situations that have the potential to cause us great harm, such as the loss of a job. Maybe we *think* we know our job is "safe" and "secure," but what if we guess wrong and are suddenly blindsided on any given Friday afternoon, right at quitting time?

Key Indicators That Your Job May be in Jeopardy

Some people hear the drum beat and others simply do not—until it's too late! Here are some warning signs that *your* job may not be quite as safe and secure as you may perhaps think it is:

- The company isn't making money and market share is stagnant or even declining.
- Layoffs, reorganizations, etc., are regular occurrences at your company.
- Your co-workers have started avoiding you.
- There is a lot of "whispering" going on.
- Your boss has begun giving you negative (or even just less-than-positive) feedback about your recent performance.
- You haven't had a raise or received a promotion in . . . well, you really can't remember when either of those things last happened!
- Lots of "star performers" are leaving the company.

Make sure *you* are paying attention to what's going on around you at work!

CHAPTER EIGHT

ROLE OF THE INTERNET

IF YOU PLAN TO SPEND ALL (OR MOST!)
OF YOUR JOB SEARCH TIME
IN FRONT OF THIS SCREEN,
BETTER GET A LOT MORE COMFORTABLE
WITH YOUR *CURRENT* EMPLOYMENT SITUATION!

Remember "the good old days" when you could go online, send out a few résumés to positions that "looked good" or "interesting" and start getting responses from potential employers almost immediately? Well, forget those days because they are long, long gone and are not likely to return any time in the foreseeable future, if recent years are any indication (and they are!).

The Internet is indeed a very remarkable tool, but like all tools, it has both its distinct advantages *and* its inherent disadvantages and limitations. Take this professional observation to heart: **Job seekers who insist on focusing all, or virtually all, of their job-hunting activities on the Internet in today's job market are doomed to failure.**

I'm sure you've run across news stories about some hapless job seekers lamenting the fact that they have applied for literally hundreds and hundreds of jobs online and have received either no responses at all, or, if they did receive any responses, they were very, very few in number and usually consisted of "we'll keep your application in our files. . . ." What is left out of news stories such as these is the fact that about three zillion other people probably applied online for the same jobs! (OK, I'm exaggerating a little bit here, but you get the point.)

Focusing exclusively, or nearly exclusively, on the Internet to get your new job is a classic example of doing the same things over and over and expecting different results! (The true definition of insanity.)

My friend and professional colleague **David Perry**, himself a top headhunter and co-author of the best-selling *Guerilla Marketing for Job Hunters* series of job-hunting books, may have said it best:

> **"Throughout history,"** he said, **"there is no record of any person ever being hired by a computer. It's people who hire people. Yet, some folks spend days or weeks searching for jobs online without ever meeting a hiring authority face to face."**

David continued by saying that this is merely confusing the *process* with actual *results*, a mistake often made by job hunters.

> **"Using the Internet to find a job is a process,"** he added. **"The results you want are a job. At some point, you have to get off the Internet, get off your duff, and go shake hands with live humans!"**

THE INTERNET IS NOT THE PROBLEM

As I just said, the Internet is just one tool in your job-search "tool box"—not THE tool, but A tool. Throughout this book I will show you (and *tell* you) how to effectively use the unparalleled power and dynamic flexibility of the Internet to locate and then *target* career opportunities. Without the Internet it is also very unlikely that we would have the virtually instantaneous communication tool that we know as email. The problem, then, is NOT the Internet, *per se*, it's how so many job seekers use it, how so many of them so *totally* rely on it to land a new job.

Many job seekers today still honestly and truly believe that the chances of their finding a new job are directly proportionate to the number of hours they spend on the Internet applying for job after job after job.[20] Today, nothing could be further from the truth!

If you spend, say, eight hours a day on the Internet applying for jobs (most of which you probably don't even remotely qualify for), sending in the *same* résumé, the *same* cover letter, to each and every one of these jobs, you will have pretty much wasted your entire day. You would have been far better served spending those eight hours doing those things that will *actually* help you land your next job! What are those things? Well, all of the tactics, strategies and various approaches featured in this book.

SEE THE PEOPLE!

One of the key characteristics of any successful salesperson—and remember, during your job hunt, you *are* a *salesperson!*—is that he or she routinely gets out to "see the people." Unless you plan to take a telemarketing (or direct marketing) approach to *selling* yourself to prospective hiring managers (not an approach at all advised, by the way), you also need to "see the people," and more specifically, those people doing the actual hiring.

Use the power of the Internet to locate the people who are hiring, as well as to learn details about various career opportunities. Then, get out from in front of your computer screen and start making contact with real *people*! As David Perry said, computers don't hire people, people hire people. So get out there and start seeing the people!

---

[20]Recent studies show that, across *all* age groups, 95% of today's job-seekers spend all (or most) of their job search time on the Internet, virtually ignoring any and all other job search activities, e.g., networking, prospecting among hiring managers and companies, etc.

CHAPTER NINE

HEADHUNTERS
CAN ONE HELP *YOU* IN YOUR NEW JOB SEARCH? (THE ANSWER MAY SURPRISE YOU!)

When you hear the term "headhunter," what is the first thing that comes to mind? How would *you* describe what you think a headhunter is, what role he or she actually plays in the job market? If you are at all like the typical job hunter your response quite likely would go something like this: "A headhunter is someone who can help you get a job, or help you find a new one."

There is, of course, a kernel of truth in this response, this perception. But to be honest about it, only a very, very *small* kernel. The fact is, **only three percent** of *all* **available jobs in the market today are filled by headhunters.** Yes, you read that correctly . . . **a full 97% of *all* jobs today are filled through other means.** (That begs the question, then, of why you would even *want* to take the time or make the effort to work with a headhunter to find your next job or career opportunity, doesn't it? Read on!)

A *true* headhunter's mission is to **IDENTIFY**, **QUALIFY**, **ATTRACT** and then **LAND** the **TOP performing talent** for a client company. (And, yes, the hiring *company* is the client in this transaction, *not* the job seeker.) Contrary to what appears to be a popular belief, a headhunter's job is NOT to help a person find a job. Moreover, he or she is NOT a career counselor; an executive recruiting firm is NOT an outplacement firm; and a "headhunting" firm certainly is NOT a staffing agency. These three types of organizations focus *exclusively* on the *candidate* and can indeed help him or her find a job. Conversely, a headhunter focuses on finding the best talent for a *company's* opening, and then determining if there could be a mutually beneficial fit between that client company's hiring needs and the candidate's skill sets, professional background and career aspirations.

OTHER MISCONCEPTIONS ABOUT HEADHUNTERS

You should also know and understand that *true* headhunters almost always focus *exclusively* on a niche market (or markets). For example, our recruiting firm, The HTW Group, specializes in placing top candidates in sales, engineering, management and research & development in the industrial sector, with most positions being, more specifically, within the overall chemical industry. So, if you are seeking an opportunity in, say, the advertising industry, not only could we NOT help you, we wouldn't even try because that industry is not within our market niche. Instead, you would have to locate a headhunter whose market niche is in the advertising industry. (Coincidentally, virtually all *true* headhunters operate in this same fashion.)

OK, let's assume that you are in fact seeking a new position in a skill set that falls within our market niche. Does that mean we can—or will—then work with you? Not necessarily. Since a company normally pays a headhunter a fee somewhere between 25% to 33% of the successful candidate's first-year base salary, the company is expecting a headhunter to present to them ONLY candidates who meet, essentially, two criteria:

- The **proposed candidate must now be doing the work** (or very similar work) **within the area of hiring interest** (referred to as "current, relevant experience").

- The **proposed candidate must have a** *proven* (and *provable*) **track record** of *quantifiable* accomplishments and achievements.

So, by re-reading the first bullet point above, you should be able to easily infer that, in general, headhunters *cannot* present an *unemployed* candidate to a hiring company, or more precisely, that they would be wasting their time if they did so. Now, what this does NOT mean is that an unemployed person can't (or won't) be considered for the open position. It simply means that no hiring company is going to pay a headhunter a fee in order to hire the unemployed person. Why? Because the company expects unemployed professionals to be going after opportunities themselves and not coming to them with a price on their head. All too often the unemployed waste far too much valuable time chasing headhunters when they actually would be better served by going directly after career opportunities themselves.

Further analyzing the first bullet point above, you should also realize that, as a headhunter, I can't (and won't!) present candidates who may *think* they have transferable skills, but actually don't have such skills at all. And that's particularly true if the candidate isn't *currently* doing a job either identical to or very, very similar to the job opening under consideration.

Let's say, for example, that we are working to fill a business development position for a company that sells industrial chemicals. You may be a great *sales* professional, with a strong, proven track record of quantifiable accomplishments and achievements selling financial instruments, but we can't (and won't!) present you on the position we're recruiting for. It doesn't matter how great your sales skills are; it doesn't matter how well you build relationships; it doesn't matter how "transferrable" *you* think your skills and background are. If you are not *currently* doing what the position requires, i.e., *selling industrial chemicals*, we simply cannot and will not present you. It's just that simple and straightforward.

Now once again, that doesn't mean that the *company* wouldn't consider hiring you. What it does mean is that they won't hire you from us (or any other headhunter, for that matter). Their comment to me would be something like this: "Skip, why do we have to pay you $20,000 for someone we have to train and take a risk on?" *They* may train you, and *they* may take a risk on you, but *not* for an additional $20,000.

Getting on, *Staying* on a Headhunter's Radar

To get on a headhunter's radar today, as well as to stay on it, your professional image, your professional *brand,* requires, first and foremost, that you have **"current, relevant experience,"** coupled with **significant, quantifiable accomplishments** and **achievements.** If you do, then seeking out a headhunter *in the correct market niche* can indeed be a wise move on your part, as well as pay you substantial career dividends.

A professional headhunter can provide you many very valuable services, all of which, by the way, are **FREE** to you, the job-seeker. (Remember, it is a *hiring company* that is the headhunter's client, not the potential candidate, and it is therefore the *company* that pays any fee(s) that may be involved in the hiring process, not the job-seeker.)

Be on the Alert for Fake Headhunters

You may get calls from or otherwise come into contact with people who represent themselves as being "headhunters," but actually are not. Their principal goal is to get a **fee** from *you!* They say that they can "market" you, can "groom" you, for a fee, to land your next job. Maybe they can and maybe they can't.

Our advice? Unless you are indeed prepared to pay a **fee** to get your next job, avoid these so-called "headhunters."

Here are just a few of the many valuable services a good headhunter specializing in your professional niche can offer you:

- *Custom* **résumé advice** and **assistance.**

- **Informed coaching** that can *significantly* improve your performance—and chances!—during **telephone** and **face-to-face interviews**.
- If you are made an offer, **assistance** and **advice** on *intelligently* **negotiating salary and/or benefits**, based on the *realities* of the current job market, not on any "gut feel" or preconceived notions.
- **Present you to appropriate hiring managers** and the **companies** they represent.
- A **thorough knowledge/awareness of open positions that make up the so-called "hidden" job marke**t, i.e., those jobs that are *not* advertised either online or at the hiring company's website. (By the way, as pointed out earlier, nearly *one-half* or more of the jobs available today fall into this "hidden" job market category!)

I'm sure you will agree that all of these services (and more!) could prove very helpful in preparing your new job candidacy. And certainly, working with a headhunter can provide you with a *tremendous* advantage over your competitors, i.e., other job seekers. But, in order to attract a headhunter's attention, to get on his or her radar, you'll have to position yourself as (and be perceived as) being among the *best of the best* in your professional field of endeavor. Why? Because those are the candidates who are getting the better jobs in today's still challenging, still very selective job market.

In addition, you will also have to exhibit, as a minimum, FOUR key characteristics. You must be . . .

- **Findable**
- **Desirable**
- **Contactable**
- **Selectable**

BE FINDABLE

You're probably familiar with the adage that goes like this: "It's not *what* you know, but *who* you know" when it comes to getting a job (or anything else of value, for that matter). In today's job market that adage has morphed into, "It's not *what* you know or even *who* you know, but rather, who knows *you* and **can you be found**!" In order to be found, I strongly advise you to develop, and then tightly control and *maintain*, your professional image and information, as well as your presence, at ***four*** primary Internet locations:

- **LinkedIn** (www.linkedin.com)
- **ZoomInfo** (www.zoominfo.com)
- **Data** (www.data.com) (formerly, www.jigsaw.com)
- **Google+** (https://plus.google.com)

LinkedIn

It is quite likely that you are already on LinkedIn, by far the most widely used and most highly respected professional networking site on the Internet. (For a more in depth, detailed analysis of LinkedIn and the many advantages it can offer you, refer back to **Chapter Five**.) If, for some reason, you are *not* currently on LinkedIn, then you certainly need to get on it!

ZoomInfo

This site is the **second most used website by headhunters and companies** trolling for top talent, and if you are not familiar with it, check it out because it can certainly pay you to take a tour of the site.

Data

This is another of the top job databases on the Web. It is also widely used daily by headhunters to find TOP candidates. Are *you* on Data.com?

Google+

(Your résumé) The fourth primary site headhunters (and hiring managers and Human Resources professionals) use to find TOP candidates is Google. Google's algorithm is such that PowerPoint presentations are readily indexed and often rise to the top in searches. So, if you put your résumé in a PowerPoint presentation and upload it to the Internet via SlideShare (www.slideshare.com), you can further increase your probability of being found.

(Your profile) Control your overall Internet presence by taking advantage of Google Profiles. Not only will headhunters search for candidates on Google, they also will oftentimes come across your name from a referral or while doing other research. Plus, nearly always, if the headhunter has any interest in you as a candidate, the first thing he or she will do is "Google" your name, in order to quickly reveal if anything relevant—or negative!—is returned in the search. Make sure your Google profiles are up to date *and* accurate—and kept that way!

BE DESIRABLE

Assuming that you have in fact been able to be found, the next step in the headhunter's decision process is to determine if you are *desirable* as a candidate. Generally, that means that you must have *branded* yourself as (and be perceived as being) someone who is in the **TOP 20%** of all candidates. (One of the inside jokes among headhunters is that they are paid by client companies to help them *hire* someone in the TOP 20% of ALL candidates and *protect* them against the rest!)

Essentially, you will be perceived, at least initially, as a *potential* TOP 20% candidate if you have accomplished the following, with the proof being contained, primarily, in your résumé:

- You must clearly have *branded y*ourself as **someone who gets results.**

- You must clearly have *branded* yourself as **someone with the qualities, background and professional skills and experience** who will *immediately* and *thoroughly* address—and meet!—the **specific need(s)** of a hiring company.

(NOTE: Employers no longer hire "generic" employees and haven't for a number of years. They hire *only* people who have *clearly* and *unmistakably* branded themselves as **someone who can make an *immediate* and *ever-increasing* contribution** to the organization.)

BE CONTACTABLE

Even though I've been in the executive recruiting business for a number of years now, and little that I encounter these days really surprises me, I continue to be amazed—no, make that *astounded!*—at how extremely difficult some candidates make it to contact them. For example, some candidates will have checked the box "Not open to receiving introductions or InMail" on LinkedIn. (Can you believe that?!) Why, then, are they even on LinkedIn? Or, perhaps they have changed their email address or cell phone number and haven't bothered to update that information in important places where they have their professional information posted online. Or—and this is an oft-occurring situation—they never bother to even check their email or voice mail, or at least they don't check them on a very regular or frequent basis.

Why is it so crucial to ensure that your contact information is kept absolutely current? It's important to keep in mind that, if a headhunter actually takes the time to contact you, the career opportunities that he or she wants to discuss with you are the absolute GEMS, and are *not* readily available to the typical job seeker. These opportunities truly can be "once-in-a-lifetime" (and of short duration) career opportunities. But, if you can't even be contacted. . . .

Or, how about this: You email a résumé to a headhunter (or, just as bad, to a hiring manger or Human Resources professional). Something in your résumé tweaked the headhunter's interest, so he or she shoots you back an email expressing a desire to perhaps pursue some career opportunities. Then, BOOM! the headhunter gets a "spam blocker" message! Realistically, how would you expect the typical headhunter (or other hiring professional) to react to this situation? Well, I'll make it easy for you and answer my own question: He or she will rapidly, and without any hesitation whatsoever, move his or her finger over the DELETE key and you (and your potential candidacy) will be history!

It is one thing if a headhunter is *proactively* trying to find you and you are merely protecting yourself and your privacy. That's quite understandable, and if the headhunter is really interested in contacting you for a career opportunity, then he or she will very likely go the extra mile to accomplish that goal. But if you have reached out to him or her and are then unable to be contacted, well, that's quite another story altogether. So, if you *want* to be contacted, then make certain that you *can* be contacted.

BE SELECTABLE

Imagine for a moment that tomorrow *you* get a call from a headhunter. Is he or she calling to offer you a job? Of course not. Unfortunately, it doesn't quite work that way. Is the headhunter trying to *sell* you something, or to get a fee from you? Absolutely not! Remember, the headhunter's client is the *hiring company*, not you, a potential candidate.

The *primary* goal of the headhunter during this initial call is to try to determine, as quickly as possible, if you are in fact a candidate that he or she would like to add to his or her inner circle, as someone he or she may want to consider for future, appropriate career opportunities. In other words, the headhunter is attempting to determine if you are *selectable*.

If you are at all interested in availing yourself of the wide variety of professional services and the very valuable assistance that a good headhunter can offer you, I strongly advise you to field his or her call with the care and consideration it deserves. It is presupposed that the headhunter already has identified you as a TOP candidate, or he or she wouldn't have contacted you in the first place. Don't blow it by projecting a lazy, lackluster—or worse, rude!—attitude during the call. Consider this call as being as vitally important to your future career success as a call from a hiring manager could be—because it is!

BECOMING PART OF A HEADHUNTER'S INNER CIRCLE

Are there any advantages to establishing an *ongoing* professional relationship with a headhunter, i.e., becoming an integral member of his or her inner circle, even if you do not now actually need—or desire—his or her services? There certainly can be, as I will explain below. But first, you must get in the headhunter's inner circle. Here is how to accomplish that, once contact is actually made with the headhunter:

- **Avoid the "shadows on the wall" syndrome.**

    Make no mistake about it: ANY call from a headhunter is an INTERVIEW! So be at the very top of your game, if and when you actually get a call from one. In **Headhunter Hiring Secrets: The Rules of the Hiring Game Have Changed . . . Forever!** (as well as in this book), I discuss the "shadows on the wall" syndrome in detail and provide numerous examples of how candidates can quickly remove themselves from further consideration by saying (or revealing) things that quickly and easily scare away headhunters, hiring managers and Human Resources professionals. For good!

    Example: During the initial telephone screen, the headhunter asks the potential candidate this question: "Why are you thinking about leaving your current position?" The candidate's answer: "My boss and I are constantly at each other's throats and I am just fed up with it. I'll take *any* job to get away from him!" I will *guarantee* that this type of response will make *any* headhunter quickly terminate the phone call and you will no longer be considered for *any* job openings he or she is trying to fill!

- **Keep money "in check."**

  If "more money" is your number one motivator for seeking a new career opportunity, it's very unlikely that a good headhunter will work with you. Clearly, any new opportunity must be competitive in terms of compensation, but experience proves that candidates who have money as their number one motivator for considering a career opportunity are far more prone to accept counter-offers from their current employer and end up not taking an offer from the hiring company, if it is made. If the headhunter even suspects that there is a possibility that a potential candidate will do that, most simply won't work with the candidate.

- **Keep your focus on the *career opportunity* and why you might be interested in it.**

  Be able to properly and clearly articulate why you would be open to considering an opportunity, if it was clearly stronger than what you are doing today. Is it due to a desire for career growth? A desire to change geographic locales? The opportunity to move to a larger, more stable firm (or smaller, more entrepreneurial firm)? Do you feel the need to establish a better, more desirable work-life balance?

- **Be able to *quickly* and *effectively* "translate" your skills.**

  As the headhunter reveals the career opportunity to you, think on your feet and start translating your skills. In other words, be prepared to show how your skills, accomplishments and achievements logically *translate* into addressing the issues, solving the problems and successfully meeting the challenges inherent in the job that the headhunter is presenting to you.

- ***Immediately* brand yourself to *become*—and *stay*—"top of mind."**

    If you are not the right candidate for the job that you are initially contacted about, don't despair. You may nonetheless still be perceived by the headhunter as a strong candidate for appropriate *future* opportunities. I always keep exceptional candidates in mind (and in my company database) for future, appropriate opportunities as they come along. And the more a candidate can do to stay "top of mind," the more likely I am to contact him or her regarding these future opportunities.

    Obviously, making a good first impression is the way to *immediately* establish top-of-mind awareness with a headhunter. But this isn't just a once-and-done process, either. To ensure that you *stay* top of mind, you must, at a minimum, *follow up* with the headhunter and then *stay* in touch, periodically, in *meaningful* ways, though not in frivolous, irritating ways, such as "keep me in mind" emails. For example, if you feel comfortable after your initial contact with the headhunter, be sure to send him or her a follow-up Thank You note or email. You might also, from time to time, refer appropriate professional colleagues to him or her for consideration.

    Here is an example of the ultimate pay-off that can accrue to the candidate who stays top of mind with a headhunter:

    One of my potential candidates stayed in touch with me for **five years** after his initial contact with me, periodically providing me with valuable industry information and a steady stream of excellent candidate referrals. When an appropriate, *unadvertised* position finally came available, this candidate was the first one I thought of! The result? The candidate was vetted for the position, sailed through the interviews and was offered (and accepted) the position. In his new role, the candidate's salary went from $75 thousand a year to $95 thousand a year!

As with most professional associations, and as I've already illustrated, you shouldn't necessarily expect things to start happening overnight once you have established contact with a good headhunter. A good *professional* headhunter is in the game for the long haul and you should be too. If the position he or she presents to you initially doesn't prove to be a good fit, if you have established a solid, reliable, *ongoing* relationship with the headhunter, as I have already stressed, he or she certainly will keep you top of mind when a more appropriate career opportunity *does* come along.

Here are some of the distinct advantages of becoming part of a good headhunter's inner circle:

- **You will be in the unique position of being able to take advantage of both *current* and *future* career opportunities** perhaps known *only* to the headhunter, and not generally available to the vast majority of your competitors, i.e., other job seekers.
- **If a headhunter has worked with a hiring company for a while**, and has established a good, solid relationship with the company, **he or she oftentimes has an inside track that can strongly benefit the job candidate**.
- If for some reason a **headhunter is unable to place you for *current* career opportunities**, having a solid relationship with him or her will **significantly improve your odds, over time, of getting the inside track to some of the best jobs available in the future.**

'Due Diligence': A Final Consideration

You can be absolutely assured that a good, *true* headhunter has done his or her "due diligence" by thoroughly checking you out *before* making contact. You certainly should do the same with a headhunter! Be sure to get his or her contact information. Then, look up the recruiting firm on the Internet. Read any reviews that may have been posted by men and women who have used the firm's services. How long has the firm been in business? What are the firm's areas of expertise, its market niche (or niches)? Is the headhunter who contacted you on LinkedIn AND does he or she have a *complete* profile? (If a headhunter isn't on LinkedIn, or if he or she is but has a very sketchy and/or incomplete profile, then you may still want to move forward but keep your antenna up all along the way.)

I am quite impressed by the candidates who do their due diligence on our executive recruiting firm, The HTW Group. To me, that means the candidate is far more likely to also do his or her due diligence on a client company before going into a job interview, thereby significantly increasing the odds that the candidate will be thoroughly prepared.

CONCLUSION

I hope that, in this chapter, I have adequately clarified for you what a *true* headhunter is, what he or she *actually* does (versus what many job seekers *think* they do), and how a headhunter *may* (or may not) be able to assist *you* in the search for your new job. This chapter certainly was *not* included in this book in order to get me new candidates, though! As you've seen, that's not the way a headhunter typically attracts new candidates at all.

Once job seekers fully understand and completely appreciate how tremendously beneficial a relationship with a good headhunter can be, they usually have just one question: "How can *I* get one interested in assisting *me* during my job search?!" I hope I've answered this question for you, if you decide to try to enlist the services of a headhunter in *your* new job search.

HOW TO FIND A HEADHUNTER

To locate a headhunter specializing in your professional niche, check out these sites:

www.mrinetwork.com (**MRI** – **Management Recruiters International** is a global network of approximately 800+ recruiting firms and 4,000 recruiters. Once on the site do a keyword search to find a recruiter specializing in your area of interest and/or niche.)

www.recruiterredbook.com (This site provides you the ability to access 13,000+ recruiters for a fee.)

www.linkedin.com (LinkedIn features the profiles and other useful information on the vast majority of recruiters worldwide.)

Chapter Ten

FINDING JOBS, PEOPLE WHO HIRE
How to Find the Really GREAT Jobs!
(As Well as the People Who are Doing the Hiring)

A company could have the very finest, most innovative and creative products in the world, but until potential buyers are made aware of the existence of these products, the company really has nothing of value, right? The same is true for you, the job hunter. You could have the most impeccable, most impressive credentials in the world, but until a potential employer (or a representative of a potential employer) becomes aware of *your* existence (as well as your availability, of course), then you really have nothing of value, either.

In this chapter I show you tactics and strategies you can utilize to effectively and efficiently locate not only the really good jobs, but also the contact information for the men and women who are doing the actual hiring for these jobs.

Unleash the POWER! of Google Search to Find *Most* Open, Posted Jobs

An excellent place to begin your search for *most*[21] open (and posted and/or advertised) jobs in today's job market is Google, or more precisely, Google search. This Google function allows you to locate jobs by type *and* preferred location. Here are the steps involved in the search:

- Go to www.google.com
- In the search cell, type this command: **site:jobs** (no space between the words), followed by the type of position you seek and then the preferred job location.

Here is how your entry should look in the search cell:

site:jobs position location

For example, let's say you are looking for an accounting position in the Atlanta, GA, area. Here is the information you would type in the Google search cell:

site:jobs accounting Atlanta GA

As this is being written, this particular search string returns links to numerous sites featuring thousands of accounting jobs in Atlanta, quite probably a lot more results than you would care to deal with and wade through. Let me show you how to significantly narrow your search.

---

[21] I say "most" here because as many as 50% to 80% of *all* open positions are not listed or advertised *anywhere*! This, of course, is where the power of effective networking, as well as the services of a good headhunter in your professional niche, can come into play to help you locate the jobs in the "hidden" job market.

Let's assume that you are a seasoned, experienced accountant and you are really interested only in *senior* accounting positions. Wading through thousands and thousands of possible positions to locate the jobs most suitable for you obviously wouldn't be very efficient—or very desirable! No problem. You would merely employ quotation marks in your search string to further narrow your search, as illustrated below:

site:jobs "senior accountant" Atlanta GA

This search will return links to sites featuring *only* senior accounting jobs, a far more manageable and much more targeted number of potential, suitable positions. Of course you can also employ the various Boolean operators (AND, NOT, etc.) in your search string to construct and further refine your job search.

Theoretically, precisely just how much you can narrow your job search really is limited only by the creativity and ingenuity incorporated in your search string. For example, let's suppose that you are searching not only for senior accounting positions in the Atlanta, GA, area, but, since it is part of your unique professional skill set, you are also interested in locating open positions requiring experience with Sarbanes-Oxley (a federal act which introduced major change to the regulation of corporate governance and financial practices) accounting practices and principles. Here is how you would could create your Google search string to locate such open positions in Atlanta:

site:jobs "senior accountant" Sarbanes-Oxley Atlanta GA

This little "secret" is simple, powerful *and* quite effective. Once you've identified positions that are potentially of interest to you, you can then begin applying online. But I strongly recommend that you NOT limit your activities strictly to online applications. You should also begin identifying the decision-makers for these positions, and there are effective ways of doing precisely that, which will be addressed later in this chapter.

Once you've targeted jobs you want to pursue using Google search, and once you've identified the applicable decision-makers, you should seriously consider using an approach that is working especially well in today's job market—the **direct mail letter campaign**, which will also be examined later in this chapter.

TURBO-CHARGE! YOUR JOB HUNT
WITH SIMPLYHIRED AND INDEED.COM

SimplyHired and Indeed.com are two of the strongest, most user-friendly sites you can use in your online (and offline) job search activities. They can literally **Turbo-Charge** your job search. Here's why. These sites aggregate and logically index job openings from both of the major job boards (www.monster.com and www.careerbuilder.com), as well as from some of the smaller job boards and various company websites, and feature them in one convenient location, i.e., on these two sites. That means you can conduct ONE major online job search rather than having to go to each individual job board. Let's examine a typical online experience using just one of these sites, SimplyHired. (Indeed.com works in a very similar fashion.)

Obviously, the first thing you need to do in order to use SimplyHired (and/or Indeed.com) is to sign up for the service, which is FREE. Simply go to www.simplyhired.com. At this time, of course, you will set up your username and password. After that is accomplished, sign in to the site.

Once you sign in to SimplyHired, below is the top part of the first screen you will see:

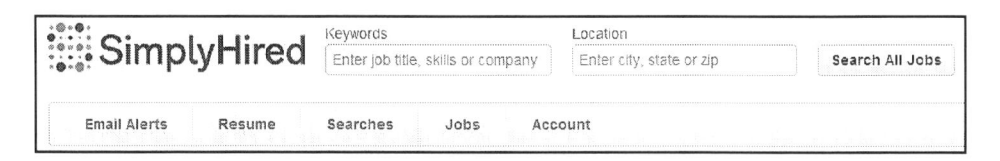

SimplyHired	Keywords Enter job title, skills or company	Location Enter city, state or zip	Search All Jobs
Email Alerts	Resume	Searches	Jobs	Account

This is where you begin your job search, by entering job title, skills or company information in the "Keywords" box. Then, you enter the desired job location, i.e., city, state or ZIP.

For example, to conduct a search for a chemical engineer position in Houston, TX, here is the information you would enter:

chemical engineer	houston, tx	Search Jobs
job title, skills or company	city, state or zip	Advanced Search

At the top of the next page is a screenshot of the information that will be returned once you click on the "Search Jobs" button.

FINDING JOBS, PEOPLE WHO HIRE

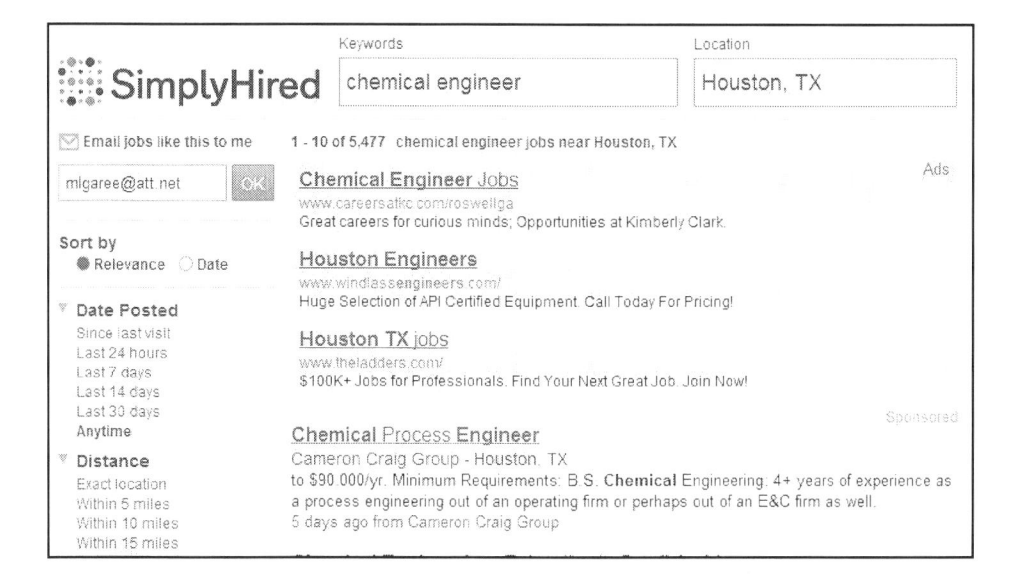

| SimplyHired | Keywords: chemical engineer | Location: Houston, TX |

Email jobs like this to me
migaree@att.net   OK

Sort by
● Relevance ○ Date

Date Posted
Since last visit
Last 24 hours
Last 7 days
Last 14 days
Last 30 days
Anytime

Distance
Exact location
Within 5 miles
Within 10 miles
Within 15 miles

1 - 10 of 5,477 chemical engineer jobs near Houston, TX

Ads

Chemical Engineer Jobs
www.careersatkc.com/roswellga
Great careers for curious minds; Opportunities at Kimberly Clark.

Houston Engineers
www.windlassengineers.com/
Huge Selection of API Certified Equipment. Call Today For Pricing!

Houston TX jobs
www.theladders.com/
$100K+ Jobs for Professionals. Find Your Next Great Job. Join Now!

Sponsored

Chemical Process **Engineer**
Cameron Craig Group - Houston, TX
to $90,000/yr. Minimum Requirements: B.S. **Chemical** Engineering; 4+ years of experience as a process engineering out of an operating firm or perhaps out of an E&C firm as well.
5 days ago from Cameron Craig Group

INTEGRATE SIMPLYHIRED WITH LINKEDIN

You are also given the option of integrating your SimplyHired account with your LinkedIn account, in order to reveal any connections between those in your LinkedIn network with people and positions returned by your SimplyHired search.

For example, when I entered "chemical engineer" and "Houston" in my SimplyHired account, a "Marketing Manager, Oilfield & Mining Chemicals" position with BASF in Houston was returned. And, when I signed in to my LinkedIn account I not only got the name of a BASF person I am already connected to on LinkedIn, I also got another link that allowed me to "See all 1,541 connections" that may have at least *some* relevance to my search.

For a headhunter this offers unprecedented power and flexibility in potential candidate searches. For example, if I have a candidate who is a chemical engineer with marketing experience, and is either already in Houston or is willing to move there, I will start networking with my existing LinkedIn connections, looking for a way to brand my candidate and get his or her information in the hands of persons of influence at BASF.

By using the power inherent in SimplyHired, rather than using a "shotgun" on my target, I can now use a "rifle" and significantly focus my efforts. I can cut through a tremendous amount of clutter and eliminate time-wasting, superfluous activities. As a job hunter so can you!

Here is how to get started, how to **turbocharge** *your* job hunt using SimplyHired and Indeed.com:

- Sign up for FREE SimplyHired and Indeed.com accounts today. (www.simplyhired.com) (www.indeed.com)
- Sign up for a FREE LinkedIn account, if you don't already have one. (www.linkedin.com)
- Conduct a test run on your SimplyHired and Indeed.com accounts to see how well they work and what marvelous things the sites can do both to *simplify* and to *speed up* your job hunt.
- Be sure to integrate your SimplyHired account with your LinkedIn account.
- Learn how to use the "Advanced Search" functions in both sites, in order to quickly and precisely refine your job searches.
- Once the positions being returned are appropriate for you, set up search agents so that new opportunities are *automatically* delivered to your email in-box every day.
- Now, study the positions that SimplyHired and Indeed.com provided you and brand yourself as someone who can do the job. (One-size-fits-all cover letters and résumés do NOT work!)
- Once you've properly branded yourself, apply online through links on SimplyHired and Indeed.com.
- Then, see who is in that company (or associated with it) from among your LinkedIn connections and begin networking with these professionals through LinkedIn. Also make it a point to join some of the same LinkedIn groups to which these professionals belong.

Job-hunting in today's job market is never easy, of course. Not only are the currently unemployed people in the market, there are also millions of currently *employed* people who say they are so fed up with their employers that they, too, are seeking to land a new job. No matter how you look at it, that's a LOT of people going after a finite number of jobs! So, any advantage that you can capitalize on will definitely be to your benefit, correct? Well, two of the distinct advantages available to you are SimplyHired and Indeed.com. Make sure you take full advantage of them!

How to Learn Who is Actually Doing the Hiring

Once you have surfaced jobs that you might want to explore further, then the obvious next step is learning the names, titles, etc., of the decision-makers for those jobs, i.e., the people who are either doing the actual hiring or those who will be influencing the hiring decision. There is a fast, efficient way to accomplish just that.

In **Chapter Five** I examined the tremendous professional networking power of LinkedIn. Like virtually all sites, though, LinkedIn also has some limitations. Two of the more (apparent) limitations are:

- You need **CONNECTIONS**; and
- In order to see *most* of those connections, you need a **PAID** account.

I say *apparent* limitations because there actually is a way to work around them: The **LinkedIn "Hack."** Using this approach you can actually view **over 95%** of *all* profiles on LinkedIn—whether or not they are in your network. And you do *not* need a paid account to do it. I explain how to do that next.

The LinkedIn 'Hack'

Google indexes *public* profiles from LinkedIn. The LinkedIn "hack" is an easy and powerful way to access those profiles in Google.

- Go to www.google.com
- Copy and Paste the following search string into Google:[22]

    site:linkedin.com ("Chemical engineer" **AND** "Georgia Tech" **AND** "Georgia Pacific")
    -intitle:profiles -inurl:profiles -intitle:jobs -inurl:jobs -intitle:jobs2 -inurl:jobs2 -intitle:dir -inurl:dir -intitle:company -inurl:company

---

[22]In this example let's use a job title of "Chemical Engineer" and "Georgia Tech" (to surface Georgia Tech graduates) and "Georgia Pacific" as the company.

The phrases *within* the parentheses are the *variables* which you can modify depending on the people you want to target. The phrases *outside* the parentheses are the *required* constants. These constants force Google to look only at people's profiles and eliminates discussions, questions, answers to questions, job postings, polls and all of the other information available on LinkedIn. (Remember: whom to get your brand in front of is our objective here.)

There are, however, **two limitations** to this approach:

- If a profile is marked "private" Google won't find it; and

- The person you are searching for must have put the key words you include in your search in his/her profile. So, for example, if you are looking for a "Georgia Tech" graduate, the person has to have used "Georgia Tech" in building his or her profile. If they used "Georgia Institute of Technology" you won't find them unless you do a second search using *those* key words. (Other Boolean operators such as OR and NOT don't work as well in this so-called **X-ray** command, so you should stick with the AND operator.)

Results of My Search

As this is being written, here are the results returned from the search string cited above:

- I find SEVEN people who either are or were a **"chemical engineer"** at **"Georgia Pacific,"** from **"Georgia Tech,"** and who have a *public* profile on LinkedIn, and who used these particular words in their profile.

- If I change **"Georgia Tech"** to **"Georgia Institute of Technology,"** I now find 15 people.

- If I want to find *all* Georgia Tech grads at Georgia Pacific, I would take out "chemical engineer" and use the following:

    site:linkedin.com ("Georgia Tech" **AND** "Georgia Pacific")
    -intitle:profiles -inurl:profiles -intitle:jobs -inurl:jobs -intitle:jobs2 -inurl:jobs2 -intitle:dir -inurl:dir -intitle:company -inurl:company

With this search string I NOW get **700** results!

- If I want to find **ALL** names at **Georgia Pacific**, I can try to find **hiring managers**, **people to network with**, et al. I would use:

    **site:linkedin.com ("Georgia Pacific")
    -intitle:profiles -inurl:profiles -intitle:jobs -inurl:jobs -
    intitle:jobs2 -inurl:jobs2 -intitle:dir -inurl:dir -
    intitle:company -inurl:company**

When I do that, because I have a very robust network, I get **70,000** results. Clearly more than I can handle, but a great start toward finding people of interest to network with and/or contact.

A way to manage this quantity of information is to go back and put in qualifying key words, such as "sales," as shown below:

**site:linkedin.com ("sales" AND "Georgia Pacific")
-intitle:profiles -inurl:profiles -intitle:jobs -inurl:jobs -
intitle:jobs2 -inurl:jobs2 -intitle:dir -inurl:dir -
intitle:company -inurl:company**

This modified search string returns **24,000** results.

So, if you've become frustrated and discouraged using the more traditional methods of trying to find just the right people to put your information in front of, then you should seriously consider using this POWERFUL, highly workable LinkedIn "hack." It can save you literally hundreds of hours of time and eliminate a great deal of frustration and wasted effort.

KEEP A *WRITTEN* LIST OF CAREER OPPORTUNITIES!

As you build your list of career opportunities you are interested in exploring further be sure to keep a *written* list.

Do NOT assume that you will remember every person and company you want to contact during your new job search—you won't! And certainly, when you begin receiving feedback (and calls) from hiring managers, headhunters and corporate recruiters, you will want to have all details of the specific career opportunity readily available to you for reference—*before* speaking to them!

CHAPTER ELEVEN

THE *STEALTH* JOB SEARCH
WHY YOU MAY NEED ONE, HOW TO CONDUCT IT

How do you go about finding a new job if you already have one? Very, very carefully, that's how! If you're currently employed and word that you're looking should leak out at your current employer, you could easily—and very quickly!—find yourself *unemployed*, making it a whole lot harder, not to mention a much more pressing issue, to land a new job.

If you are a currently employed man or woman you definitely would be well advised to conduct what I refer to as a **STEALTH job search**, in order not to jeopardize your current job and unnecessarily risk your future career prospects. You must always keep in mind that, if the wrong person learns of your plans, you could quickly be called in to your boss's office to explain your "indiscretions."

Who would leak such information about you? Actually, just about anyone, and they could do it either quite innocently or with definite malice aforethought. Why? Jealousy. Envy. In an attempt to curry favor with the boss. Really, for any number of reasons. Remember, too, any secret you have is no longer a secret once you tell just *one* other person!

Am I being paranoid here? No, just reporting on human nature. Am I saying that, if you are looking, you should trust *no* other person, not even your best friend at work? Yes, as a matter of fact, that is *precisely* what I'm saying! Keep the fact that you're looking strictly to yourself, period.

KEEPING YOUR STEALTH JOB SEARCH STEALTHY

While no system is foolproof, the best ways to ensure that your stealth job search remains under the company's (and your boss's!) radar include the following:

- As already stated earlier, **make sure that *ALL* of your job search activities, i.e., making photocopies, "polishing" your résumé, "surfing" the job boards, etc., are conducted *on you own time*, using your *own equipment* and on *your own premises***—not on your current employer's! Do NOT call in sick or fabricate meetings outside the office to attend job interviews. If you need time off, take vacation time or personal days. If questioned about such authorized time off, merely say that you have to deal with *personal* matters and leave it at that.

- **Never, never, never use your current employer's telephone number as your contact number.** Use your home telephone and/or your cell phone number as your contact number. (That doesn't mean, though, that you conduct your job search activities on your cell phone while on company premises.)

- **If you don't already have a personal email address, e.g., yourname@gmail.com, etc., then get one!** It's FREE! Never, never, never use your current company email address in your new job search. (Many companies can—and do—routinely and regularly monitor employee email correspondence and usage.)

- **Check the "anonymity level" of any online sites where you will be posting your résumé and/or making application.** (LinkedIn can normally be considered a free-fire zone because most professionals have a presence there and that presence usually is perceived as merely innocent professional networking activity—unless, of course, you include something like this in your LinkedIn profile headline: "Open to new opportunities" or "Seeking new opportunities.")

- **If you are reluctant to use your home address on your résumé, then consider using a more general address.** For example, if your address is 123 Flower Street, Cleveland, OH, using "Suburban Cleveland, OH" is certainly acceptable during the early stages of the job search.

- **Disguise the name and location of your current employer on your résumé by providing a *general* description and location.** State Farm Insurance Companies, headquartered in Bloomington, IL, for example, could become "A major personal lines insurance group of companies headquartered in the Midwest."

- **Network very, very carefully.** As a general rule, you should limit your networking activities to those professionals who are *outside* of your current employer. On the other hand, it's certainly acceptable to approach others, say, at professional meetings or after-hours business get-togethers. Do NOT, however, say something such as, "I hate my current job and will go about anywhere just to get out of there!" Rather, say something along these lines: "While I am certainly doing well at my current position, I am always open to genuine opportunities to take my career to the next level. Do you have any suggestions or know anyone I should be talking to?"

Under no circumstances appear desperate or negative! Desperate, negative people make most others *extremely* uncomfortable and makes them want to get away from that person as quickly as possible and around more positive people.

- **Select your references very, very carefully.** Normally, you won't be able to provide the names of bosses or professional colleagues at your current employer as references. Instead, consider providing the names of *previous* bosses and/or professional colleagues. In the (remote) event that a hiring manager with whom you have interviewed for a new job insists on references from your current employer, simply tell him or her that you can indeed provide such references—once a genuine offer is made!

- **Watch what you say on or post to your online social sites, such as Facebook, Twitter, et al.** While you may be laboring under the impression (false!) that such social sites are "personal," in fact, many times they are anything but!

Should You Tell Your Current Boss You're Looking?

If you can believe it, some employment experts suggest that it can be perfectly acceptable for employed people to tell their boss that they are looking for a new job—if they have a "good relationship" with their boss! While I am not necessarily trying to gainsay these "experts," I do have one nagging, very crucial question: What if you guess *wrong* about your *perceived* relationship with your current boss?! Wow! That could really backfire on you, couldn't it?

Obviously, if you are currently employed, telling your boss about your new job search is your call, but I would strongly suggest that you would be far better off erring on the side of caution on this issue. Unless the boss is, say, your brother-in-law, or your sister-in-law, then I say wait until you have a genuine offer of a new job before you say *anything*. (Now that I think about it, if your boss *is* your brother-in-law or sister-in-law, that may be even more of a reason NOT to tell him or her about your new job search!)

The point of this entire chapter is that you should use extreme caution and exercise prudence and good judgment during your entire stealth job search.

Remember, trying to improve your professional lot is NOT "sneaking," it is NOT being "disloyal" or "unappreciative" or "ungrateful" toward your current employer! Here is what it is: Looking out for yourself, your family and your own career. Remember, if you don't manage your own career, someone else certainly will try to—including your current employer!

THINKING OF TELLING *YOUR* BOSS YOU'RE 'LOOKING'? TAKE A CUE FROM THE CEO OF YAHOO!

At what point during her new job search do you suppose **Marissa Mayer**, who took over as CEO of Yahoo several years ago, advised *her* boss at Google that she was "looking"?

You can be assured that it was *not* during the time she was actively considering her new post (and being secretly courted by the Yahoo Board of Directors). Oh no, this savvy young executive amply demonstrated that she certainly knew how to play the "hiring game," and play it well.

She advised her boss at Google that she had been looking just **30 minutes** before she actually walked out the door to take over as the new Chief Executive Officer of Yahoo!

Chapter Twelve

'PROSPECTING' FOR 'GOLD'!
Contacting Hiring Managers, Human Resources Professionals & Headhunters

"There's gold in them thar hills" was the clarion call during the California Gold Rush days in the mid-19th Century. And you know what? There actually *was* gold in "them thar hills"! Tens of thousands of men (and quite a few women) set out to get their hands of some of it too!

Unfortunately, though, most ended up with *no* gold. When these folks learned that the gold wasn't simply lying on the ground, there to be picked up and taken away, and that they actually had to *work*, and work hard, to get at the gold, they soon gave up in frustration and went away empty handed. Only those who had a *plan*, and took the time to investigate where the gold most likely would be found, and only those who were willing to work hard to get at the gold, ultimately ended up with any. In many ways, the Gold Rush is an appropriate metaphor for a successful job hunt.

If you've followed my advice up to this point in the book, you should by now have a pretty idea of where the "gold," i.e., the most-sought-after jobs, is likely to be found. You should also have a good, solid plan for getting at it, or at least getting at the people whose responsibility it is to dole it out to worthy candidates. So, with that in mind, let's look at the ways you can (and should) begin making these contacts and prospecting for *your* gold—your new, better, different job.

Key Contact Methods/Approaches

Once you have determined which available career opportunities come the closest to matching what you perceive to be your *ideal* job, and have identified (to the extent possible) the decision-makers involved in the hiring process, then the next obvious step is to make actual contact with these decision-makers. There are, of course, a finite number of initial contact methods/approaches you can employ to accomplish this goal:

- **Online job applications (the "job boards")**
- **Telephone prospecting**
- **Email contact**
- **United States Postal Service (USPS)**

In this chapter I will cover the key things you need to know about each of these methods/approaches. No one method/approach is necessarily better or more effective than any of the others. Rather, you will find (as I have found through the years-long, unforgiving crucible of simple trial and error in a day-to-day business environment) that usually a good, appropriate mixture of these methods/approaches will work best and most effectively in landing your next career opportunity.

Keep this in mind, though: The **principal goal** of each and every contact you make is **to schedule an interview** with the hiring professional. Usually, the initial interview will be on the telephone, with either the hiring manager himself/herself, or perhaps someone from Human Resources who does the initial applicant screening.

> The *primary* goal of *each* and *every* contact with a company or a hiring professional is to land the all-important **JOB INTERVIEW**!

ONLINE JOB APPLICATIONS

Regardless of his or her current employment situation, i.e., employed, under-employed or unemployed, here is how the typical man or woman *consistently* goes about finding a new job today . . . they . . .

- **Spend hour upon hour in front of their computer** surfing the job boards, posting for job after job after job. Oftentimes, it makes little if any difference if they are even remotely qualified for the positions. All they know is that they *need* a job or they *want* a new job.
- **Send the same generic résumé and the same generic cover letter** (if they even bother to send one at all) to virtually each and every posting.
- **Soon get discouraged and frustrated** when they hear absolutely nothing back from *any* posting.
- **Continue to send résumé after résumé** to **posting after posting.**
- **Become even more discouraged** and **frustrated.**

As I pointed out in **Chapter Eight**, the Internet (or more specifically, the job boards on it) *must* be viewed as just another tool in your job search toolbox—*not* the **first**, **last** and **only** tool! The problem most frustrated and discouraged job hunters face today is that they do indeed begin *and* end their job search with the job boards, never even considering other very useful, sometimes far more appropriate and effective tactics and strategies, let alone actually trying them. Don't you make that same mistake.

Don't Play the 'Online Lottery'

What do I mean by the term "Online Lottery"? Let me briefly explain by giving you an example of how a hiring company recently used one of the major job boards (which shall go unnamed here) that was touting its "new technology" to fill just ONE of its open positions.

The major job board claimed that, through its relationships with media outlets, as well as its unique social media positioning, it could "push" ads to locations throughout the Web and more effectively and efficiently winnow down a usable pool of fully qualified candidates for participating hiring companies. And indeed that is precisely what the job board was able to do for this hiring company.

The first cut of potential candidates for just the *single* job opening the company was trying to fill consisted of **50,000** applicants! These 50,000 applicants were then further assessed using the job board's "new, sophisticated software" to pare down the list to just **50** people. This short list of candidates was provided to the hiring company, candidates were contacted, interviews were set up and, ultimately, the successful candidate was hired.

The hiring company said it was ecstatic with the job board's results and very impressed with the quality of the candidates produced. And, of course, the candidate who ultimately got hired was equally ecstatic. But how about the other 49,950 job seekers who were never even in the running?!

In this particular example, which is very typical of the results realized today with online applications, the odds of winning the position were just **one in 50,000**—and that only considers the applicants who made it to the initial pool of 50,000! Not very good odds at all, I'm sure you will agree.

The Internet Job Boards—with a Twist

Let me share a little known headhunter "secret" (approach) with you, one that still utilizes the Internet job boards, but with a uniquely different, far more effective twist. It's a secret I love to share with job hunters, but I have to warn you, in order for this approach to work, you must first have positioned yourself, professionally *branded* yourself, as a candidate who is clearly and unmistakably *exceptional* at what you do. That is, this secret will *not* work if you are viewed as a mediocre or even an average candidate. I will also warn you that I get mixed responses—actually, *very* mixed responses!—from those job hunters with whom I share this approach and suggest they consider using it.

Some job seekers say, "Wow! That's a GREAT idea! I never would have thought of doing something like that!" Still others say such things as, "You have got to be kidding me. That is something I would *never* do!" Plus, the feedback I get from those who *do* try it ranges from, "I tried it but it didn't work" to "I landed an interview with it!" to "I just got hired!"

With these caveats in mind, then, let me outline the simple **FIVE-STEP approach** that you may want to consider using in *conjunction* with the job boards. It can prove to be an approach that can get you out of the job-hunting doldrums (or prevent you from landing there in the first place!) and out of playing—and continuing to *lose* at—the "Online Lottery." It can get you well on your way to finding your new, *ideal* job.[23]

STEP 1
Go to the job boards and find an open position for which you are *fully qualified*.

STEP 2
Do NOT, however, APPLY FOR THE POSITION ONLINE! Instead, find an *internal sponsor* for the position, someone who will represent you and your candidacy.

Many companies offer a referral bonus to employees who recommend someone who ultimately gets hired at the company.

Such bonuses can be substantial, too, ranging from $500 to $3,000. So, if you see an opening with a company that you are

---

[23] If you are a currently employed person conducting a "stealth" job search, you will of course want to make sure that you protect your anonymity where possible and appropriate.

a good, appropriate fit for, i.e., you genuinely have the credentials/experience/skills that are required, you can use the *proactive* networking approach featured in **STEP # 3** to identify someone who works in that company, get them to review your résumé and credentials and, if they feel you would be a good fit, ask them if they would be willing to sponsor you and submit your information internally. What's in it for them? Of course it's the referral bonus!

STEP 3

Use **LinkedIn** to find someone in the company within your network or, if your network is relatively small, use the LinkedIn "hack" to find someone within the desired company. (Refer back to **The LinkedIn "Hack"** featured in **Chapter Ten**.)

If, for example, you want to investigate a sales position at **Georgia Pacific** (a manufacturer and supplier of chemical additives for the papermaking process), and you would like to learn the names (and have access to the LinkedIn profiles) of salespeople within the company, here is the copy to place in the Google search box:

site:linkedin.com (***"sales" AND "Georgia Pacific"***) -intitle:profiles -inurl:profiles -intitle:jobs -inurl:jobs -intitle:jobs2 -inurl:jobs2 -intitle:dir -inurl:dir -intitle:company -inurl:company

Note: That which is in **bold italics** are your ***variables***.

Or, say you wanted to find *salespeople*[24] OR *business development* staff at Nalco, a global leader in water, hygiene and energy technologies and services. The copy you would place in the Google search box is shown at the top of the next page.

---

[24] Because salespeople are usually more money motivated than the average employee, they can make great internal sponsors. Why? Because they want a shot at earning the referral fee paid by the company, if you are in fact ultimately hired in part because of their sponsorship of you!

site:linkedin.com (*"sales" OR "business development"*) ***Nalco***
-intitle:profiles -inurl:profiles -intitle:jobs -inurl:jobs -intitle:jobs2 -inurl:jobs2 -intitle:dir -inurl:dir -intitle:company -inurl:company

At the time this is being written, Google search returned about **24,000 people** who are potential *referral* candidates you can reach out to and possibly use!

STEP 4

Begin calling the **referral candidates** you have identified. (Below is an example of an effective script to use.)

(YOU)

"Susan, this is (your name). **I know your time is valuable and this will only take three minutes. Do you have three minutes, or should we schedule a better time to speak?"**

(SUSAN)

"I have three minutes but that's it. What is this about?"

(YOU)

"**I noticed that your company has an opening for a mechanical engineer at its Chicago facility. Now, I know that, since the position is posted, I either need to go to HR or apply online.**

Many large companies like yours have employee referral programs, where if someone is referred and hired the referring employee gets paid a couple of thousand dollars. Is this the case at your company? (If she answers in the affirmative, continue with the script. If not, thank her and move on to your next contact.)

"**Susan, if I were to send you my résumé, and indeed you felt that I was 'XYZ Company quality material,' would you be willing to introduce me in to the company? The value of your doing so ensures that I get reviewed by a real**

person and not by a computer, and the value to you is that you could get the referral bonus. Would you be open to me sending my information to you for review?"

Does this internal sponsor approach actually *work*? you're probably asking yourself at this point. In my professional experience, it works **about half the time**. That is, about half the time the person you speak to will be willing to review your résumé and about half the time they won't. When you encounter someone who is not willing to be your sponsor, simply move on to the next person on your list.

STEP 5

After you have found an internal sponsor, **do NOT then apply online!** That will cause any referral bonus for the current employee to be null and void. Only apply online once someone in Human Resources contacts you and specifically directs you to do that.

BACK TO BASICS: PICK UP THE TELEPHONE!

Just for the record, I live in the same busy, frazzled, crazy world that *you* live in today. I know how extremely difficult—if not *seemingly* impossible!—it can be to get a real live person on the telephone these the days because of the ubiquitous use of voice mail. (Notice that I said *seemingly* impossible because it is *not* impossible. It only sometimes seems that way!)

We have a saying at The HTW Group that goes like this: When all else fails, **PUTT** (**P**ick **U**p **T**he **T**elephone)! When you do that, of course, you can anticipate encountering essentially THREE obstacles/challenges, all of which, by the way, *can* be overcome (Hey, we overcome them each and every business day at The HTW Group!):

- **Voice mail** - Sometimes referred to as, "that blasted (or words to that effect) voice mail."
- A tenacious **gatekeeper**.
- **Resistance** from the **person called** (if you actually get him/her on the line).

Let's take a closer look at how you can effectively deal with each of these obstacles/challenges and get where you want to go: To talk to a decision-maker about a job you're interested in exploring further and set the stage for an interview.[25]

As I just stated, rarely are you ever able to reach a real, live person at any business you call today. (**Exception:** If the company is in the business of trying to sell *you* something!) That's particularly true with most of the larger companies, of course. Almost always you will be greeted by the company's voice mail system. You know the drill . . .

> **"Thank you for calling ABC Company. Your call is very important to us** (Does anyone actually *believe* this today?!)**. Please listen closely as our menu has recently changed. If you know your party's extension you may dial it at any time. . . ."** *ad nauseum.*

Sometimes, though definitely not always, you can dial "0" and a company operator or customer service representative will come on the line. If you do indeed actually get a real live person on the line, you may have made it to first base! Why? Because you may be able to get this person to give you the extension of the person you're attempting to reach, and the next time you can call him or her directly! Here is what you could say to accomplish that:

> **"Good morning, I need to reach Lucille Barnes in** (department)**. Would you please give me her extension so I can call her directly?"**

The chances that the operator will comply with your request? Fifty-fifty, probably, but remember, like so many employees today, the operator or customer service representative might be willing to comply. He/she may already be overwhelmed answering calls just like yours every day. The more he/she can eliminate in the future, the fewer calls to field! Just human nature.

If you can't, however, coax the direct extension out of the operator or customer service representative, then you will have to go to Plan B, which is, your call is transferred to Ms. Barnes's extension and one of three things is then likely to occur:

---

[25] I am using fictitious hiring manager "Lucille Barnes" in the examples featured in this section, but the general approach is the same for a headhunter, a Human Resources professional or any other hiring professional.

- You **immediately get Ms. Barnes's voice mail** (most likely occurrence); or,

- An **administrative assistant (and perhaps a secretary) answers your call** (somewhat likely occurrence); or,

- Surprise! **Ms. Barnes herself actually answers** her own phone (most unlikely occurrence)!

What do you do in each of these cases? What do you say? If you want to be ultimately successful in getting Ms. Barnes's attention, you will need a plan and be prepared to execute the plan, regardless of the situation you may encounter.

On the following pages we will more closely examine the reactions/responses you can reasonably anticipate encountering in each of these situations, i.e., when you reach the voice mail of the hiring manager, get the resistant gatekeeper on the telephone, or—surprise!—you actually make telephone contact with the person doing the hiring for the position you seek.

I will also show you how, with practice and perseverance, plus having a well-thought-out and well-executed plan, you *can* overcome such obstacles and challenges.

I am quite well aware that, for most people, just the thought of dealing with the situations (and people) you're quite likely to encounter during telephone prospecting can and quite often does induce significant hesitancy, reluctance and anxiety. (In the sales professions this behavior is referred to as "call reluctance," driven primarily by anxiety and the genuine fear and dread of the response/reaction they *expect* to receive when sales prospecting by telephone.[26])

Let me stress once again that, while you are in a new job search, you absolutely, positively, *must* consider yourself a *salesperson*. The "product" you're selling is yourself and the skills, talents and valuable experience you have accumulated and earned during your career. So, you do indeed have something of high value to offer and sell! Savvy hiring managers and hiring companies will fully recognize that fact. The ones who don't, or the ones who turn out to be rude and abusive to you? You probably wouldn't want to work for them in the first place.

---

[26]TOP salespeople quickly learn how to overcome "call reluctance" and become very successful. Just coincidentally, so do TOP job candidates!

How to Find the Time to Telephone Prospect If Currently Employed

The *good* news about telephone prospecting for your new job if you are currently employed is that you won't have to spend virtually every waking moment during normal business hours doing it. The *bad* news is that the amount of time you will be *able* to conduct telephone prospecting will, by necessity, be somewhat restricted. (Unless you want to risk having your employment status abruptly changed by telephone prospecting from the office of your current employer!)

Here is how you can fit telephone prospecting into your schedule—without risking your current job:

- If you are in the **same time zone** as your targeted contact, call over your lunch hour—away from your current business office, however. Since most hiring managers today do not work anything like a 9 to 5 schedule, you can also try contacting them either early in the morning, before their work day (and yours) officially begins, or after the official work day ends for most employees.

- If you are in a time zone **behind** your targeted prospect, call early in *your* business day before heading off to your job.

   For example, if you are in the Pacific time zone and your targeted prospect is in the Eastern time zone, you will usually have at least a two-hour window in the morning to make your calls, i.e., from 5 a.m. to 7 a.m., Pacific time, because, during this same time frame, it will be from 8 a.m. to 10 a.m. in the Eastern time zone, a time during which *most* businesses will be open.

   Just *reverse* the process if you are in a time zone **ahead** of your targeted prospect, i.e., start calling *after* your business day ends but *before* theirs does.

Typical Voice Mail Message Left

Back to Ms. Barnes. Let's first address the type of voice mail to leave if you encounter her voice mail. (Assume the position Ms. Barnes is attempting to fill is for a paints and coatings sales professional in the Phoenix, AZ, area.) If you are at all typical, you'll quite probably leave a voice mail like the following example: (I get voice mails *exactly* like this every single business day!):

> "Hi, Lucille, my name is (your name). **I am very interested in the job you have advertised in Phoenix. Please give me a call at 123-456-7890. Thanks! Hope to hear from you soon."**

What's wrong with a voice mail message like this? Actually, there are a number of things wrong, *really* wrong—and extremely counter-productive—with a voice mail message like this one!

First, I'm assuming that you don't actually *know* Ms. Barnes, correct? Even though we live in a somewhat casual world today, keep in mind that some people still take offense at the presumed familiarity of someone they don't know personally or professionally addressing them by their first name. If, after you have actually talked to Ms. Barnes, she tells you to call her "Lucille," great. But until that time, I strongly recommend that you take the tried and true *professional* approach and refer to her as "Ms. Barnes." That way, you avoid any potential, unnecessary risk of alienating a person you are, above all else at this point, attempting to *influence*, right?

Second, unless you are absolutely certain beyond any reasonable doubt that Ms. Barnes has advertised *one* and *only* one job, and that the *one* job actually is in Phoenix, how could she possibly be expected to know *which* job you're referring to in your voice mail message?! Why would you expect her to care enough at this point to even try to learn *which* job you're calling about? (**FLASH!** She won't care enough. Guaranteed.)

Third, the fact that *you* are "very interested" in the job you're calling about is of little or no concern to Ms. Barnes at this point. At this very early stage in the game, she is listening *exclusively* to her own FM station—**WIIFM** (**W**hat's **I**n **I**t **F**or **M**e)!

And finally, does it make any sense whatsoever to expect Ms. Barnes to actually return your call? Why would she? What did you say in the voice mail message that would cause her to actually even *consider* calling you back?! (I'll go ahead and answer that question for you: NOTHING!)

Let me cite just one more example of a *classic* voice mail that I (and other hiring professionals) get day in and day out:

> **"Hi, this is** (your name). **I sent you my résumé the other day and I was just following up to make sure you got it. Please call me at 123-456-7890."**

Unless your voice mail message gives the recipient what we at The HTW Group refer to as **"cause for pause,"** leaving a meaningless, strictly self-centered and self-serving message such as the ones cited above is nothing more than a gross waste of *your* time and the time of the recipient. Plus, the odds are overwhelming that you will *not* receive a response—from *any* hiring professional!

Voice Mail Message Left by *True* Professionals

Now that you know the type of voice mail message *not* to leave, let's examine a voice mail that *can* have results, the type that is left by *true* professionals who obviously know what they're doing. While nothing works each and every time, a voice mail message along these lines works more often than not, possibly resulting in what you seek, a call-back. (I'll use "Ms. Barnes" again):

> **"Good morning, Ms. Barnes. My name is** (your name) (*slowly* spell out your name). **I see on CareerBuilder that you have a need for an industrial sales professional selling paints and coatings in the Phoenix area. I am currently employed by one of your competitors and my passion is selling paints and coatings to accounts such as** (name a few of the more well-known).
>
> **Chances are, if I am not a good fit for this position, I certainly know a number of other professionals it could pay you to contact.**
>
> **Again, this is** (your name). **My number is 123-456-7890.** (Slowly repeat your name and telephone number.)

Can you see how a voice mail message like this would have at least the *potential* for giving Ms. Barnes "cause for pause"? Do you see how the focus is predominantly on Ms. Barnes and *her* professional needs and desires, not on yours?

There are of course no magic words when it comes to leaving a voice mail message, or when composing any other type of communication involved in a job search, for that matter. The key points to take away from this section are the following:

- Be very *specific* **with regard to the position** (and location) you are interested in exploring further.
- **Emphasize that you have** *current* **and** *relevant* **experience** and **expertise** in the type of position you're investigating with a prospective employer.
- **Provide a** *benefit statement* **in your message**, i.e., what's in it for the person (and his or her company) trying to fill the position.
- **Keep the primary focus** of the message on the professional needs and desires of the **hiring manager and his or her company, the headhunter,** et al., not on yourself and *your* professional needs and/or desires.
- Design your message so that it does indeed give the recipient **"cause for pause"**!
- Keep your message **brief**.

> Voice mail messages left during the job search **should not exceed 17 seconds.** If they are much longer, they simply won't be listened to!

GETTING AROUND THE GATEKEEPER

Now, let's take a look at the approach you should take if you encounter a gatekeeper, particularly a *tenacious* one, once your call is transferred to Ms. Barnes's extension. Here is how the person answering Ms. Barnes's telephone can usually be expected to respond:

> "Good morning, Lucille Barnes's office, Charles speaking. How may I help you?"

A couple of things to notice here. First, "Charles" is apparently on good enough professional terms with Ms. Barnes to refer to her by her first name. Second, by saying, "How may *I* help you?" indicates that Charles sees himself as *the* gatekeeper for Ms. Barnes, or at least an *important* gatekeeper for her. So he is on guard and you should be too. Here is how you could respond:

> **"Good morning, Charles.** (Your name) **here for Lucille, please."**

What?! Didn't I just advise you to err on the side of professionalism and refer to Ms. Barnes as . . . well . . . Ms. Barnes?! Why the sudden switch? A very good reason: By referring to her as "Lucille" you are *implying* (even though it's not true, and it doesn't *have* to be true, either!) that there is some sort of personal or professional relationship between you and Ms. Barnes. Unless Charles is really on the ball, to be on the safe side and perhaps avoid incurring the wrath of Ms. Barnes, he may simply connect you with her! And after all, isn't that the goal of your call, to actually speak to Ms. Barnes?! Sure it is!

More likely, though, because Charles has probably already been strongly admonished by Ms. Barnes to carefully screen all of her calls, particularly ones concerning employment, he can be expected to come back with something like this:

> **"What is this in regard to?"**

Oh, well, at least you *tried*! At this point you will of course have to state the reason for wanting to speak to Ms. Barnes. So, being able to think quickly on your feet, you will want to say something like this:

> **"I need** (not "want"!) **to speak to her about the paints and coatings sales position she is trying to fill in Phoenix. I am currently** (if true) **working in this capacity for one of your competitors and I know** (not "think" or "believe") **she would appreciate learning how I might be of value and assistance to her and your company."**

Now, Charles can be expected to be fully ready for this kind of response because, chances are, he may have heard it many, many times before. He knows *precisely* how to counter this statement:

> **"You need to call HR."**

An "amateur" job hunter usually responds to this off-putting, though really quite common, objection by saying something inane, such as this:

> **"Well, I *have* called HR and I am either constantly put in to voice mail or put on hold for 15 minutes. Or, they**

tell me to go online and fill out an application. I don't want to waste my time doing that."

On the other hand, a *true* professional will remain totally unruffled and respond with a comment like this:

> "**Sure, I can call HR and I will be glad to do that, Charles. But being in sales** (since in this example the position *is* a sales position) **I know the best way to 'make the sale' is to talk directly to the person who is doing the 'buying.'"**

For a *non-sales* position, you might instead say something like this:

> "**Sure, I can call HR, and I will be glad to do that, Charles. But being in the same business as you and Ms. Barnes, I know how vital it is to have top-notch people on your team. I currently am among the very top performers in my company, and I can bring this same performance level to you. I need just a few minutes to discuss this further with Ms. Barnes. If she has no further interest in me, so be it. Maybe I can then recommend some other great people she could also benefit from considering."**

Now, unless good old Charles is really, really on the ball, he is probably not going to be very sure where to go from here in his script. Obviously, you've given *him* "cause for pause." He certainly will know he is dealing with a professional, someone who seems to know what he/she is talking about, and not just "another person looking for a job." Use any hesitation he shows at this point to attempt to establish at least some rapport with him. You might quickly add, for example:

> "**By the way, Charles, how long have you been with** (name of the company)**, and what do you find most exciting and interesting about *your* job?"**

The idea here, of course, is to use methods and dialogue that can begin making a quasi-ally of the gatekeeper, to try to establish at least some level of rapport with him or her. If you can do that, it will pay you dividends if you find it necessary to place another call to Ms. Barnes at some point in the future.

At this point, I know that some of you reading this are probably thinking that a conversation and/or approach like this would *never* work in the "real" world. Well, I beg to differ because it actually *does* work! Not each and every time, of course, but certainly often enough to continue using it.

At The HTW Group we use this approach, or certainly ones very similar to it, each and every business day whenever we call in to companies to reach out to top talent to discuss career opportunities with them or to discuss hiring needs with hiring managers.

Let me assure you that virtually no one we encounter during our attempt to contact top talent or hiring managers in companies exactly "rolls over" for us. We are continually met with resistance of one kind or another. You will be too, but I've just shown you how you, like us, *can* overcome that resistance and get where you want to go more often than not!

THE RESISTANT HIRING MANAGER, HEADHUNTER, ET AL.

Miracle of miracles! When you place a call to a hiring manager, headhunter, or Human Resources professional with whom you want to discuss a career opportunity, guess what?—he or she actually answers the telephone himself/herself! Hey, it does happen sometimes, just not very often these days. (When this *does* happen, it happens most frequently before the official business day—and the daily business onslaught—begins or after it officially ends for the hiring professional, and when most of the staff usually aren't in the office, but he or she often is.)

> To successfully counter the resistance you *will* meet when trying to directly connect by telephone with a hiring manager, headhunter or a Human Resources professional, take a cue from top *salespeople*: **Be persistent but patient** and professional, **present a "value proposition"** (what's in it for them), **establish rapport** if you can. If none of this works, simply move on to your next contact and plan a follow-up email or direct mail letter if you still have interest in the position.

If there ever is a time where you *definitely* need to have a plan, and be fully prepared to *execute* that plan, it is when (and if, of course) you do actually get the hiring manager, headhunter or Human Resources professional on the line! Because hiring professionals, especially hiring managers, today are so often harried and otherwise overworked and overburdened in most companies, it's quite likely that you'll be met with a very abrupt, not-all-that-friendly of a greeting like this (we'll use "Ms. Barnes" again):

> **"Lucy Barnes."**

An "amateur" job hunter almost always will be thrown off script when met with such abruptness and no-nonsense tone and demeanor, and will usually end up stuttering and stammering and blowing his or her chance to establish a meaningful dialogue with a hiring manager. A *true* professional, on other hand, will be *well prepared* with an appropriate response and *confidently* come back with something along these lines:

> **"Good morning, Ms. Barnes. I am in the same business as you and I know how valuable your time is so I won't waste it."**

Pause and wait for any response Ms. Barnes may have to your opening comment. For example, she might come back with . . .

> **OK. Who is this and what is it about? I'm really quite busy.**

Or, she may leave you listening to dead silence on the other end of the line. In either case, you can then say something like this:

> **My name is** (your name) **and I am** (or have recently been) **a top salesperson for one of your competitors** (do NOT name your current company at this point). **If I could show you how I can bring *significant* value to you in the sales position you are trying to fill in Phoenix, wouldn't it make sense for us to schedule a meeting?**

The degree of professional "pain" Ms. Barnes is feeling as a hiring manager until she fills the Phoenix sales position, will, more than anything else, drive her response. If she has been inundated with applications, telephone calls and emails regarding the position, chances are, she will try to get you off the line as quickly as possible. If that's the case, she can be expected to shoot you the old **"You have to contact HR"** line. You would then come back with essentially the same dialogue you used with "Charles":

> **"Of course I would be glad to call HR. But, if your company is anything like mine** (small laugh or a chuckle here can take some of the tension out of the conversation)**, I suspect that you get a ton of applications from**

people who aren't even qualified for a sales position, right? Rather than having to wade through a bunch of these applications, if you will give me just 15 minutes of your time, I think we can save both of us a lot of time and effort. If I don't prove to be a good fit for your sales position, I can highly recommend some other top salespeople you might want to consider."

If Ms. Barnes is herself a *true* professional, and she is indeed feeling some professional "pain" until her sales position is filled with a top candidate, she more than likely will come back with a comment like this:

"What company are you working for now?"

If you are currently employed and you feel comfortable revealing that information at this point, then simply tell her the name of your current employer. If not, then you could say:

"I'm sure you can understand the necessity for keeping this information confidential for the time being, but let me assure you that it is one of your major competitors. I will certainly be glad to reveal the name of my employer if it appears you have some genuine interest in me as a candidate, and likewise, if I feel your company is a good fit for the next step in my career."

Is such a response playing hard to get? Absolutely not! If Ms. Barnes is indeed a *true* professional you'll more than likely earn her respect with such a comment, not her disdain. If you have gotten this far with Ms. Barnes, you definitely will be making some significant progress. She may then say,

"Well, tell me a little bit about yourself and what you are now accomplishing for 'one of our major competitors.'" (Her way of being coy with you, but at least she is willing to give you a little more time to sell yourself to her!)

To which you then respond to her comment with the **90-second elevator speech** you will have developed for use during the interview phase of your new job search. More about this in **Chapters Fourteen** and **Fifteen**, but for our purposes here, let's use this *condensed* version:

"I have been with my current company ten years and have a master's degree in chemical engineering. I am responsible for selling and providing excellent service to our paints and coatings customers in the Tucson metropolitan area.

"When I was assigned the sales territory five years ago, we had about $2 million in annual sales. Today we are approaching $10 million in annual sales. Overall customer satisfaction levels have increased from 75%, when I took over the territory, to nearly 95% today.

"I have been in the Top 20% of all salespeople in our company, on the basis of total annual revenue generated, since my second year in the business.

"This is just glimpse of the expertise and experience I can put to work for you and your company.

"Do I sound like the kind of salesperson you'd like to consider for your operation in the Phoenix area?"

Obviously, you would have to tailor this condensed version of your 90-second elevator speech to fit your own credentials, accomplishments and achievements. But as you are considering this example, make sure to focus your attention on the possible reasons *why* this would be a good condensed elevator speech to use:

- **First**, you have *quantified* **your accomplishments and achievements**, with *dollars* and *percentages*, rather than merely saying something like, "I have consistently been among the top salespeople in my company year in and year out."

- **Second**, you have been **able to *position* yourself** in *less than a minute*!

- **Third**, you have placed the **primary focus** of your comments **on the hiring manager** and *her* **professional needs**, not on yours.

- **And finally**, you did what every successful salesperson does (and remember, during the job search you *are* a salesperson!)—**you asked for the order**, i.e., "Do I sound like the kind of salesperson you'd like to consider for your operation in the Phoenix area?"

If you can get a hiring manager as resistant as "Ms. Barnes" apparently is to engage you in a conversation, no matter how brief, you will have accomplished a lot. Plus, you will have set the stage for further discussion—if you manage to strike some responsive chords with her during the conversation. And, if you diligently practice and then take the approach suggested here, you can indeed expect to strike some responsive chords with her (or any other hiring professional).

Again, there are no magic words or phrases to use to be successful during telephone prospecting. And certainly not every hiring official you contact will pay you the courtesy of hearing you out, as Ms. Barnes did in our example dialogue. In fact, some people will be downright rude. To that I say, "So what? Who cares?" Simply do what a successful salesperson does each and every business day: Forget about it and move on to your next telephone contact. You probably wouldn't want to work for a company that hires such rude, short-sighted people in the first place, right? Right!

I know that, in general, the suggested dialogue and approaches I've recommended in this section *do* work because we use such dialogues and approaches each and every day in the recruiting business. Use words that feel comfortable to you, but make sure you adhere as closely as possible to both the spirit and the methodology recommended in this section. At first you might feel a little uncomfortable, but if you practice, practice, practice, these approaches will soon become second nature to you. Count on it!

YOU ARE NOT A 'SUPPLICANT,' SO DON'T ACT LIKE ONE!

No matter whom you personally talk to (either on the telephone or in person) during your new job search, keep in mind that, *if you have positioned yourself as clearly being among the TOP candidates in the job market*, you will have earned proper respect and courtesy. Don't settle for anything less, or act like a "supplicant" because, clearly, you are not!

Incorporating Email Into Your Prospecting Activities

Properly constructed and well-timed email correspondence can—and *should!*—serve as an integral part of an overall, well-orchestrated **personal marketing *package*** during your new job search. In the following sections I examine how you can *effectively* use email during your job search to contact hiring officials, as well as in your follow-up activities with them. I also show you how to construct your emails so that they will stand a far, far better chance of actually being *read*, and *responded to*, than the typical email message constructed and sent by the typical job seeker.

Before you can begin sending email messages, however, you must first know the email addresses of the persons you want to contact, or rather, how to *find* those email addresses, so I will start with that subject.

How to Find Email Addresses

Just as you would never want to send a direct mail letter addressed "To Whom It May Concern" during a job search, you'll certainly want to make sure that you also address your job-prospecting (or follow-up) emails to a *specific* person, ideally, the hiring manager (or other hiring professional). You may have been able to surface at least some of the email addresses you need for prospecting when you did your preliminary targeting for career opportunities. If you still need some email addresses, though, there are a number of very efficient, *effective* ways to discover email addresses today.

- **Google.com.** Oftentimes, the easiest way to solve any problem is to use the simplest, fastest approach. That definitely *can* be the case when it comes to finding email addresses. Simply go to Google.com and type in this search string (with the quotes): "Julia James, ABC Company, Los Angeles, CA." (If you also have the specific street address or POB number of the business, that can also help you narrow the search.) Chances are, you *will* come up with one (or more) email addresses for Ms. James using this method.

- **The hiring company.** Since you already know the name of the company with the position you're interested in, go to the company website and see how the email addresses of various employees and/or officers of the company are configured. For example, usually, though certainly not always, the configuration used is normally something like this: FirstName.LastName@CompanyName.com. So, in the case of "Ms. James" in the previous bullet point, her email address (if her company uses the configuration just cited) could be expected to be something like the following: julia.james@abccompany.com.

- **General Internet search.** As is the case today with just about *any* subject you care to explore, you can find numerous other methods and approaches for finding email addresses simply by typing this search string in your Web browser's search engine: "How to find email addresses." You will be hit with literally scores of references as the result of this search, but be forewarned: While many of the references are FREE, some are not. Don't end up paying for something you can likely get FREE!

TESTING EMAIL ADDRESSES

Now, to test if this is indeed the correct formatting for email addresses within the targeted company, go to www.mailtester.com and enter the email address you intend to use for the recipient of your email. (Enter your own email address at www.mailtester.com to see how it works.)

If you can't verify an email address on www.mailtester.com, try this approach:

- Pick one email address and put it on the "To" line in your email client program.

- Then, go to the "bcc" line and enter as many variations as you can think of for the email address. **(Important: It is *critical* that you place these email address variations on the "bcc" line and *not* on the "cc" line.)**

- When you hit "Send" you will then be able to determine which is the *correct* email address because it will be the only address to receive the message; all the other variations will be returned as "delivery failure."

How to Get Your Email Opened—and READ!

As we saw in the section on telephone prospecting, virtually no one answers the phone anymore. Very few respond to your voice mail messages. And—surprise!—very few people answer your emails! So, the question becomes: How *do* you as a job seeker not only get your message into the hands—and the minds!—of today's busy, frazzled, distracted hiring managers and other decision-makers, but also, how do you get them to open *and* actually *read* your emails?

I'm sure that it will come as no great shock to you that, in today's still competitive job market, hiring managers get dozens—if not hundreds!—of emails each and every business day. (I get about 300 emails a day, on average, myself.) So, I have no illusions about how difficult it is to break through the clutter facing hiring managers and other decision-makers today, and you shouldn't either, of course. Nonetheless, there *is* an approach that you can use to *significantly* increase the chances that *your* email will be among the few that actually *are* opened—and read! It's an approach The HTW Group coaches all its candidates on, and it works often enough for you to seriously consider using it during your new job search.

Here are the basic considerations of the approach:

- Use a *compelling* email **subject line** that will *significantly* improve the odds that your email will actually get opened by a hiring manager or other decision-maker.

- Make sure you that you **properly brand yourself** and use the **right kind of message**, i.e., a message that clearly and quickly conveys what you can do for the *hiring manager* and his/her *company*, not what they can do for you, in the **body copy** of the email.

- Make your email communications an **integral part of your overall "touch plan**," i.e., the contacts (telephone, email, direct mail, etc.) you make with a given hiring professional during your job search.

- Send the email to the *correct* **email address**.

- Ensure that your email communications are just a ***part* of an overall, well-orchestrated, personal marketing package**.

Now, let's examine each of these basic considerations involved in my recommended approach to effective email marketing.

The Subject Line

By far, **the most important part of your email is the subject line**. If the subject line is not strong enough to get the email opened, then obviously, it doesn't matter what message is actually contained in the body of the email, does it? The email simply will *not* be opened!

Here are some examples of the types of subject lines that will practically *guarantee* that your emails will ***not*** be opened (and therefore *read*):

- Skip Freeman's résumé and cover letter
- Response to your job posting
- I heard you were hiring
- Your Plant Manager position

And of course the list goes on and on. Most of these types of subject lines face one of two fates: They instantly get hit by the DELETE key or they are *automatically* forwarded to human resources, where they can easily—and very quickly!—disappear into a black hole.

Here are some examples of subject lines that are far more likely to get your emails opened:

- Quick note regarding your August 5th news release
- Your article in Engineering Technology
- Savvy driver of new business
- Backlog increasing? I can help
- Is XYZ's new product affecting ABC's market share?
- Decreasing fiberglass scrap by 27 percent

Subject lines such as these work because they suggest *powerful, current* topics that are relevant to the email *recipient* (in this case, the hiring manager and his/her company). In other words, these subject lines suggest not what's in it for *you*, but rather, what's in it for the hiring manager and his/her company! Big difference.

Certainly, you're interested in the company hiring *you*, but guess what? That's not what the company is interested in at all! As a matter of fact, keep this in mind: No company—and I do mean *no* company!—is in the business of hiring you or anyone else. Remember, the business *every* company is in is **making money**, or at least it better be or the company won't survive. So, it's entirely up to you to convince a potential employer of one of two things (or both):

- That you can *make* **the company money**; or,
- That you can *save* **the company money**.

Usually, everything else is merely unwanted, unwelcome "noise" to a hiring manager and his/her company.

BODY OF THE EMAIL

Assuming that the subject line of your email is indeed so compelling that it gets the email opened, you will then have to *deliver*, in the body copy, that which is *promised* in the subject line. That is, you will have to ensure that you *properly* and *quickly* brand yourself as someone the company simply *must* at least *consider* hiring, as well as stress what, *specifically*, you can do that will benefit the *company* in the message portion of your email. (By the way, make sure all of your emails are "above the scroll." Emails that look novel-length almost always are immediately hit with the DELETE key because hiring managers simply don't have the time, or the patience, to wade through lengthy emails.)

> Avoid writing a *War and Peace*-length email message! Recent studies recommend that an **email message** used in conjunction with a job search **be *less than* 500 words**. A **LinkedIn InMail should be *less than* 250 words**.

On the next page are two email messages.[27] The first email is the typical email most job seekers send to hiring managers and other hiring professionals (I get this kind of email every day!). The second is how our executive recruiting firm coached a candidate to rewrite her email to give it much more focus and impact. (By the way, she ended up getting an interview and was subsequently HIRED for the position she sought!)

---

[27] This candidate was applying for a position with a Nashville, TN, entertainment firm.

THE TYPICAL JOB-HUNTING EMAIL SENT

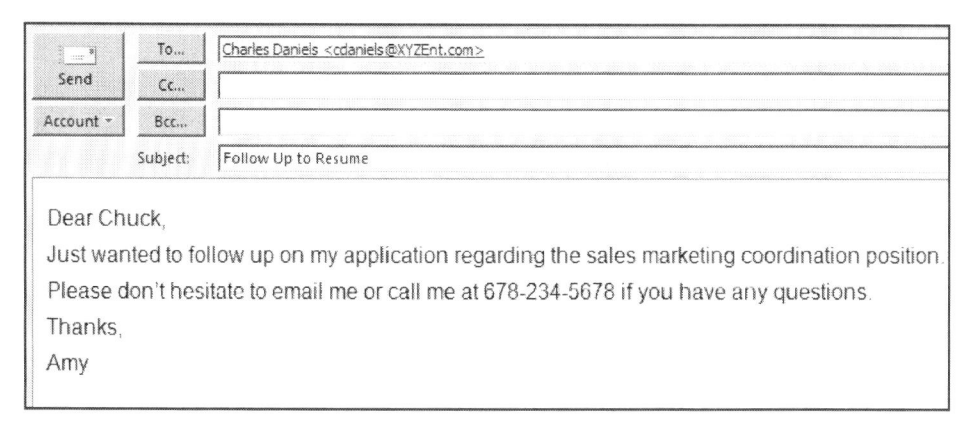

To: Charles Daniels <cdaniels@XYZEnt.com>
Cc:
Bcc:
Subject: Follow Up to Resume

Dear Chuck,

Just wanted to follow up on my application regarding the sales marketing coordination position. Please don't hesitate to email me or call me at 678-234-5678 if you have any questions.

Thanks,

Amy

REVISED, REWRITTEN VERSION
(WHICH WON AN INTERVIEW
AND SOON THEREAFTER THE JOB!)

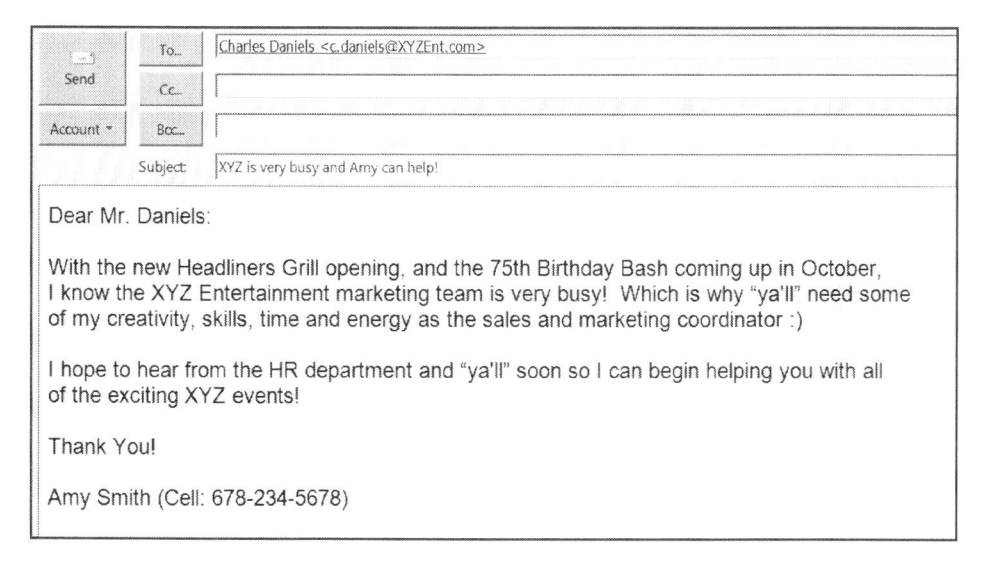

To: Charles Daniels <c.daniels@XYZEnt.com>
Cc:
Bcc:
Subject: XYZ is very busy and Amy can help!

Dear Mr. Daniels:

With the new Headliners Grill opening, and the 75th Birthday Bash coming up in October, I know the XYZ Entertainment marketing team is very busy! Which is why "ya'll" need some of my creativity, skills, time and energy as the sales and marketing coordinator :)

I hope to hear from the HR department and "ya'll" soon so I can begin helping you with all of the exciting XYZ events!

Thank You!

Amy Smith (Cell: 678-234-5678)

If *you* were a hiring manager or other decision-maker, which of these two emails would *you* be most likely to a.) **READ**; and b.) **RESPOND TO**?

MAKE YOUR EMAILS PART OF AN OVERALL 'TOUCH PLAN'

As is the case with *every* element of your overall personal job marketing plan, and as I have just pointed out, an email should be an integral part of your overall "touch plan." In order to successfully reach a hiring manager or other decision-maker, you should "touch" them about every **ten days** with some type of planned, creative communication/contact. I have found that this frequency generally brands a candidate as being persistent and assertive without being overly aggressive, tedious or bothersome. This presupposes, of course, that these touches consist of messages that convey an attempt to deliver **value to the hiring manager and his/her company**, not as suggestive of what the company can do for you, the candidate.

'TOUCH PLAN' HELPS YOU BREAK THROUGH 'CLUTTER' & 'NOISE' SURROUNDING HIRING MANAGERS

Marketing 101 teaches that, on average, in today's oftentimes still somewhat frenetic job market, it takes about **SEVEN** "touches" (meaningful contacts) to get a hiring manager's or other decision-maker's attention.

Most candidates usually give up after just *three* touches, and then wonder why they weren't successful!

MAKE SURE YOUR EMAILS ARE JUST A *PART* OF YOUR OVERALL MARKETING PACKAGE

No one thing, no one approach, will ever get you where you want to go in today's job market, and of course that's also true when it comes to your email messages. They must be just a part, albeit an *integral* part, of your overall, consistent, personal marketing *package*. In addition to your emails, that personal marketing package should be comprised of your telephone calls (and voice mails), LinkedIn invitations, InMail, connections made with administrative assistants to hiring managers, and yes, even "snail" mail communications.

How do I know the approaches and techniques outlined in this book actually work? Because, as a headhunter, I use them each and every business day to effectively reach out to hiring managers and other decision-makers to successfully market job candidates. Think about it, if this approach *didn't* work, I would soon be out of business!

Use the approach outlined in this section to start breaking through the "clutter" and "noise" to effectively reach a hiring manager or other decision-maker. Start branding yourself as someone who can bring real value to the hiring company, rather than automatically being branded by a hiring manager as being "just another candidate." Learn how to be perceived as someone who is *persistent* without being overly aggressive. If you do all of these things, I guarantee that you will *significantly* stand out from your competition (other job seekers) and gain substantial momentum toward getting the new job you seek!

Some Other Things to Keep in Mind About *Business* Email

While business email doesn't necessarily have to strictly comply with as many of the rather stringent rules applicable to more *formal* business correspondence, such as a business letter, it still should be treated as "official business" correspondence. As such, you should keep a few general "rules of the road" in mind:

- Make sure there are no **misspellings** or **grammatical errors** in your message (these happen far more often than you might imagine).

- Always include a **salutation,** e.g., "Dear Ms. Jones," etc., and if you do use this formal construction, use a *colon* (:) after "Dear Ms. Jones:" *not* a comma (,) or—heaven forbid!—a semi-colon (;), as a surprising number of people do.

- Even though we currently live in a Twitter and text messaging world, always **spell out** *all* **words**. For example, do *not* use "txt" for "text," etc.

- If your email program allows you to assign an importance rating to each email, **don't automatically assign a "High Importance" rating to every email** you send to the same hiring official. It's usually acceptable to assign such a rating to the *initial* email you send, but, if you assign a "High Importance" rating to every *subsequent* email you send to the same hiring professional, you will very quickly reach the point of diminishing returns. That is, if *every* email is of "High Importance," then arguably, none of them are.

- If your email program allows for it, **create your email in HTML format**. That way, you can make full use of text formatting options, e.g., bold face, Italics, etc. If the email recipient has his/her email program set up to view emails in HTML format, that's great. If not, you've lost nothing.

THE OLD STAND BY – 'SNAIL MAIL,' (AKA THE U.S. POSTAL SERVICE)

Ever hear the old saying about how everything that is *old* can eventually come back around again as *new*? Well, in the digitally connected world we live in today, the old is the U.S. Mail, which in recent years has indeed somewhat come back around again as new. Well, if not new, then certainly different enough from the types of correspondence/contact most of us have grown used to for it to stand out. (When, for example, was the last time *you* actually received a business *letter* at your office, or even a personal letter at home?)

You can use this difference, this *exception* to "normal" communications methods, to your distinct advantage during your new job search. I'll explain how you can accomplish that in this section. But first, I want to briefly revisit the overwhelming role the Internet continues to play in job-hunting today.

Earlier in this chapter I briefly touched on how, relying on the Internet exclusively (or nearly exclusively) to land your next job almost always results in a lot of wasted time and energy, not to even mention a high degree of frustration. In the recruiting business this job-hunting approach is referred to as **"post and hope."** Not so very long ago, a job seeker actually *could* have some realistic *hope* of getting *some* results from his or her postings to jobs on the Internet. Today, not so much.

In the "good old days" of online job-hunting, you could reasonably expect to apply for a position on the Internet, i.e., the job boards, have a real, *live* person review and evaluate your résumé and then receive at least *some* type of response:

- An email, letter or postcard telling you that your résumé had in fact been received, reviewed and would (perhaps) be kept on file for future reference.

- An email asking you to complete an additional online application, which *could* have meant that you were possibly advancing to the next step in the hiring process.

Or maybe, just maybe, you would actually receive a phone call and have a phone interview!

Here is the scenario that typically unfolds today when you post for a job on the Internet:

- Hundreds, and sometimes thousands, of résumés are received for many open positions, particularly the GREAT positions. (Two examples: One position our recruiting firm recently posted received 809 online applications. One of our clients recently told me her company received over 1,700 applications for just *one* position it posted.)

- Virtually all résumés, especially in the larger companies, are "read" exclusively by computers, at least during the initial stages of applicant consideration.

- Usually, only résumés that contain the appropriate key words for any given position will bubble to the top of the initial computer "read." If your résumé does *not* contain these key words, it is doomed to stay buried forever, no matter how many times you might subsequently apply for the position.

- Even if your résumé makes the first cut by the computer, if you happen to be the 800th applicant, and the company finds the candidate of its choice in, say, the first 200 applicants, you will hear nothing further from the company—even if you just happen to be the most qualified (on paper, at least) candidate to apply!

- And, if your résumé somehow does rise to the top in the initial search by the company's computer, you can still have a long, long way to go. Since staffing levels in Human Resources have been significantly cut in recent years, and with a commensurate increase in the number of résumés received per job opening, best case scenario, the limited number of résumés that ultimately *do* get read by a human being will get a mere 20 to 30 second review, if that.

- Sometimes you *may* receive a *computer-generated* response telling you that your résumé was received. But, more often than not, you don't receive any response at all.

- If you are very, very lucky, you may actually receive an email asking you to fill out an online application, again often never hearing back.

Human Resources departments at companies today want you to think and believe that the *only* way to get a job is to find their posting and make an application online. Thus, like lemmings, 95% of all job seekers find a posting online, apply and then "hope" they hear back. The fact is, "post and hope" is *not* a very viable job-hunting strategy!

How to Use the U.S. Mail to Reach Today's Hiring Managers

There is a way—an *effective* way!—of circumventing the Internet, breaking through all the "clutter" surrounding hiring managers and companies today and actually getting hired. I warn you, however, there is one very important stipulation you must first agree to:

You will have to be willing *and* prepared to do things differently from 95% of today's job seekers.

As this is being written, launching a **direct mail campaign** using the U.S. Mail is one of the top Headhunter Hiring Secrets working in the current job market, and it powerfully brands you as someone who is, in fact, *unique* and *different*. Here are the **SIX steps** involved in this tactic:

STEP 1

Know, *specifically*, what you are good at and be able to brand yourself in regard to how you can **make a company money** or **save a company money**—or **BOTH**!

STEP 2

Identify appropriate **companies** (best free tool is www.zoominfo.com).

STEP 3

Identify appropriate **people** to target. (Refer back to the LinkedIn "hack.")

STEP 4

Craft your **direct mail letter** using the techniques outlined below.

STEP 5

Follow up with an appropriate **phone call** (or voice mail).

STEP 6

Follow up any voice mail left with an appropriately worded **email**.

Since I have already covered steps 1, 2 and 3 in some detail in previous sections of this book, **I will focus on steps 4, 5** and **6 in this section**. Let's begin with the crafting of the **direct mail letter (STEP 4)** to be used in your job search campaign.

The Direct Mail Letter

There are **FIVE** critical components of a *successful* direct mail letter:

- The **headline.**
- **Lead-in** (or transition) **sentence** between the headline and bullet points.

- **Bullet points**.
- Statement of "**accomplishments/achievements**" geared toward *making a company money* or *saving a company money* (or BOTH).
- A **Post Script** (P.S.).

The direct mail letter shown on the next page illustrates how all of these components work together. This direct mail letter is one used by one of our executive recruiting firm's candidates. He was applying for a technical sales position with a leading paint and coatings company.[28] (He got hired!) Let's examine each of these components in more specific detail.

HEADLINE

XYZ CHEMICAL COMPANY HAS THE STRONGEST ENGINEERED CERAMIC PIGMENT TECHNOLOGY IN THE MARKETPLACE!

I think you will easily see *why* this headline (which should be in **bold face** and *centered* immediately after the salutation but before the body copy) *immediately* captured (and focused) the attention of the hiring manager. This is the kind of headline *you* need to create for *your* direct mail letter, making it applicable and appropriate to your professional specialty and the new position you are seeking, of course.

WARNING: Make sure *your* direct mail letter is targeted to a *specific* hiring manager, company and position. In other words, **Do NOT use a one-size-fits-all, generic one**, e.g., "To Whom It May Concern," etc.

LEAD-IN SENTENCE

Make sure your **lead-in** (or transition) **sentence** (which is located immediately after the headline) is a clear, concise and logical link between the headline and the first set of **bullet points** used in the letter. Here is the lead sentence used in our candidate's job-winning direct mail letter:

> And that is **why we should connect . . . because I can bring to you:**

Notice how well he tied in the headline and the first set of bullet points with his lead-in sentence. There is a clear, logical, smooth segue from one element (headline) to the next (first set of bullet points).

---

[28] Feel free to turn to the next page, read the letter, and then come back to this page to see *why* it worked so well!

190 Camden Hill Road
Dallas, TX 75210
678-123-4567 | chris.lastname@gmail.com

Date

Mr. Tom LastName
President and CEO
XYZ Chemical Company
123 Williams Drive
Cincinnati, OH 45257

Dear Mr. LastName:

XYZ CHEMICAL COMPANY HAS THE STRONGEST
ENGINEERED CERAMIC PIGMENT TECHNOLOGY IN THE MARKETPLACE!

And that is **why we should connect . . . because I can bring to you:**

- A blend of both **technical** and **sales skills**
- A strong background in **resins, additives** & **paint formulation**
- Experience in **paint applications**, **equipment** and **troubleshooting**
- The ability to help a customer incorporate new technology more quickly by virtue of having led a team of chemists in the role of technical director

Additionally, some documented successes include:

- Currently in sales/business development with $250 million division of a specialty chemicals company focused on value-added sales of raw materials into paint & coatings:
    - Achieved 121% of revenue budget in 2014.
    - YTD, at 95% of 2015 budget, currently the **highest in the company.**
- Sherwin Williams – **Developed a new waterborne latex emulsion** that brought in $260K in sales in year one and **$4.1 million in year two**. Additionally, led a team in solving a customer's application problem, saving a $2 million account **and increasing margins by 3%.**

As stated on a recent performance review, *"Strongly adds both to the top line & the bottom line: to the top line by driving new business; to the bottom line because he doesn't have to bring technical support to the field to support his business development efforts as many salespeople do."*

Mr. LastName, I look forward to speaking with you regarding how I can add value to *your* team.

Sincerely,

Chris LastName

P.S. I will call you on Tuesday, November 10th, at 9 a.m., CT, to arrange a time for the two of us to talk. If this is not a convenient time, then please ask Mary to call me on my cell phone (678-123-4567) and suggest an alternative time.

BULLET POINTS

As you can see, the candidate got immediately, directly and concisely to the point regarding what he could bring to the table in the position with the first set of bullet points:

- A blend of both **technical** and **sales skills.**
- A strong background in **resins, additives & paint formulation.**
- Experience in **paint applications, equipment** and **troubleshooting.**
- The ability to **help a customer incorporate new technology more quickly** by virtue of having **led a team of chemists in the role of technical director.**

Long introductory paragraphs simply will *not* be read by most of today's busy hiring managers. Most have neither the time nor the patience to plow through long sections of copy. Bullet points usually will be read, though—if they are presented in the fashion that they are in this sample direct mail letter.

STATEMENT OF 'ACCOMPLISHMENTS AND ACHIEVEMENTS'

Then, notice how the candidate briefly outlined his **"Accomplishments & Achievements,"** all of which, by the way, were intentionally geared toward *making the company money* and/or *saving the company money* (or **BOTH**):

Additionally, some documented successes include:

- Currently in sales/business development with $250 million division of a specialty chemicals company focused on value-added sales of raw materials into paint & coatings:
- Achieved 121% of revenue budget in 2014.
- YTD, at 95% of 2015 budget, currently the **highest in the company.**
- Sherwin Williams – **Developed a new waterborne latex emulsion** that brought in $260K in sales in year one and **$4.1 million in year two**. Additionally, led a team in solving a customer's application problem, saving a $2 million account **and increasing margins by 3%.**

Again, I'm sure you will agree, in these bullet points, this candidate quickly and clearly demonstrated how he could **make the company money** *and* **save the company money**!

The P.S.

And finally, let's briefly examine the P.S. used in the candidate's direct mail letter:

> **P.S.** I will call you on Tuesday, November 10th, at 9 a.m. CT, to arrange a time for the two of us to talk. If this is not a convenient time, please ask Mary to call me on my cell phone (678-123-4567) and suggest an alternative time.

Even though to some a P.S. may appear to be nothing more than a frivolus tack-on to a letter, in actuality, the importance of a good, effective P.S. simply cannot be overstated. Study after study shows that a **well-constructed P.S. can increase readership of a letter an astounding 75%**! Plus, when one reads the P.S. and realizes that someone is actually going to call them, you usually have their attention and they normally will then read the rest of the letter. (It is critical, of course, that you call them when you say you will!)

Want to Make *Sure* Your Direct Mail Letter 'Registers'?

Virtually *any* business *letter* received by a hiring manager will stand out simply because it is such a unique method of correspondence today. If you want to practically *guarantee* that your direct mail letter stands out, and will stand the greatest chance of being remembered by the hiring manager, then send it **registered** or **certified** mail, with a return receipt requested through the U.S. Postal Service. (**NOTE:** Certified mail is the least expensive of the two methods of delivery.)

Follow-up Phone Call

The first and foremost point to make about the follow-up phone call **(STEP 5)** after sending your direct mail letter to a hiring manager is this: **If you do NOT follow up with a phone call, at the time and on the date you indicated you would in your direct mail letter, you will effectively *eliminate* yourself from further consideration.**

> **Never, never, never say something like this when you place the follow-up telephone call to your direct mail letter:**
> "Hi, this is (your name), and I am calling to follow up on the letter I sent you. Did you get it?"

Of course, just as I indicated in the section on telephone prospecting, the chances that you will actually get the hiring manager on the line with your first phone call are usually very slim. But just for the sake of illustration, let's assume that you do indeed get him or her on the line when you call. Here is what you should say (using the actual name of the hiring manager, of course!):

> **"Mr./Ms. Hiring Manager, this is** (your name) **calling you this morning at 9 a.m.** (if that's the time you said you would call, of course), **as I indicated I would in the letter I sent you several days ago. Is now a good time for us to speak for a few moments, or should we compare calendars and perhaps schedule a more convenient time?"**

If your direct mail letter did indeed give the hiring manager "cause for pause," he or she may come back with something like this:

> **"Now is as good a time as any, I suppose, and I do remember receiving your letter. Refresh my memory a little bit about the position you're seeking and why you feel you are the right person for it."**

If the hiring manager's response is *anything* along these line, now is the time to *sell* yourself and restate your qualifications (your "value proposition") once again to him or her. So, make sure you are *prepared* to do that *before* placing the call! Simply restating and re-emphasizing key points from your direct mail letter may suffice at this point. If the hiring manager wants to learn more information about you, be assured that he or she will ask you during the telephone conversation.

At the very least, unless you get totally shut down, you will have opened up a dialogue with the hiring manager. Where you take it from there will separate you from other, more typical job seekers, those who are merely "looking for a job, any job."

> **In the follow-up telephone call to your direct mail letter do NOT ask for the job!** The goal is to establish a dialogue with the hiring manager and, if possible, arrange an in-person interview with him/her.

Follow-up Voice Mail[29]

What do you do if you *cannot* get the hiring manager on the line when you make your follow-up telephone call to the direct mail letter you sent to him or her? Try these tactics:

- **Attempt to get in touch with the hiring manager's administrative assistant**, and if you do get this person on the line, tell him or her that the hiring manager was expecting your call at (the time you said you would call). You may be put right through to the hiring manager . . . or not. If not (for whatever reason, i.e., "She is in a meeting . . ." "She has someone in her office and can't speak to you now . . ."), then attempt to learn when you might be able to reschedule the call.

- If you *cannot* get in touch with the administrative assistant, then **leave a voice mail** along these lines:

    "Mr./Ms. Hiring Manager, this is (your name) **calling you today at** (the time you said you would call), **as I indicated I would in the letter I sent you a few days ago. I have a proven track record of success in** (restate your general qualifications, achievements and accomplishments). **I will call you back on** (time and day). **My number is 678-123-456."**

> **Do NOT ask the hiring manager to call *you* back** when (and if) you leave a voice mail to follow up your direct mail letter. He or she simply will NOT call you back. YOU must take the initiative and call him or her back—at the time and day you indicate you will!

---

[29] Also part of STEP 5

Follow-Up Email

If, after attempting to directly contact a hiring manager using the tactics and strategies outlined in **STEPS 4** and **5**, you are unable to do so, then consider making one more attempt, by sending the email featured on the following page.

A few points to consider about this follow-up email:

- You're *gently* bringing the hiring manager *up to date*, i.e., reminding him/her that you have previously made contact, but have been unable to reach him/her.

- You are merely *re-stating* your credentials and what you have to offer the hiring manager and the company, not what they can do for you. You are *not* placing your entire résumé in the body of the email!

- You are very subtly *asking for the order*, i.e., a meeting. You are NOT asking him/her to call *you*, even though, by including your contact telephone number, it's obvious that that option is indeed open to him/her.

Making Contact

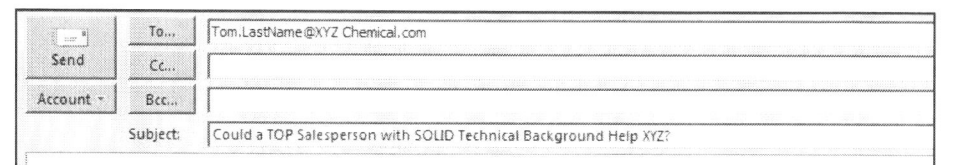

To: Tom.LastName@XYZ Chemical.com
Subject: Could a TOP Salesperson with SOLID Technical Background Help XYZ?

Dear Tom.LastName:

The short answer to the question posed in the subject line is a resounding YES!

A few days ago I sent you a certified letter outlining what I have to offer you and XYZ Chemical. I also left you a couple of voice mails. While I certainly have no intention of becoming a "pest," I would like to once again briefly summarize my **background** and **experience** for you:

- A blend of solid **technical** AND **sales** skills.
- Strong background in **resins, additives** & **paint formulations.**
- Experience in **paint applications, equipment & trouble-shooting.**
- Ability to **help customers incorporate new technologies quicker**, by virtue of having **led a team of chemists** as a **technical director.**

Some **documented successes** at my current employer, a $250 million division of a specialty chemical company, include:

- Achieved 121% of last year's revenue budget.
- YTD, at 95% of current year's revenue budget—the highest in the company.

Shouldn't we compare schedules and spend a half an hour or so discussing how we may be of mutual benefit to each other?

My cell phone number is 123-456-7890.

Thank you and look forward to the opportunity to visit with you soon!

YOUR NAME

Reaching the Point of Diminishing Returns

How many times (beyond the SEVEN "touch" points) should you continue to attempt to contact any given hiring manager? The short answer is this one: Until you actually reach him or her! Realistically, though, the number of times you try to reach any given hiring manager will depend in large part on a couple of things:

- **How much *genuine* interest you have in exploring a particular career opportunity.** (If the position is just one that you think you might find only moderately interesting, then obviously, you're not going to waste a great deal of time attempting to investigate it further.)

- **Whether or not you think there are *legitimate* business reasons you have not been able to get in direct contact with the hiring manager**, e.g., you simply keep missing each other on the telephone, he or she has actually been out of the office, etc. If you have any reason to believe that the hiring manager is simply avoiding you, however, then don't waste an inordinate amount of time. Instead, just move on to the next career opportunity you want to explore and don't look back.

There is a thin line between being persistent and taking the initiative and simply becoming a pest. If you adhere to the "seven touches" principle you will more than likely be perceived as persistent. Attempted contacts after seven touches, however, can quickly degenerate into your being perceived as clearly a pest. Plus, by that time, you quite likely will have reached the point of diminishing returns in your efforts.

No Magic Approach

Just as there aren't any magic words or phrases that can absolutely *guarantee* that you'll get where you want to go in a new job search, there also isn't any one magic approach that will do that, either. Rather, all the methods of approach featured in this chapter work *best* when used in conjunction with each other and in some logical, meaningful combination. You should consider all of these recommended prospecting approaches as important tools in your entire marketing/prospecting tool box.

Chapter Thirteen

THE INBOUND MARKETING PLAN
How to Have the Really GREAT Jobs (And The People Who Do the Hiring) Find *You!*

In the 1989 film *Field of Dreams,* while walking in his cornfield one day, farmer Ray Kinsella hears a voice that whispers, *"If you build it, he will come"* (referring to deceased baseball great "Shoeless" Joe Jackson, a player Ray's father idolized), and then he sees a baseball diamond. Ray did end up building a baseball field and . . . well . . . you probably know the rest of the story (or you can download the movie and watch it!).

If *you* "build it," i.e., your professional image, using the various methods and approaches outlined and recommended in this book, will anyone actually come looking for *you* in today's still highly competitive job market? You bet they will! There is, however, one very important caveat involved, if you expect headhunters,[30] hiring managers and Human Resources professionals to *actively* seek you out and initiate direct contact with *you* (instead of *you* always having to initiate the contact with them!):

> **You must have positioned yourself—professionally *branded* yourself—as *clearly* and *unmistakably* being in the "Top 20%" of ALL available candidates for any given position (and be *perceived* as being among this rarified group by hiring professionals).**[31]

How do you accomplish this goal? Through the quality and thoroughness of your LinkedIn profile, the quality of your résumé and *targeted* cover letter, the specific accomplishments and achievements you've made in your career up to this point, the degree of your involvement in and professional contributions to your profession, to name just several key considerations.

> It is normally among the **Top 20%** of **ALL** candidates that hiring managers, headhunters and in-house corporate recruiters aggressively focus their recruiting efforts for hard-to-fill positions, or those positions which usually aren't advertised—*anywhere*, i.e., the "hidden" job market.

---

[30] Refer back to **Chapter Nine** to review how you can best attract the attention of headhunters so that they will initiate contact with you if a suitable career opportunity comes along.

[31] The fact is, even if you don't happen to be in the "Top 20%" of all candidates, you still don't have to accept your career "fate." You still can have a steady stream of genuine *and* useful career opportunities and information coming directly to you each day. (Just make sure that, if you are currently employed, this information doesn't come to you at your current employer's office!)

In order to take *maximum* advantage of a constant inflow of career information, as well as various career opportunities inherent in it, you must first ensure that you have . . .

- **Branded** yourself as a professional who has both *current* and *relevant* experience for any positions/career opportunities which may interest you or that a hiring professional may contact you about.

- **Positioned** yourself as a candidate who can clearly and unmistakably a.) *make* **a company money**; b.) *save* **a company money**; or ideally, c.) **accomplish** *both* **goals**.

- **Created** (and have diligently maintained) a powerful profile on **LinkedIn**, one that has IMPACT, as well as one that is designed to make it easy for headhunters like me (and, of course, hiring managers and Human Resources professionals) to contact you with career opportunities that may be appropriate for you to consider and not generally available to other job seekers.

SITES THAT CAN GET JOBS, CAREER OPPORTUNITY NEWS COMING DIRECTLY TO YOU!

Four sites that you should *immediately* investigate and consider including in your repertoire of great sources of job/career opportunity news are these:

- www.indeed.com – This is one of the easiest job sites to navigate on the Internet, as well as one of the most widely used by job seekers. To get started searching for job/career information, you merely provide the information for the "What" (job title, keywords, company name, etc.) and the "Where" (City, State, ZIP). You can post your résumé on the site and set up automatic alerts on career opportunities you want to consider.

- www.googlealerts.com (offered in FREE and paid versions) – At this site you can have up-to-date, relevant job information coming directly to you on a daily basis. (Currently, I have a number of alerts set up on this site to get frequent alerts about companies that are hiring top professionals who are in my recruiting firm's market niches. I use this information to network with the hiring companies, as well as with professionals who may be good potential candidates for the job openings. Obviously, you, as a professional seeking new career opportunities, can use such information for job leads in your professional niche.)

- www.google.com/alerts - Like googlealerts, which, by the way, is *not* owned by Google, this site, which *is* owned by Google, can keep a steady flow of current, relevant job/career information coming to your email in-box, either on a daily basis, or even on an "as it happens" basis.

- www.bizjournals.com/search - This site allows you to keep fully and completely up to date on and informed about what is happening across the spectrum in business circles. By knowing what companies are growing, emerging new products and markets, etc., you will be able to more efficiently and effectively prospect for jobs and career opportunities. You will be able to find people in these companies whom you can link in with on LinkedIn, use the information to launch a powerful direct mail campaign, etc.

- www.nicheboards.com – As the site name implies, you can also consider posting your confidential résumé on niche boards, which can more tightly focus the information you will be receiving.

Take Control of Your Career, Your Destiny

Most people dread change, or at least most have some degree of fear about making a change—any change—in their lives. Certainly, that's understandable, but in today's economic climate, that can also have devastating results when it comes to your job, your entire career.

Make no mistake about it, despite continued improvement, a degree of uncertainty remains in the economy in general and in the job market in particular. Not only are salary increases lagging for the currently employed, opportunities for promotion have also dried up considerably in some companies. Today, many companies still are—and have been for some time—running lean and mean, and many seem intent on maintaining that approach—indefinitely. Budgets continue to be slashed, divisions, teams and offices are being reduced in size or eliminated completely in some cases. "Pink slips" are still very much a real threat.

NOW is the time to take charge and FULL control of your own career destiny, and that's particularly true if you are currently employed. It definitely is true that it is almost always easier to get a new job when you already have a job!

Don't unnecessarily expose your career prospects to the fickle whims of a current employer. Don't be caught unaware. Don't risk being blind-sided by your current employer. And certainly, don't commit to riding it out with your current employer, out of some misplaced sense of loyalty—a loyalty, as I've already indicated, that quite probably will *not* be reciprocated. Why? Because on any given Friday, perhaps in the not-too-distant future, without *any* prior notice whatsoever, your company may suddenly decide that both *you* and your *job* need to go!

ADVANTAGES OF AN 'INBOUND MARKETING PLAN'

Besides the obvious convenience of having great career opportunities directly and regularly coming to you, setting up an Inbound Marketing Plan also effectively addresses a key axiom in today's job market that has been previously mentioned:

It used to be said that, "It's not *what* you know that helps you get a job, but rather, *who* you know."

Remember, today, the *new* axiom is . . .

> "It's not *what* you know, or even *who* you know, that helps you get a job; but rather, who knows *you* and can you be *found?!*"

By making sure that you have a high profile and a well-developed (and maintained) presence on LinkedIn and similar sites, which are literally first-stop shops for hiring managers, headhunters and in-house corporate recruiters in search of TOP talent, you certainly can meet this important new requirement!

Part III
Starting to Reap The Rewards of Your Job-Hunting, Prospecting Efforts

If you've carefully followed and diligently applied the tactics and strategies, as well as the various methods and approaches I've recommended up to this point, you have already accomplished a great deal more than the typical job hunter. Now, guess what? You *will* begin to see your efforts pay off! You *will* start receiving some *positive* feedback—some ACTION!—from headhunters, hiring managers and Human Resources professionals you've made contact with during the job-prospecting phase.

After all, I'm assuming that the career opportunities you explored during your prospecting phase were in fact *real* positions, correct? (If they were not, then I strongly recommend that you go back to the beginning of the book and do some serious reviewing!) That means, of course, that potential candidates *will* start to be contacted, assuming the hiring professionals are in fact in earnest about filling the positions! (A relatively safe assumption.)

Which particular candidates would you expect to be among the very *first* contacted by hiring officials? Easy answer here: Those who gave the hiring official the aforementioned "cause for pause," that's who! On the preceding pages of this book I've cited many unique, creative methods for you to employ to accomplish this goal. In Part III, I'm going to show you how to capitalize on that accomplishment. I'm going to show you not only how to *prepare for*, but also, how to *excel at* the next crucial stages in the entire hiring process—the interview stages.

CHAPTER FOURTEEN

THE TELEPHONE INTERVIEW
IT'S BACK TO THE TELEPHONE! (BUT THIS TIME YOU'LL BE ON THE *RECEIVING* END!)

Chances are, if you're currently employed, and have been at your job for any length of time, it may literally have been *years* since you have had a job interview. And if that's indeed the case, it's probably safe to assume that you may be a little "rusty" on the process. Like so many factors involved in a job search in the current job market, today the interview process probably bears little if any resemblance to the one you may remember when you landed your current position.

Not so many years ago—before the job market went south during the Great Recession—here is essentially how the interview process usually got started and unfolded:

- You responded to an online job posting that looked "interesting" to you, and before long, if you were even remotely qualified, the hiring company might well contact you to arrange for an onsite face-to-face interview, if the position was local, or at least to arrange for a telephone interview, if the available position was not in your geographic locale. (Of course the hiring company would take a harder, closer look at you if travel expenses were involved in getting you to an onsite face-to-face interview.)

- If an onsite face-to-face interview was indeed set up and you were able to successfully clear that hurdle, you may have been asked back for a second, and possibly, even a third interview. Certainly, though, by the third interview, you would either have been clearly eliminated or be in the final running for the position. If the companies were aggressively hiring (and many were), they tended to make hiring decisions in a somewhat timely manner and not leave candidates hanging for too long.

Of course that was during a time when jobs were plentiful and the number of available positions was more in sync with the number of qualified candidates available to perform them. No longer is that true, of course. Today, with unemployment (and *under*-employment) still remaining an issue for many people, virtually *any* open position can—and quite often *does!*—generate numerous applications, many from men and women who are in no way even remotely qualified to perform the job. As a result, here is how the interview process normally proceeds for the typical job seeker in *today's* job market:

- You go online and locate job openings that appear "interesting" to you, so you fill out an online job application, include your résumé and fire both of them off.

And you wait, and you wait, and you wait. Usually, because your application and résumé are among many other applications and résumés, it is extremely unlikely that you will ever receive *any* response back from the hiring company, unless it is an automatic, computer-generated, one-size-fits-all, generic response like this: "We have received your application . . . and we will contact you if we have further interest in your candidacy. . . ."

- In the remote event your application and résumé somehow surface to the top (or near the top) of the heap because of your unique qualifications, high demand for your skill set, proper use of keywords, etc., you *might* receive a call from a Human Resources screener. Don't get too excited, though, because this screener has one primary job: To *eliminate* you from further consideration as quickly as possible, in order to whittle down what quite probably is a sizable pool of applicants to a much more manageable size. How do they accomplish this? They wait for you to make some kind of *faux pas* during the telephone screening process! (By the way, because of lack of preparation, naïveté, inexperience, etc., most applicants end up doing precisely that!)

- If—and this is a BIG "if"!—you are able to clear the initial telephone screening by the Human Resources professional, then you *may* be moved to what may be the next step in the process: A telephone interview with the person doing the actual hiring for the open position. And, if you clear this hurdle, you *may* be invited in for the far more meaningful face-to-face interview with the hiring manager!

- If—and again, this is also a BIG "if" in today's job market—you do land a face-to-face interview, don't start packing your bags to move to your new job. You still have a *l – o – n – g* way to go before you have any realistic shot at the job! Why? Because if you pass the litmus test of a first face-to-face interview, you may be required to submit to another, and then another, and another . . . and still not have any really good idea where you actually stand in the running. That's how much some companies today are still dragging out the entire hiring process.

TELEPHONE INTERVIEW

A rather bleak scenario, I'm sure you will agree. But, as I have stressed again and again throughout this book, as long as you have positioned yourself as being among the TOP candidates in today's job market (and continue to be perceived as such by hiring professionals), your experience with the entire hiring process in general, and the interview process in particular, can easily turn out being anything but typical. But to reemphasize, that presupposes that you do the following:

- **Cleary** and **unmistakably brand yourself** as definitely being among the **TOP candidates** in your profession.

- **Position yourself**, through your résumé, your cover letter, your LinkedIn profile, as well as in all of your other online presence, and in virtually every single piece of correspondence/documentation you deliver to a potential employer, as *clearly* **being THE solution to any and all problems the company wants/needs to addres**s by filling the position for which you are applying.

If you accomplish—and then *maintain*—this professional image, this professional *posture,* chances are quite good that you can entirely circumvent the first step in the hiring process—the bottleneck created in the initial application phase, i.e., going online and posting for a job or jobs and getting lost in the shuffle. Indeed, as you have learned throughout this book, if you do position yourself in this fashion, you could end up in a very enviable position: Having headhunters, hiring managers and Human Resources professionals seeking *you* out for suitable career opportunities!

A Few Thoughts About... 'Canned' Responses to Interview Questions

One of the recommendations that most job seekers most often resist is to use *rehearsed* (aka "canned") responses to interview questions that can be predicted with near certainty.

The reasons most often given for this resistance include:

- The answers don't feel (or sound) right.
- I do a lot better in interviews when I "wing it."
- I fear a job interviewer will be able to "see right through" such answers and know they are "canned."

All very understandable fears and concerns. They also just happen to be unfounded and largely without basis—provided you approach the issue of *rehearsed* responses with the right preparation, commitment and frame of mind.

Do you have a favorite TV show, movie or play? Remember this: every single word and sentence of dialogue featured in these shows, movies and plays are not the "genuine" words of the actors and actresses. Still, the dialogue is believable, right? You easily get drawn into the story being told because the actors and actresses convince you that the dialogue and the story line are "real."

Now, I can anticipate what you're going to say and think: Yes, but these people are professional actors and actresses and I am not! Well, during the job search you better become at least a *semi-*professional actor or actress, if you plan to succeed!

The key to accomplishing this feat? Practice, practice, and rehearse, rehearse, then practice and rehearse some more.

Most of your competition (other job seekers) will fumble and grope their way through their answers to key interview questions, thereby hastening their *exclusion* from further consideration. You, on the other hand, by giving informed, intelligent, *rehearsed* answers to these same questions, will *significantly* stand out as a savvy professional, and markedly increase your chances of ultimately winning the job!

One of the Best Kept Secrets About Job Interviewers

Men and women who do job interviews are issued a script, and they must *memorize* this script, *before* they are ever allowed to interview even a single job candidate. Each script contains essentially the same questions . . .

Just kidding, of course! It only seems that way to most job seekers. The point is, you *will* be asked the same questions, or at least the same *types* of questions, over and over again, by different people, during the various stages of the *entire* hiring process. You should therefore both *anticipate* this *and* be prepared to provide appropriate, effective answers to such questions.

Keep in Mind: *Each* Step in the Interview Process is an *Exclusionary* Step—*Not* an *Inclusionary* One!

One of the key new "rules" of the "hiring game" introduced in **Headhunter Hiring Secrets: The Rules of the Hiring Game Have Changed . . . Forever!** was that, contrary to what most people think, the hiring process is *not* one of *inclusion*, but rather, one of *exclusion*! That is, hiring professionals are *not* trying to determine which candidates to include in the hiring pool, they are trying to determine which candidates they can *exclude* from the pool, so they can quickly winnow down the number of candidates to a very select few.

The Initial Telephone Screen: First Step in the *Exclusion* Process

Literally 99.99% of the time your very first contact *from* a hiring manager, headhunter or Human Resources in-house recruiter will be a telephone call. This initial call is intended to accomplish one *primary* goal: To screen you *out of* the potential hiring pool of candidates.

You read that correctly: to screen you *out* of the pool, *not* to try to include you *in* the pool!

(Remember, today's job market is still essentially one of *exclusion*—not, as so many job hunters continue to incorrectly perceive, one of *inclusion*.)

"Amateur" job hunters, or the ones who have taken little or no time to prepare for the new job hunt, usually fall quickly and easily into the screening-out process, too. There are several reasons for that:

- They do *not* screen incoming calls, so they are **not adequately prepared when a call from a hiring professional comes in**. As a consequence, they usually answer the phone with something like this: "Hell – O – O." Then, when the hiring professional identifies himself/herself and mentions the position under consideration, these job seekers may come back with, "Now, who is this again? What is this about? Did I apply for *that* position. . . ? I don't remember that." Great first impression, huh? Very professional!

- Since these job seekers are unprepared (obviously) to properly field questions that they *should* anticipate in the initial screening call, when asked a question such as, "Tell me a little bit about yourself and why you are interested in this position," they are quite likely to answer, "Well, I sent you my résumé, didn't you get it? Everything you need to know about me is in there." (Don't believe it? Happens all the time!)

- These job seekers apparently are still laboring under the impression (FALSE!) that the hiring professional must sell the position to them, the *candidates*. Doesn't work that way anymore, folks, and hasn't for years and probably won't for the foreseeable future, either.

I could go on and on about the incredibly self-defeating (and *incredible!*) things job candidates oftentimes say during this all-important initial phone screen by a hiring professional, but I'm sure you get the point.

Here is how polished, *professional*—and savvy—job seekers handle the initial phone screen:

- They *NEVER* **answer any unexpected call** from a potential hiring professional. Instead, **they screen each call** *before* **responding**. That way they can get organized and prepared *before* discussing a career opportunity.

- They set up a **professional voice mail greeting** on the phone(s) they have designated as their official job-hunting phone(s). The greeting can be something as simple as:

  "You've reached the voice mail of (your name). **Please leave a message and I will return your call as soon as possible. Thank you."**

- When they return the hiring professional's call, they are ready, willing and able to intelligently answer any questions, as well as to specifically discuss the career opportunity. If they are unable to reach the hiring professional when they return the call, they leave this voice mail:

  "(Mr./Ms. hiring professional)**, this is** (your name) **returning your call regarding the** (name of position) **position at** (name of company). **I am excited about discussing this career opportunity with you soon. My number is 123-456-7890. Thank you!"**[32]

PRIMARY PURPOSE OF THE INITIAL TELEPHONE SCREEN

As the name implies, the initial telephone screen has one *primary* purpose: To either screen you in to the hiring process, or, far more likely, to screen you out of it. You should still be optimistic when you do receive this initial call because *something* about you and your qualifications gave the hiring professional enough "cause for pause" to contact you in the first place. Plus, I just showed you how to make sure you will be fully prepared to respond to this call, in order to *significantly* improve your chances of being screened-*in* to the hiring process.

---

[32] Leave only ONE voice mail message. If the hiring professional took the time to call you, the chances are pretty good that he or she will return your call soon. You may follow up with subsequent calls, but do NOT leave another voice mail message.

Telephone Interview

Normally, though certainly not always, the person who will be making the ultimate hiring decision will *not* be the one conducting the initial telephone screen. Some headhunters like to do their own candidate screening (I do), while others prefer to hire someone else to conduct the screens for them. In the corporate world, rarely does the actual hiring manager conduct the initial telephone screens. Usually, this is handled by Human Resources personnel whose sole (or primary) job is to conduct these initial candidate screens. They then pass along the names of the "survivors" to the hiring manager.

If you pass this initial telephone screen you will normally be moved to the next stage in the interviewing process, usually an "official" telephone interview with a hiring manager, if he or she agrees with the initial screener's opinion that you are a candidate worthy of a second look.

Under no circumstances, however, should you view this initial telephone screen as anything but an *official* interview, even though, technically, it usually is not one. If you think to yourself, well, this call really doesn't count because I won't be talking to the one doing the actual hiring, think again. If you don't get past the person doing the initial screening, there won't be any other interviews, official or otherwise. So always be on your toes!

How the Typical, Initial Telephone Screen is Conducted

Let's take a look at how the typical, initial telephone screening process unfolds, when conducted by a Human Resources in-house corporate screener responding to applications the company wants to consider further (as opposed to an in-house corporate recruiter making recruiting calls to candidates they have identified through LinkedIn, etc.).

After some introductory—and usually quite *brief*—chit-chat, the screener can normally be expected to get right to the point. He or she will also usually be working from a prepared script and have a list of pertinent questions (the same ones they use for *all* candidates to be screened, by the way) and will not want (or be able) to spend much time with any single candidate because, typically, they will be making a LOT of calls. So it's best to keep *your* answers to these questions sufficiently comprehensive but nonetheless brief as well.

Telephone Interview

Below are examples of the types of questions you should anticipate at this stage in the process, as well as the recommended ways to answer them:

(SCREENER)

"Now, just to clarify, you are applying for the (name of position), **correct?**"

(YOU)

"Yes, that's correct."

(SCREENER)

"And are you currently employed? I notice on your résumé that you have not named your current employer.

(YOU)[33]

"Yes, I am currently employed, and the reason I have not indicated the name of my current employer on my résumé is because I don't want to risk doing anything to jeopardize my current job while I am exploring other career opportunities. I can tell you, however, that I currently am employed by one of your company's 'major competitors' (laugh)."

(SCREENER) (Should laugh too, but no guarantees.)

"OK, I can understand and appreciate that.

"Tell me a little bit about what you currently do for 'one of my company's major competitors,' then."

(YOU)

"I am a senior salesperson in the (name of territory) territory for the company. In this position I am responsible for seeing that our customers have 'just in time' access to the products and services they need to remain a top competitor in the industry. Two of my

---

[33]If you are *not* currently employed, then obviously, don't say that you are. Still, something about your application caught the company's eye or they wouldn't be contacting you! So capitalize on this opportunity to *sell* your worth to the company during this initial telephone screen.

Telephone Interview

client companies are 'X' and 'Y.' I'm sure you have heard of them, and certainly know their reputation for top quality products and services."

(SCREENER)

"And how long have you been in this position, and what has been your track record to date?"

(YOU)

"This is my seventh year in this position. When I first took over the territory, three years ago, our company was realizing about $5 million in annual sales. Today, I have moved that figure to nearly $10 million and increased my company's market share by 20% during that same period."

(SCREENER)

"Well, that certainly sounds impressive. So, why are you looking for a new position if you're doing so well?"

(YOU)

"Fair question, and I will certainly be glad to answer it.

"Let me assure you that I love my current job and am satisfied that I work for a great company. But I believe I owe it to myself and to my family to look not only at a job, but at an overall career as well. And it definitely appears to me that the (position name) position at your company could very well be the next logical step in my career development.

(SCREENER)

"What is your current salary, and what salary would you expect from our company if you were the successful candidate?"

(YOU)

"My current salary is certainly competitive in the industry. And, while salary is of course always a factor to seriously consider with any new position, it's not the *only* factor, I don't think. I am confident that, if your

company were to find me the candidate of choice, and likewise, if I believe that moving to your company would be the next logical step in my career progression, I would certainly expect the salary to be fair and competitive."

Let's pause here for a moment. You will just have been asked the BIG question—the SALARY QUESTION, and obviously, if you follow my recommended response above to the question, you will appear to have clearly side-stepped the issue, at least for the time being. Sometimes this works and sometimes it does *not* work.

Remember, the person doing the candidate screens may (or may not) know the salary range for the position. If he/she does, and has been advised to *automatically* screen out any candidates who are nowhere near the salary range for the position (either way below or way above), or candidates who will not divulge their current salary, you may want to come clean at this point and you may not. If you do decide to take the come clean approach, I suggest that you merely provide a range, e.g., "in the mid- to high-70s."

Why am I suggesting that you not state your *specific* salary at this stage of the hiring process? Two primary—and very legitimate—reasons:

- **Once you state your *specific* salary you may easily have painted yourself into a corner.** If the figure you cite far exceeds the salary allotted for the position, you will *automatically* be eliminated from further consideration. State a salary that is low, or even ridiculously low, and you certainly have left money on the table that you probably will *never* be able to recoup—if you become the candidate of choice and salary negotiation gets serious.

- Isn't being asked—and sometimes, even implicitly commanded—to reveal your current and expected salary in the very early stages of the hiring process **similar to another poker player asking you what cards you have in your hand, so that they will know whether or not to place a bet?**! Or, let's reverse the process here. What would you expect the reaction of the company (or the hiring professional) to be if one of the first questions *you* asked about the position was, "Now, how much is the salary for this position?" You would be out of the running in a heartbeat!

The position you ultimately decide to take on the salary question, which you can expect to come up early and often during the entire job search, will of course depend largely on how badly you really want the position, how really desperate you are to find a new job.

Whenever candidates we present to our hiring company clients do indeed take our advice never to state, *specifically*, the amount of their current salary, they usually encounter one of two situations:

- **They face the risk of being perceived by the hiring professional as someone who is merely "playing games"** about the salary issue and effectively being eliminated from further consideration.[34]

- If the hiring professional is himself/herself a savvy professional, he or she clearly understands that the hiring process is indeed a "game," and that the salary question is merely an integral part of that game. **Most will simply move on with the interview** (at least for the time being) and **come back to the salary question later, if and when he/she develops serious interest in the candidate.**[35]

---

[34] I have had hiring managers contact me after interviewing candidates our firm has presented and say something to this effect: "If a candidate won't tell me his or her current salary, or what he or she will require for the position under consideration, I won't waste any more time 'playing games' with them." Hey, it sometimes happens! Best advice? Move on to the next career opportunity!

[35] This is particularly the case if the candidate has clearly positioned himself/herself as a TOP candidate and is also perceived as being such by the hiring professional.

Establish Reasonable Salary Expectations Early on in Your New Job Search

The issue of salary, or more precisely, your salary *expectations*, will come up early and often in your new job search. And, unless you want to be summarily *excluded* from further consideration, it is a topic that the hiring manager (or other company representative) should bring up, not you! So, in order to be fully prepared to deal with this issue, you need to do your homework early on in your new job search.

The principal reason salary becomes an almost immediate issue is simple: The hiring manager (and the company he or she represents) wants to determine, as quickly as possible, if your salary expectations are at least in the ballpark, so that he or she doesn't waste any time on you if your expectations are (in his or her opinion) ridiculously out of line with what the company expects to pay for the position. You, on the other hand, have the same goal: To determine if the company is in *your* ballpark.

While there are many sites on the Internet that can assist you in accurately determining a fair and competitive *current* salary for virtually any position(s) sought, I highly recommend these two sites as excellent places to begin your research:

www.salary.com

www.glassdoor.com

Navigating through both of these sites is quick and easy and you can conduct your search by a number of key factors: Job title, locale, company name, etc.

Do NOT take the simplistic approach that many job seekers take . . . Well, I now make "X dollars" and I expect *at least* a 10% increase in salary, therefore the salary that I will require in a new job is at least "X dollars." Far too many factors go into establishing a competitive salary figure to rely on this approach—factors such as geographic locale, size of the hiring company, the hiring company's salary and benefits administration policies and procedures, current job market conditions, supply and demand, etc., etc., etc.

Take the time to do the necessary and appropriate research and you will be prepared to *intelligently* negotiate salary—if and when a job offer actually comes your way!

Throughout this book I have pointed out the many built-in advantages you will have if you have positioned yourself among the TOP candidates in the job market. Salary is yet another key area of differentiation. Today, job candidates who are merely run of the mill or someone just "looking for a job, any job" are rarely in a position to negotiate salary in any meaningful way. You, on the other hand, certainly may be!

I am going to make the assumption that, when you were conducting your early targeting research, you limited your serious inquiries to hiring companies that you know, from your salary research, offer salaries that certainly are in the range of consideration for you.

Let's be realistic here too. Both parties to this salary issue, i.e., the hiring professional and the potential candidate, have—or certainly *should* have—a pretty accurate idea of the salary range that will be involved in any position under consideration. If the candidate did his or her homework, then he or she knows what a realistic salary range will be for any given position. And you can bet that hiring professionals certainly have a very, very good idea of the amount of salary it is likely to take in order to attract top candidates for the positions they are trying to fill.

Before most hiring professionals make serious contact with a potential candidate they already have a relatively high degree of certainty that the candidate's current and/or most recent (and expected) salary will be "in the ball park." Otherwise, they wouldn't waste their time contacting the candidate!

Savvy hiring managers and other hiring professionals understand and respect the many nuances and considerations involved in the salary issue, and that's particularly true when a currently employed person they are considering is involved. They understand that you, the candidate, are selling your skills, talents and experience, and that obviously, you want to make the very best deal possible for yourself. The hiring professional, on the other hand, is trying to make the same very best deal for himself/herself and/or the hiring company.

Now, back to the initial screener call.

(SCREENER)

"What do you know about our company, if anything?"

Telephone Interview

(YOU)[36]

"Well, actually, I know quite a bit about your company, being in the same industry, of course. I know, for example, that your company is a leader in (names of products and/or services), **and that you are entering your** (number) **year in the industry. That says a lot to me, since our industry is so very competitive.**"

(SCREENER)

"Assume for the moment that you become the candidate we ultimately select for the position. How soon could you leave your current employer?"

(YOU)

"I would expect to give two weeks' notice, if we are ultimately able to come to an agreement on this position."

(SCREENER)

"I've looked at your résumé and I can definitely say that it is quite impressive. What is *not* on your résumé that I should know?"

(YOU)

"Well, let me assure you that there is nothing 'negative' about me or my professional career that I have omitted from my résumé. (Laugh)

"A résumé, of course, can only give a glimpse of a professional, his or her major accomplishments and achievements. Unfortunately, it cannot let the reader actually 'see' the real person and what he or she has to offer in the way of personality, commitment to excellence and values and judgment. In order to get a glimpse of those characteristics, you really have to

---

[36]This is where having done your homework on a prospective employer will pay off. If you are not asked a question like this, you've lost nothing. If, however, you *are* asked this question, and you are *prepared* to give an intelligent answer to it, you will automatically stand out from the vast majority of your competitors, i.e., others vying for the same position.

actually meet the person behind the résumé. I would like that chance—the chance to meet with the key decision-makers for this position."

(SCREENER)

"Well, perhaps you will get that chance.

"Now, do you have any questions for me?"

(YOU)

"Yes, I do. What are the next steps in the process? I definitely am interested in pursuing this position and having the opportunity to show you that I can bring the same high-level performance and achievement to your company that I am now delivering for my current employer.

(SCREENER)

"Well, we are currently contacting the candidates we are most interested in at this point. We will then determine which of these candidates to pass along to the person doing the actual hiring. If there is further interest in your candidacy you will be contacted.

(YOU)

"Great! I will look forward to hearing from you soon!"

THE *MOST* IMPORTANT INTERVIEW QUESTION IS ASKED BY YOU!

At the end of virtually each and every interview (including the initial telephone screen) you quite likely will be asked a question like this:

"Do you have any questions for me?"

If you give an inane answer such as, "No, I think you've answered all of my questions," you are quite probably dead in the water, right there, right then! (By the way, just for your information, this is *precisely* what the overwhelming number of candidates say when asked this question!)

Ask for the **"next steps"** in the process!

Does everything always go this neat, this smoothly, during the initial screening call? Of course not, but these initial calls can be expected to be about as highly structured and tightly focused as is the case in this example, if for no other reason than the fact that the screener must make so many of these calls. If he or she were merely to "wing it," or in any way waste time on every call, the task of making these calls could quickly become overwhelming!

THE SCREENER CALL FROM A HEADHUNTER, CORPORATE RECRUITER

When a headhunter or in-house corporate recruiter (and sometimes, even hiring managers, particularly in the smaller companies) *actively* recruits for top talent, i.e., a candidate's name and credentials have surfaced through an online presence or from a candidate's personal contact with the hiring professional through a telephone call, email, direct mail letter, etc., this initial screening call tends to be somewhat longer and much more focused on the individual candidate. The actual length of this initial screening call, as well as the direction it takes, however, depends in large part on how well the candidate fields such calls.

Within the first 30 seconds of my screening calls, for example, I can pretty quickly and accurately assess the quality of a candidate (and so can a good corporate recruiter or hiring manager). Let's just start with how he or she answers my call. If they answer it this way:

(CANDIDATE)

"**Hello.**" (And then dead silence until I say something)

(ME)

"**Hi, this is Skip Freeman. I am an executive recruiter returning your call about the chemical sales position I have open in Denver. Is this John?**"

(CANDIDATE)

"**Who is this again? What is this about?**"

(ME)

"**This is Skip Freeman. You left a voice mail message on my phone a few days ago expressing some degree** of interest in a sales position I am trying to fill for a client."

(CANDIDATE)

"I did? I called *you*? I don't remember calling you. . . ."

I wish I could say that I rarely get a response like this from candidates I call about career opportunities, but I can't. I get this type of response quite often, actually—and so, by the way, do corporate recruiters and hiring managers! And, hey! these candidates are your "competition" in today's job market! That means it really doesn't take much at all in the way of professionalism to *significantly* stand out from this "competition." So it's definitely to your advantage to learn—and then to use—the *correct* way to respond to a hiring professional's call.

Here is the type of candidate response that will make me (and, you can be absolutely assured, corporate recruiters and hiring managers, too) *want* to learn more about you and your qualifications, as well as your possible suitability for a particular position I am attempting to fill for a client company:

(CANDIDATE)

"Good morning! John Smith speaking. How may I help you?"

(ME)

"Good morning, John, this is Skip Freeman returning your call from a few days ago. I am an executive recruiter reaching out to top candidates for a sales position I am trying to fill in the Denver area."

(CANDIDATE)

"Hey, Skip! Thanks so much for returning my call. I genuinely appreciate having an opportunity to discuss the Denver position with you, as well as the opportunity to show you how I can bring real value to the hiring company. . . ."

See the difference? If *you* were a hiring professional, which candidate would *you* want to spend a little time with on the phone, in an attempt to determine if there is perhaps a good fit between him or her and the position you are attempting to fill?

TELEPHONE INTERVIEW

Regardless of who actually makes these initial screener calls to you, as a candidate you should have one principal goal: To go to the next step in the interview process, which usually is a telephone interview with the person who will be doing the actual hiring for the position.

TWO IMPORTANT CONCEPTS TO KEEP IN MIND DURING THE INTERVIEW PROCESS

Let me briefly pause at this point to address two very important concepts to keep firmly in mind throughout the entire interview process:

- **"Shadows on the wall"**
- **"Leading the witness"**

Both concepts were introduced in the first book in the Headhunter Hiring Secrets series of career development/management publications, ***Headhunter Hiring Secrets: The Rules of the Hiring Game Have Changed . . . Forever!*** If you've already read that book, then you are familiar with the concepts. If not, let me briefly examine the concepts and show you how crucial they can be to a successful interview experience.

'SHADOWS ON THE WALL'

Remember when you were a child and your parents put you to bed for the night? Then, suddenly, the wind picked up and began making those huge trees outside your bedroom window sway back and forth, casting scary shadows on the wall. As a child you were of course frightened by the shadows. You really didn't know why! There was just something about those shadows, the noise of the wind, the darkness outside your window, that made you pull the covers over your head—or call for Mom or Dad to bring you a drink of water (even though thirst certainly wasn't your main concern at the time). Anything to make these uneasy, frightening feelings go away!

Well, guess what? From time to time, some hiring managers and other hiring professionals still experience these "shadows on the wall" in their offices—when they are interviewing candidates. How? Primarily by what the candidates sometimes say in response to perfectly routine interview questions. Let me give you an example:

> (HIRING MANAGER) (Assume the interview has been going very well up to this point)

"Tell me how you feel about the possibility of moving all the way from San Diego to Denver."

(CANDIDATE)

"Well, to tell you the truth, I would move all the way to the Antarctic to get away from the boss I have now."

ALARM! ALARM! ALARM!

The hiring manager suddenly sees "shadows" on his/her office wall, and they were initiated by the candidate's incredibly self-defeating answer to the question about a move to Denver! Now, the hiring manager fears *any* further *consideration* of this candidate for the position. After all, if the candidate feels this strongly (and *negatively*) about his current boss, and quite apparently has no hesitation whatsoever to freely comment on it, he easily and quickly could become a behavior problem for the company.

Interview soon over, candidate *eliminated* from further consideration!

Think this type of thing doesn't really happen? Think again. It happens all the time—even to highly qualified, *prepared* candidates. It can be the result of simply falling into a (false) sense of well-being after having established good rapport with the hiring manager, or merely the result of a brief lapse of professionalism. Whatever the cause, unfortunately, it definitely happens with some degree of regularity. Don't *you* make this mistake!

'LEADING THE WITNESS'

By virtue of the fact that they conduct so many candidate interviews of one type or another on a regular basis, most headhunters and in-house corporate recruiters usually are quite skilled interviewers. Hiring managers? Maybe, maybe not, and that's usually true because most hiring managers rarely spend much time interviewing candidates during their entire career. So, this is where the concept of "leading the witness" comes into play and can serve you well when interviewing with a hiring manager (either on the telephone or in person).

Whether or not a hiring manager is even consciously aware of it, he or she is attempting to learn **several key things** about you, the candidate, during *any* interview:

- **Can you *do* the job**, i.e., are you adequately prepared, either by education or experience (or both) to actually perform the tasks involved in the particular job under consideration?

- **Do you *want* to do the job**, i.e., do you have a genuine desire and willingness to perform the specific tasks involved in this *particular* job, or are you intending to use it merely as a stepping stone to the job you *really* want to do?
- ***Will* you do the job**, i.e., can you be fully expected to hit the deck running from day one and keep running for as long as necessary?
- **Are you a good *cultural fit***, i.e., will you actually "fit in" here at our company, here in our division? We're pretty (serious-minded, fun-loving or whatever people), are you?

A hiring manager may or may not ask you specific questions to elicit the information he or she needs, in order to address these concerns and considerations. That means you, the candidate, must learn how to phrase answers to the questions the hiring manager *does* ask, in order to address these concerns *for* him or her. Let me give you an example of how that might work.

Suppose the hiring manager asks you this question:

> "Where do you see yourself, say, three years down the road, if you are the person I select for this position?"

Think about this question: What is the hiring manager *actually* asking you? Isn't the *real* question this:

> "Do you *want* to do the job—this *specific* job?"

Of course it is! And you should therefore phrase your answer to the hiring manager in such a way as to *lead* him or her to learning the answer to the question that *actually* should have been asked. Here is how you could answer this question and accomplish that goal:

> "I have ambition, of course, but I try never to let my desire to get ahead in my career take a back seat to making sure to take the time to gain strong, valuable experience with my current job. That way, I always have a strong base upon which to build my overall career. If I am your candidate of choice, I plan to excel

at this job and would certainly be in it for the long haul.

"If you, as my boss, feel it is time for me to take on more responsibility and authority, I want to be completely ready!"

Wouldn't *you* find this to be a satisfactory answer to the *real* question being asked by the hiring manager? I know that it's certainly far superior to saying something like this (as some people actually say!): "In three years I intend to have *your* job."

That's what "leading the witness" is all about and how you should put this concept, this tactic, into regular practice, whenever appropriate and necessary, throughout the *entire* interview process.

The principal goal of each and every *telephone contact* with a hiring official or screener is to get to the **FACE-TO-FACE** interview—as soon as possible. Know how many recorded cases there are of a candidate being hired for a fulltime position during a telephone interview? You guessed it . . . ZERO! (Contract positions are *sometimes* filled with just a phone call.)

PREPARING FOR THE CALL

Provided you pass the initial telephone screen, the next step in the interview process is the telephone interview conducted by the hiring manager himself/herself. (If you have been working with a headhunter, he or she will normally facilitate and coordinate the telephone interview with the hiring manager.) Typically, this telephone interview will last about 30 minutes and be considerably more comprehensive than the initial telephone screen. Here are some very important things to consider as you prepare to participate in the telephone interview:

- **Take the call in a *quiet* place** where you will *not* be interrupted or disturbed. (Absolutely no background noise!)
- **Have a pen and paper handy** so that you can take notes during the interview. (No, you will NOT remember all the important details, questions, etc.)

- If you will be participating in the interview using your cell phone, **make sure it is FULLY charged**! (Yes, I've had candidates doing telephone interviews and their cell phone "died" midstream! Not a way to make a good first impression with a hiring manager.)

- **Avoid making distracting noises during the interview**, e.g., sniffling, coughing, clearing your throat, etc. If you must sniffle or cough, or clear your throat, cover the mouthpiece on your phone so the interviewer won't hear it! (I've had the "pleasure" of having to interview people who had to stop and cough practically every other word. Very, very distracting! Very, very unprofessional!)

- **Have a list of questions you intend to ask during the interview**, if you get the opportunity. (No, you will *not* remember the questions you want to ask if you don't write them down!)

- **Make sure you have anticipated the questions that you are *most* likely to be asked** by the hiring manager during the telephone interview—and have carefully and *thoroughly* rehearsed appropriate answers to them. (See boxed item at the top of the next page for the most frequently asked questions for those men and women who are *currently employed*.)

I know what you may be thinking at this point: Hey, all of these things are just really common sense, aren't they? Well, sad to report, oftentimes, common sense really isn't all that common.

QUESTIONS YOU SHOULD ANTICIPATE BEING ASKED—AND HOW TO ANSWER THEM!

Just because you cleared the first interview hurdle, the initial telephone screen, and have now landed a telephone interview with the man or woman who will do the actual hiring, don't you dare relax! The primary goal of the telephone interview with the hiring professional is precisely the same as it is for each and every other step in the entire interview process: to *eliminate* you from further consideration, as quickly and as efficiently as possible. So be on the alert at all times during each and every interview phase!

THE TOP 5 INTERVIEW QUESTIONS *CURRENTLY EMPLOYED* JOB CANDIDATES ARE ASKED

While the actual questions can be worded in a variety of ways, here are the TOP 5 questions *currently employed* job candidates are asked during the interview phases:

1. Tell me about yourself.
2. Why would you consider leaving your current employer?
3. What is your current annual salary? AND/OR, What are your salary expectations for this position?
4. Who are you, as a professional, and what, specifically, are your experience and qualifications for this position?
5. What are your *long-range* career goals?

Many of the questions you can anticipate being asked by the hiring manager, at least initially, are designed to feel you out, to see if you are really as good as your credentials indicate you are. True professionals who are well prepared *and* well rehearsed can easily parry these initial thrusts by the hiring manager. "Pretenders," on the other hand, quickly fall into the hiring manager's carefully set trap and are therefore quickly eliminated.

Here is just a sample of the *types* of questions you should anticipate the hiring manager asking you during the telephone interview, as well as how it is recommended that you respond to these questions:

(HIRING MANAGER) (After the requisite bit of chit-chat at the beginning of the interview)

"So, tell me why you are considering leaving your current job. From your résumé it looks to me as though you are progressing quite well."

(YOU) (No matter *what* the actual reason(s) may be for your wanting to leave your current company)

"I really love my current job and my current company. But I believe it is time to take my career to the next

level by moving to a larger company, one that is a leader in the industry.

"I know that your company is indeed a leader in our industry and I notice that you are currently working on some exciting new ideas and products. I saw, for example, where your company just recently introduced a new (type of product or process) that I would love to have been involved with.[37] It's this kind of thing that makes me excited about the possibility of working for a leader in the industry."

(HIRING MANAGER)

"Yes, my team was heavily involved in that project and we are very proud of our accomplishments.

"Now, tell me, what is your current salary, and what kind of salary would it take to get you onboard, if we decide to go that way?"

(YOU) (Facing essentially the same "salary question" dilemma you faced with the screener during the initial telephone contact, of course.)

"Well, I make a very competitive salary at my current job, and I feel confident that, if I am your candidate of choice, and likewise, if I conclude that this is a career opportunity that I must seriously consider capitalizing on, I am sure your company will also offer a very competitive salary."

Again, let's briefly pause here at the "salary question," which, as I've said, will almost always come up during the very early stages of the interview process. Why? Well, for one thing, the hiring manager knows the salary range that he or she must live with, in order to fill the position. Plus, even though he or she probably has a pretty accurate idea of what your current salary is, the hiring manager still will make an attempt to get you to show your hand, particularly when it comes to your *expected* salary. Why? Because the hiring manager is trying to determine,

---

[37] In order to be able to mention something new, unique or different about the hiring company, though, you must have first done your homework! A simple, fast and easy way to do this is by checking out the company's website *before* the telephone interview, paying particular attention to news releases, etc.

as early as possible, if it is even worth his or her time to consider you further.

For example, if the hiring manager knows that $60,000 is the very top annual salary that can be offered for the position, and reasonably presumes that your current salary is somewhere in the mid- to high-$50s, then he or she likely will retain you in the candidate consideration set, all other things being equal, i.e., you have the right qualifications, experience, etc. But what happens if you tell the hiring manager that your *expected* salary is in the mid- to high-$60s? You quite likely just priced yourself out of the hiring manager's market and you will be *excluded* on the spot—unless you are an *exceptionally* qualified candidate and the hiring manager might be willing to go to the mat to recruit you for the position.

Again, the best advice is to resist citing *specific* salary figures (either current or expected) at this point in the process. If the hiring manager *insists* that you address the salary issue at this point—and some certainly will—then cite a salary range, e.g., "mid- to high-$50s" (or whatever the figure is). Usually, this will satisfy most hiring managers, though certainly not all of them.

I will also reiterate at this point that it's important for you to keep in mind that you are trying to negotiate the best deal for yourself—just as the hiring manager is attempting to do for himself/herself and the hiring company. Once you reveal your "hand" you essentially give away any subsequent salary negotiating power you may have had. If you actually get to a genuine job offer, *that* is the time to negotiate salary, not at this early stage of the game. You should keep that in mind and the hiring manager certainly already knows this fact, or at least he or she should know it. (And if the hiring manager doesn't know this, then perhaps you are dealing with the wrong hiring manager and company!)

As already stated, quite a few hiring managers certainly do know, understand and appreciate how the entire hiring "game" is played, and that includes the salary issue, so many of them will simply roll with your savvy answer to the salary question and move on with the interview—provided they still have a strong interest in you as a candidate.

Now, back to the telephone interview, and let's assume that this hiring manager is one who *will* roll with the answer you've just given to the salary question.

Telephone Interview

(HIRING MANAGER)

"Well, OK, let's set aside the salary issue for the time being.

"Tell me a little bit about yourself and give me some specific examples of the types of experience you've had thus far in your career.

(YOU) (Let's assume you are applying for a senior chemist position, with an emphasis on paints and coatings)

"Well, I have a master's degree in chemistry from Northwestern University, and my area of specialty is paints and coatings.

"During the ten years I have been with my current company, I have had the opportunity to be involved in some very exciting, ground-breaking projects. For example, the team I currently lead just last year developed what is shaping up to be a revolutionary concrete patch. Because of the unique color additives included with the product, our patch blends in nearly perfectly with existing concrete surfaces, etc., etc., etc."

In other words, this is where you provide a *synopsis* of your professional accomplishments and achievements. Of course the hiring manager has already seen your résumé and has a good idea of what you've *stated* are your experience and qualifications or you wouldn't be receiving this call. The hiring manager's goal here is to see how well *you* tell the story in your own words, and equally important, to see if you tell the *same* story as the one told in your résumé.

Another question that you may be asked during this telephone interview is the "long-range plans/goals" question. It usually is phrased along these lines:

(HIRING MANAGER)

"Tell me a little bit about where you want to be in your career, say, five years down the road."

Remember the previous section in this chapter on **"leading the witness"**? Where one of the things a hiring manager tries to determine during an interview is whether or not the candidate actually wants to do the *specific* job under consideration, or if the candidate is merely viewing the position as a brief stepping stone to bigger and better things? Well, this is a prime example of that type of question, and the advice I gave you in the "leading the witness" section equally applies here.

(YOU)

"Well, I'll readily admit that I have ambition, but that said, I still try never to let my desire to get ahead in my career take a back seat to making sure that I take the time to gain strong, valuable experience with my current job. That way, I always have a strong base upon which to build my overall career and the progression of it. If I am the candidate selected, I plan to excel at this job and am certainly in it for the long haul.

"If and when you, or whoever else might be my boss at the time, feel it is time for me to take on more responsibility and authority, I want to be completely prepared, completely capable and ready!"

If you satisfactorily answer questions like this that are posed during this telephone interview, then the hiring manager is likely to begin winding down the interview by saying something like this:

(HIRING MANAGER)

"Well, I've asked you a lot of questions, now it's your turn. Do you have any questions for me?"

As has already been pointed out, here is how an embarrassing number of candidates will inevitably answer this question, which is really one of the *most* important questions during *any* interview:

(YOU)

"No, I think you've pretty well covered everything and answered all my questions."

Anytime I have ever had a candidate answer this key question from a hiring manager in this manner—despite the fact that the candidate had been thoroughly coached on the *correct* way to answer it!—they were *immediately* washed out of the process. A typical response to me from the hiring manager, when I make a follow-up phone call to him or her to learn how the interview went with our candidate, usually goes something like this:

> "Skip, your candidate did pretty well during the interview until, at the very end, when I asked him if *he* had any questions for me. He said he didn't, and to be honest about it, that bothers me a great deal. Why doesn't he have any curiosity? I know I'm not perfect and that there probably were things about the job that I didn't cover, or cover well enough. Why didn't he notice these things? Why didn't he ask me to clarify or amplify?
>
> "I think I will have to pass on him."

Petty? Shortsighted on the part of the hiring manager? I don't really think so, to be honest about it. Don't you make this same mistake and jeopardize what might otherwise have been a very successful interview by dropping the ball on this question.

Well, then, how should this question be answered? Here is one way:

> (YOU)
>
> "**You certainly have been very thorough, and I genuinely appreciate your taking the time to explain the position to me. I do, however, have a couple of questions**" (then, using the "crib sheet" you prepared in *advance* and in *anticipation* of this very question, ask the hiring manager to tell you a little more about a process, product, company procedure, etc.).

After the hiring manager has addressed your closing interview questions, then it's time for the "zinger" question from you! Remember what that question is? Here, once again, is that all-important question:

> (YOU)
>
> "**Thank you for clarifying these issues for me. And now, I simply have one more question for you: What are the *NEXT STEPS* in the process? I am very excited about this career opportunity and I know I can make a substantial contribution to the great team you have already assembled.**

If you have managed to make a *very* favorable impression on the hiring manager during the telephone interview, and if he or she is one who feels comfortable making quick decisions, he or she may come back with something like this:

(HIRING MANAGER)

"I will be interviewing candidates for the next week or two, and then I will decide which ones to bring in for an in-person interview.

"Based upon what I have learned from you today, I feel comfortable setting up an onsite visit with you, if you want to pursue this further."

(YOU)

"Great! Yes, I definitely want to pursue this position further."

(HIRING MANAGER)

"OK. Let's do this: I'll check my schedule and see when a good time would be to have you come in to my office. I'll call you back within a few days. Is that all right with you?"

Or, perhaps you *did* make a very favorable impression with the hiring manager, but he or she always plays it close to the vest, so he or she may say:

(HIRING MANAGER)

"I will be interviewing candidates for the next week or two, and then I will decide which ones to bring in for an in-person interview. If you are among this group I will call you to arrange an interview time."

Were you just blown off with the hiring manager's response? Not necessarily. He or she may simply be the type of person who wants to interview *all* the candidates who made the screener cut *before* making *any* decisions about which candidates, if any, to bring in for face-to-face interviews.

On the other hand, if you were advised by the hiring manager that he or she intends to bring you in for a face-to-face interview, that doesn't mean you've got the job, either. All it means is that you cleared yet another hurdle on the way to (perhaps) ultimately landing the position. That's it. To be sure, you're making progress, but you still have a long way to go to the finish line!

WHAT ARE *YOUR* NEXT STEPS AFTER THE TELEPHONE INTERVIEW?

You've successfully completed the telephone interview with the hiring manager, and based upon the positive (or at least not negative) feedback from him or her, you're feeling pretty good about your chances at this point. You've even done something most other candidates who were also interviewed didn't even *think* about doing—you sent a Thank You note or email. Now what? What are *your* NEXT STEPS in the process? Two things, actually:

- **You're going to wait** . . . and then wait some more.
- You're going to **keep on keepin' on**.

How long of a wait until you hear something back from the hiring manager who interviewed you on the telephone? That depends entirely on the individual hiring manager and how much "pain" he or she is feeling as the result of a job going unfilled.

In recent years many hiring managers have themselves been considerably under the gun to perform exceptionally well or face ending up on the other side of the desk. That means many if not most are certainly hesitant about making any fast hiring decisions that could possibly come back to haunt them and their companies.

You could hear back from the hiring manager in days, or perhaps weeks. Or, perhaps never—unless you follow up with a phone call or some other method of contact. And that is why you are going to primarily concentrate your efforts on the second step of *your* next steps, to keep on keepin' on.

For some inexplicable reason, some job hunters actually stop, or at least begin to slow walk, their job-hunting activities once they get what they perceive to be a good "bite" from a hiring manager and/or a hiring company. Never, never, never take this approach, no matter how GREAT you think your chances might be of actually landing the job you're seeking!

A savvy job hunter understands and appreciates that a successful job search involves generating *genuine* career *opportunities* (plural)—lots of them! The idea is to end up with several (or more!) really good career opportunities to choose from as the job search heads toward its culmination. That means you have to continually be doing the things suggested and recommended in this book to generate these opportunities. And if you do this, the opportunities *will* come, believe that!

How Many Times Should You Follow Up After a Telephone Interview?

You sent a follow-up Thank You note or email after your telephone interview with a hiring manager. You waited two or three weeks after that and then placed a follow-up phone call (and had to leave a voice mail because you couldn't reach the hiring manager directly) and/or sent a follow-up email, yet you have heard nothing from the hiring manager. You still have no idea where you stand, if anywhere, with regard to the position. What should be your next step in the process?

To be honest about it, if, after these follow-up steps, you've still heard nothing, you probably should conclude that you are no longer in the running for the position. Any additional follow up at this stage will only make you look desperate, and that's certainly something you want to avoid.

Remember, you, too, are a professional. You, too, are currently making (or have recently made) *significant* contributions to your profession and your time is also valuable. As I reminded you earlier, you are NOT a supplicant, someone who needs a job so badly that you will practically beg for it, so don't even think about acting like one. You have valuable skills and experience that you are ready, willing and able to employ for select employers. If any particular position doesn't seem to be a good fit, for either you or for them, then simply move on to the next career opportunity you have generated through your job search activities.

How to 'Smoke' The Other Interviewed Candidates!

IMMEDIATELY send a **THANK YOU! note** or **email** following your telephone interview (and **following each and every other interview you may have**)! In this note or email you should *briefly* restate your "value proposition," i.e., what you can do for the hiring manager and his/her company. Not only will the vast majority of other interviewed candidates *fail* to do this simple thing, most will not even *think* about doing it!

Chapter Fifteen

The Face-to-Face Interview

You've Got Your First Onsite Job Interview (aka the **Face-to-Face** Interview) Maybe in Years! Now What?!

Once you successfully get by the telephone interview with a hiring manager, the next step in the interview process, if you are in fact selected to go to the next step, is the all-important **face-to-face** job interview, usually conducted onsite at the hiring company's offices. Quite understandably, because it may literally have been years since your last onsite job interview, you're probably more than just a little bit nervous and anxious.

While this first face-to-face interview is hardly the last step along the route to successfully competing for a position, you have every right to be proud of your progress to this point. Depending on the level and type of position, many other candidates were eliminated from further consideration during the initial telephone screen. Still more were eliminated during the hiring manager's telephone interview. You can be assured that only a select few candidates have been called in for a face-to-face interview. Celebrate the fact that you are among this select few, but keep your eye on the ball too! Get ready for your next crucible.

In this chapter I am going to show you both how to adequately prepare for the face-to-face interview *and* how to **ACE the interview**! If you follow my advice and suggestions, not only will you stand head and shoulders above the other candidates to be interviewed, and who will *not* be nearly as well prepared as you, you will also be in a completely different league!

Pre-Planning for the Face-to-Face Interview

Overall Dress, Appearance and Grooming

Chances are, you will have at least a week to ten days (or more) before you are scheduled to go in for your face-to-face interview with the hiring manager. Use this time wisely to adequately and thoroughly prepare for the interview. Important things to consider in the overall **dress and grooming** category **when planning ahead and preparing for the day of the interview**:

- **Clothing.** Obviously, to the extent possible, you'll want to blend in with the company's overall environment and culture, but determining precisely how to do that is not as straightforward as you might at first suppose. A good way to learn the company's dress code is simply to call the front desk and ask the receptionist how both men and women dress in the company. Make sure you ask for specifics, and don't settle for a description such as "business casual" because that term can have so many different meanings across companies.

In most cases, when in doubt about how to dress appropriately for an interview, neither men nor women can go wrong by wearing a darker, conservatively cut business suit and a white (or light colored) shirt or blouse. Men should also wear a conservative tie.

- **Jewelry, other accoutrements.** Both men and women should go light on jewelry, such as wristwatches, earrings, finger rings, bracelets (ankle and arm), brightly colored scarves and/or other accessories that can sometimes prove unnecessarily distracting.

  If you men currently sport earrings, it's advisable to leave them at home. While it certainly has become much more acceptable these days for men to wear earrings, some people still find men's earrings distracting, so remove them for job interviews and simply avoid possibly offending a hiring manager by wearing them.

- **Hair.** If it's still two weeks away from when you men normally get your hair cut, get it cut now. Women, if you are a few weeks out from your hair dresser, move your appointment up, if possible. And oh, do you now have colored streaks in your hair, or have it colored in some outrageous color? Lose the streaks and/or the outrageous color *before* the interview!

- **Shoes.** Are those scuffed, unpolished shoes I see on your feet, men? You could wear the finest clothing, but if your shoes are not clean and shined, you can still look like a street person! Women? You also make sure *your* shoes are shined, although usually that isn't much of a problem for you because, unlike most men, you probably have more than one (*perhaps* two) pair of dress shoes!

- **Makeup.** Women, be sure you are conservative in your application of makeup, i.e., no brightly colored lipstick, not too much rouge, etc. Men? Don't even think about it.

- **Facial hair.** Men, it's OK to have a *conservative* mustache and perhaps even a short, well-trimmed beard.

- **Teeth**. Brush especially well before going in to the interview. If possible, take a bathroom break upon arrival at the company office and do it then. Be sure to use mouthwash too! Also, If you can arrange it, schedule a trip to your dentist and get your teeth whitened before the scheduled interview date. Oh, and did I mention to be sure to use mouthwash?

- **Fingernails.** Women, schedule a visit to the nail salon, but choose a conservative, low-key color, if you apply color at all to your nails. Men, it's OK for you to go to the nail salon too, but no color on the nails, please.

- **Aftershave, deodorant and cologne.** If you use aftershave and/or cologne, don't take a bath in it. Apply it sparingly. Better yet, don't apply it at all. I actually encountered a situation once where a candidate did not get hired simply because the fragrance of perfume she wore reminded the hiring manager of a former employee she couldn't stand! (Hey! Whoever said life was fair?!)

Most of us mere mortals will never be mistaken for one of the "beautiful people," but with just a *little* extra effort, all of us can look pretty darned good. Make sure you make that little extra effort *before* the face-to-face interview. It can pay you substantial dividends!

Do Your Homework Well
in Advance of the Interview

Remember all those notes you've been taking (and keeping) on hiring professionals you've contacted and the companies they represent? (What?! You haven't been keeping notes of your job search activities and contacts?!) Now clearly is the time to review them (or *prepare* them, if that's the case), so that you will be *completely* prepared when you go in for the face-to-face interview. I also recommend that, once you prepare these notes in some sort of logical format, you place them in an attractive, *professional-looking* binder that you can discretely refer to during the face-to-face interview, if that should become necessary.

THE HIRING COMPANY

As incredible as it may seem, many job hunters do more in depth research about the next vehicle they plan to buy than they do about a company that could end up playing a key future role in their professional career. Don't you be among these short-sighted folks.

I'm going to assume that you generated at least some general information about the company during your preliminary job search targeting activities. But before you go in to the face-to-face interview, you will want to be sure that you do some more in-depth research, so you will be as thoroughly prepared as possible. The best place to begin this research is on the company's own website, paying particular attention to the company's Mission Statement (if it's featured on the website, and it almost always is), company news releases and published articles, and of course the "sell" copy usually featured throughout the site.

Here are some key areas you should focus on in this more in-depth research:

- **Unique or "revolutionary" products and/or services offered by the company**, all of which will be prominently displayed and mentioned on the company website. (It doesn't really matter if the products and/or services touted by the company itself actually *are* "revolutionary" or unique, only that the *company* positions them as being so!)
- **Relative position within the industry**, e.g., overall ranking on the basis of sales volume, market share, etc.
- **Historical/future perspective.** What are the origins of the company? Where does the company seem headed, both from its own perspective and/or from the perspective of investors and analysts, if it is a public company?

THE HIRING MANAGER

Not only is it crucial that you know as much as possible about the hiring *company* you'll be interviewing with, you also need to learn as much as possible about the person who will be interviewing you, usually the hiring manager. As I said about your hiring company research, you may already have generated some useful, basic information about the hiring manager when you were conducting early job targeting activities, but before the face-to-face interview, you'll also want more in-depth information about him or her, if it's available.

Why? Simple reason: **People tend to hire people they like—and people who are most like them!** And what makes us like other people? Well, if they seem to be interested in us, as well as know at least a little something about us, that's an important first step.

To learn more about the hiring manager visit (or revisit) Google, LinkedIn and ZoomInfo. Nowadays, nearly everyone has at least *some* information about themselves on all three of these sites, particularly on Google. You might, for example, discover a brief biography that has been published somewhere on the hiring manager. If so, you may be able to learn details about his or her career, where he or she went to school, outside interests, etc. Does he or she currently write a blog (a whole lot of people do these days, particularly those in middle management who are trying to get ahead themselves)? If so, make sure to read at least the latest one and be prepared to make a comment about it, if the opportunity should arise during the interview.

> The more you can learn about the hiring manager *before* the face-to-face interview the more likely it is that you will be able to quickly establish rapport with him or her. Why is this important? **Because people tend to hire people they *like* AND people who are most like themselves!** The way to get other people to like *you* is to show some interest in *them*!

You should also check out anything that might be related to the hiring manager on the company's website, e.g., was he or she recently promoted? Any other significant accomplishments? Depending on the job level of the hiring manager, this kind of information may or may not be featured on the company website, but it's certainly worth checking, anyway.

YOUR 90-SECOND ELEVATOR SPEECH

Should you prepare what's known as the 90-second elevator speech, that brief dialogue which you employ to tell a hiring manager (or his/her representative who may greet you in the lobby) what you have to offer the company on either your literal or figurative "elevator ride" to the interview office? Even though there are some employment experts who are suggesting that the elevator speech has become an anachronism, I beg to differ. Regardless of whether or not an actual elevator ride awaits you when you first arrive at the hiring manager's office, there nonetheless will almost always be a brief period of time before the actual interview begins. This is when you most likely will get ice-breaker questions, such as . . .

"Well, tell me a little bit about how you think you might be able to help our company."

Obviously, this is just *one* way this ice-breaker question could be asked, but regardless of *how* it is actually phrased, the *real* question is almost always . . .

"Tell me in just a few minutes why I should spend anytime at all interviewing you for this position."

Some job hunters will immediately decide that this ice-breaker question is really just informal chit-chat and decide to wing the answer. Not a wise decision. Every step along the way, every question, no matter how innocent it may *appear* to be, every response you will be asked to give to these questions, should be well considered, well orchestrated and well rehearsed.

> A 90-second elevator speech is really your "verbal calling card." You use it to tell **WHO** you are, what your **SKILLS** and **EXPERIENCE** are, and how you can employ these skills and this experience for the benefit of the hiring company.

That is not to say, however, that you should come across as some type of automaton. Rather, what I am saying is that it is always a good idea to know where you are at virtually every step of the way during your job search, as well as where you want to go and how you intend to get there. A well-developed, well-thought-out elevator speech is just part of this total preparation.

Think of your 90-second elevator speech as your verbal "calling card." It is a brief statement summarizing who you are, what you have to offer, and how you can be a solution to a hiring company's problems and/or challenges. As is the case with virtually every aspect of communication, both verbal and written, during the job search, there are no magic words.

That said, here is an example of an effective 90-second elevator speech:

> "I am a very successful salesperson specializing in chemical sales to Fortune 500 clients. During each of the last ten years I have been with my current company, I have been in the top 10 percent of all salespeople in our company, on the basis of total sales volume. This year, for example, I am on pace for sales exceeding $10 million.
>
> "Part of the reason I am successful is because I take the time to listen—really listen—to what my clients and prospects both need and want, and then I make sure that I deliver it.
>
> "If given the opportunity, I would like to put my sales skills, as well as my determination to always be among the top salespeople, to work for you and your company."

Reading this elevator speech aloud, at a normal speaking pace, takes about 45 seconds (longer in the South, shorter in the Northeast), or one-half of a 90-second elevator speech, so obviously, you could add to it, but you probably shouldn't subtract from it. The point is, the 90-second elevator speech can be less than that time limit, but under no circumstances is it a good idea to *exceed* that time limit. Otherwise, it can easily become a long-winded, boring diatribe.

Use your own words when you develop your 90-second elevator speech, of course, and obviously, tailor it for your professional niche. Just make sure you have one ready when you go in for the face-to-face interview.

AT LAST! THE DAY OF THE INTERVIEW

If you've done everything I have advised during your pre-planning activities for the face-to-face interview, you should be feeling *very* well prepared when you arrive at the hiring company's office on the actual day of the interview. And speaking of your arrival, let's get the first crucial consideration out of the way right up front.

IF YOU'RE LATE, YOU WON'T BE SEEN AS GREAT!

No matter how GREAT you might look on paper, or even how GREAT your interview skills may prove to be during the face-to-face interview, if you show up LATE for the interview, you definitely will NOT be viewed as GREAT in any sense of the word! Quite the contrary, actually. Let me illustrate this point to you by relating a recent example of how not being on time for an interview can cost a candidate and cost him or her dearly.

Woody Allen *Almost* Had it Right!

Here is what comedian Woody Allen had to say about SUCCESS:

"75% of success is just showing up."

Not to put too fine a point on it, what he *should* have said is this:

"75% of success is just showing up . . . ON TIME!"

And that is especially true when it comes to succeeding at the face-to-face job interview!

I recently had an *exceptional* candidate literally blow a face-to-face interview because he didn't arrive at the interview **on time**! (It didn't matter that the candidate had what he thought was a legitimate excuse for being late, i.e., he got lost!). The candidate made such a poor first impression with the hiring manager because he didn't arrive at the scheduled interview time that the interview got off to a disastrous start and degenerated from there. As a matter of fact, the entire interview lasted a mere 20 minutes, when usually, a face-to-face interview lasts at least an hour and sometimes even longer.

Here is what the hiring manager told me over the telephone during the after-action report:

> **"Skip, there is no question about this candidate having a very good track record and great credentials,"** she said. **"But this is a sales position I am trying to fill. Is this the kind of performance I can expect if I hire him? How many clients could he alienate by not showing up on time? Maybe none, and maybe he usually is on time for appointments. Still, I simply don't want to take a risk on hiring him."**

End of story, end of candidacy for our candidate! How could all of this been avoided? Well, just for starters, since the candidate had to fly to the job interview, he should have arrived the night before the interview, not the day of it, as he did. And, if he had done that, he could have then scouted out the business office the night before so that he wouldn't have gotten lost the day of the interview!

Picky? Unfair? An unusually harsh reaction or a total lack of understanding from a hiring manager? Yes, yes, and NO! Today's hiring managers are far more leery of making poor hiring decisions than at any time in recent memory. If they consistently make poor hiring decisions, they won't be in the hiring business long in today's job market!

WHILE YOU'RE WAITING TO BE INTERVIEWED

Sometimes you will be whisked right in to the hiring manager's office to begin the interview almost immediately upon arriving at the hiring company. More typically, however, you will find yourself sitting in the waiting area for five to ten minutes while the hiring manager prepares to interview you. This might be a good time for you to excuse yourself and head for the nearest restroom, where you can take care of the business a restroom is primarily intended for AND to freshen up. Make sure your hair is combed, your shirt (or blouse) is tucked in, (and, men) your tie is straight, there is no food on your face, etc.

Once you return to the waiting area, be sure to keep your guard up. Even though you might not be aware of it, eyes and ears are definitely on you. Certainly take the opportunity to visit and exchange pleasantries with any nearby employees (such as the hiring manager's administrative assistant, for example), but watch what you say (and do) because if it's anything even *borderline* negative or questionable it *will* be reported back to the hiring manager—right after you're gone!

LIGHTS, CAMERA, ACTION!

Finally, after all your careful planning and preparation, you're ushered in to the hiring manager's office and the interview gets underway! You are "center stage" and all attention is directed toward you! This is "where the rubber meets the road"! This is your 60 minutes (give or take) "audition"! If you blow it here, you're history!

But *you* are not going to blow it! Oh, you may be a little bit nervous, but because you've followed my advice and recommendations throughout this book, you will also be far, far better prepared than the overwhelming majority of your competition, i.e., other candidates to be interviewed.

Face-to-Face Interview

Indeed, you should be able to ACE the interview! How do I know you are going to be able to ACE it? Because in this section I am going to tell you . . .

- The **types of questions you should anticipate**, as well as the best **ways to answer them and stay in the game.**
- How to avoid casting "shadows on the wall."
- How to "lead the witness," if necessary.
- **How to effectively conclude the interview** from your perspective, your point of view.
- **How to properly conduct yourself and *effectively* interact with the hiring manager**, thereby clearly demonstrating that you will indeed be a good cultural fit for the organization.

Getting the Ball Rolling . . .

If the hiring manager was not the person who greeted you on your arrival, and you did not therefore have the opportunity to use your 90-second elevator speech on him or her, more than likely, you will now have the opportunity to do that. Usually this opportunity will come about when the hiring manager asks you something like this:

(HIRING MANAGER)

"Well, thanks for coming in today, (your name). **To get things rolling, tell me why you think you might be qualified to do this job. Tell me what you think you can do for me and my company.**"

For illustration purposes, let's assume that the position you're applying for is a sales position. Let's use a variation of the 90-second elevator speech featured earlier in the chapter to answer the hiring manager's question:

"**Well, as you may recall from my résumé, I am a very successful salesperson who specializes in chemical sales to my current company's clients, some of which are Fortune 500 companies, so they are quite demanding in their expectations. I guess that's why they are in the Fortune 500, right?** (small laugh)

"During each of the last ten years I have consistently been ranked in the top 10 percent of all salespeople in our company, on the basis of total sales volume. This year, for example, I am on pace for sales exceeding $10 million. When I was first assigned to my current territory it was only generating about $2 million in annual sales revenue.

"Part of the reason I am successful is because I take the time to listen—really listen—to what my clients and prospects say they need and want, and then I make sure that I deliver it. That makes it a 'win-win' situation for everyone involved.

"If given the opportunity, I would like to put my sales skills, as well as my determination to always be among the top salespeople, to work for you and your company."

(HIRING MANAGER)

"Fair enough. Now, let me ask you some questions that will help me learn a little bit more about you, as well as help me determine if I think you might be a good fit for this position, OK?"

Now, from this point on, and throughout most of the rest of the interview, the hiring manager will be asking questions that are designed to help him or her determine if you should be *excluded* from further consideration—OR *included* for perhaps a second or third look later on in the hiring process.

> The *principal* goal you should have during the face-to-face interview is to *stay in the game*, to make it to the next step in the process. In other words, to avoid being *excluded* at this point!

The odds are that most, if not all, of these questions will have been asked of virtually all candidates interviewed *before* you, and will also be asked of virtually all candidates who may *follow* you. If you've been paying attention and following my advice up to this point, there will, however, be a BIG difference between how *you* field these questions and how most of the other candidates will field them. You, having been adequately prepared for and anticipating these questions, can shine during the interview. Most of your competition, i.e., the other interviewed candidates, simply will not.

Now, let's take a look at some of the specific types of questions that I can *guarantee* you will almost always be asked during the face-to-face interview.

THE 'TELL ME ABOUT YOURSELF' QUESTION

To many job seekers the "tell me about yourself" question appears to be nothing more than a throw-away, a warm-up question. And in a sense, it *is* a warm up question, but be assured that it is *not* a *throw-away* question! Indeed, it is **one of the most critical questions to consider, and then to formulate an appropriate response to, when preparing for a job interview.** Blow the answer to the question and you risk irrevocably and immediately coming across as just another run-of-the mill candidate and could quite possibly end up blowing the entire job interview. Nail the answer and . . . well . . . good things certainly can be expected to follow.

As I point out in **Headhunter Hiring Secrets: The Rules of the Hiring Game Have Changed . . . Forever!**, the question really does NOT mean, at least in the traditional sense, well . . . "tell me about yourself"! Those job seekers who are not well prepared usually see it as being *precisely* that, however, and often respond with something like this:

> "Well, let's see. I grew up in rural Minnesota and I graduated from college in 2000, and I really am a BIG baseball fan, etc., etc., etc., *ad nauseum.*"

Trust me on this: When asked at the beginning of a job interview to "Tell me about yourself," the hiring manager is NOT asking for a condensed *personal* biography or your life story! Rather, your answer to the question definitely needs to be *laser-focused* on the specific task at hand: **Getting the position for which you are applying!**

A *THREE-PART* ANSWER WORKS BEST

Our executive recruiting firm, The HTW Group, coaches candidates we present to our hiring company clients to take a THREE-PART approach to answering this key question. I refer to this approach as the ***pre-planned, prepared* marketing statement approach**, with each part, of course, being delivered *consecutively* to comprise the entire answer to the question.

Parts One and Two can normally be used from interview to interview, while **Part Three will need to be *customized* for each unique career opportunity**. Let's briefly examine the makeup of each of the three parts.

Part One

Normally, the first part of the answer will consist of a **one-sentence statement of your career history**, i.e., **essentially the condensed version of your entire career history**. But that's not as challenging as perhaps it might first appear. Here is an example of how Part One can easily be constructed:

> "I am a five-year veteran of LAN/WAN administration and systems engineering, with substantial experience using a variety of contemporary business software systems."

Part Two

This part consists of a **one-** OR **two-sentence** *summary* of a *single* **career accomplishment** that you are especially proud of and one that can reasonably be expected to capture the hiring manager's attention. It must also be an accomplishment that can be easily explained and/or illustrated. It must also absolutely highlight a *bottom-line* impact for the potential employer. Here is an example:

> "Recently, as a long-term contract employee at a local regional bank, I learned that the bank was about to install a particular software system and was planning to use outside consultants for the project. I let them know that I had done a similar installation at my last assignment, outlined how we could get the job done with in-house staff and successfully complete the installation for $55-$65K *less* than it would have cost with outside consultants."

FACE-TO-FACE INTERVIEW

Part Three

This final part is the most dynamic, as well as the part that must be *customized* to fit the particular career opportunity being sought. It needs to be a **one-** OR **two-sentence** *summary* of *specifically* **what you want to do in your next career move** AND it **must be relevant to the position being sought.** Here is an example of how Part Three might be constructed:

> "For the next step in my career, I would like to move away from contract work and find myself as a direct employee of a large firm, where I can join a substantial IT team and be involved with a group that focuses on email and network security applications, while having access to the knowledge base that would come with a large, diverse IT group."

OR, here is yet another example of how Part Three might be prepared:

> "For the next step in my career, I would like to find myself as a direct employee of a small- to medium-sized firm that is looking to hire an in-house IT generalist. That way, I can continue growing my career by getting exposure to multiple IT areas, such as networking, help desk, security, and user application issues. As the firm's IT needs grow, I would love to apply my past team project management skills to managing the members of a small, growing IT team."

As you can see, two very different endings but ones that can perfectly match what two different employers may be looking for in a candidate.

PUTTING IT ALL TOGETHER

Let's assume that Suzanne Smith is applying for a chemical engineering position with XYZ, Inc., and at the beginning of the job interview, the hiring manager asks, "Well, Suzanne, in order to get the ball rolling, tell me a little bit about yourself." Here is how Suzanne might answer the question, in order to brand herself, right off the bat, as certainly not being just an average, run-of-the-mill candidate:

"I am a chemical engineer with eight years of experience, four of which were in process engineering at Clorox, working on improving plant productivity, and four in specialty resin chemical sales, where I help customers develop new products that improve their competitiveness in the marketplace. (Part One)

"Recently, through networking, I learned of a company that had great products—except for their concrete coating line. I knew that we had a resin that would enable the company to develop a faster-drying concrete coating, thereby improving the company's ability to compete more effectively in its market niche. I called on the decision-makers, got their interest, worked with R&D and helped them develop a product line that resulted in $2 million in new sales for the company in the first year, which meant $400,000 in new sales for us. (Part Two)

"For the next step in my career, I would like to be with a larger firm with more resources, so that I can continue to drive business and grow sales for both the company and my customers in a wider variety of applications. Once I have proven myself and earned the right to get promoted, I would like to use my skills to lead and develop a sales team." (Part Three)

Does Suzanne's answer adequately address all THREE criteria (parts) recommended in an answer to the "tell me about yourself" question"? Indeed it does! First, she provided a *brief* history of her career up to that point. Next, she cited a *significant* career accomplishment, and it was one she knew the potential employer certainly would—or should!—be very interested in learning more about because it (or a related accomplishment Suzanne might have come up with) could potentially and positively affect the *hiring company's* bottom line. And finally, she made it abundantly clear as to what her future career goal was, and it certainly was relevant to the position for which she was applying.

Just for the record, if you read Suzanne's answer at a normal speaking pace, you will notice that it would take about one minute to deliver. Yet significant to note, during that brief time, she clearly and immediately branded herself as a true professional, one who knows the value of what she has to offer the potential employer. Plus, she communicated that information in a very convincing, believable manner. You can accomplish the same thing—if you anticipate this question (and I can absolutely assure you that you *will* be asked the "tell me about yourself" question in one form or another during virtually *any* job interview!) and adequately prepare your answer to it.

By taking the three-part approach to the "tell me about yourself" question recommended here, you will *automatically* set yourself apart from the overwhelming majority of your competition, i.e., other candidates seeking the same position. You will *automatically* brand yourself as certainly not being just another average, run-of-the-mill candidate.

Why?

Because the vast majority of the other candidates can be expected to take the approach mentioned earlier to answer the question: "Well, I grew up in rural Minnesota . . ," and quite likely, the hiring manager's eyes will start to glaze over . . . his/her mind will begin to wander . . . he/she will start thinking of ways to conclude the interview as quickly as possible, in order to move on to the next candidate, maybe someone who actually has something valuable to offer the hiring manager and the hiring company.

'GOTCHA!' QUESTIONS

There are certain questions that you can almost always anticipate being asked during the typical interview.[38] For the most part, these questions are designed with one purpose in mind: To trip you up, to see if you will make a *faux pas* severe enough to get you *excluded* from further consideration. In **Headhunter Hiring Secrets: The Rules of the Hiring Game Have Changed . . . Forever!** I coined a term for these questions— "gotcha!" questions. Because if you answer them in any way that casts "shadows on the wall" of the hiring manager's office, you *will* be excluded from further consideration. Count on it.

Below are some of the more common types of "gotcha!" questions you can anticipate, as well as how you should respond to them:

---

[38]Significant to note, however, is that these questions will not usually come one right after the other, as featured in this section. Rather, they will be interspersed among many other questions you'll be asked during the interview, e.g., questions about your technical knowledge and skills, etc. The idea, of course, is for a skilled interviewer to catch you off guard and see if you will make a *faux pas*!

Question: "Tell me about your current boss. Any issues?"

How you may be *tempted* to respond: "Well, he and I certainly don't see 'eye to eye' on just about everything. As a matter of fact, the kindest way I can describe our relationship is to say that it is 'contentious.'"

SHADOW ON THE WALL! The hiring manager is going to think, if this candidate is this openly critical of his or her current boss, how long will it be before I become "the bad guy/gal" and he or she starts impugning *my* integrity? I'll pass on this candidate.

How you *should* respond: "My boss has taught me a lot since I have worked for him. We don't always agree on everything, but we have worked out a professional relationship that helps both of us accomplish what we need to accomplish and get the job done right."

What the hiring manager may be thinking: I suspect this candidate probably has some "mixed" emotions about his or her current boss, but at least he or she has enough integrity to project a positive attitude. That's a plus.

Question: "What do you like least about your current job? What do you like most about it?"

How you may be *tempted* to respond: "Actually, I can't think of a thing I *like* about my current job. When I first started the job I used to be excited about going to work, but for the last couple of years I dread going to work. I can't wait for the opportunity to get out of there!"

ANOTHER SHADOW ON THE WALL! Bad attitude!

How you *should* respond: "One of the things that sometimes bothers me at my current job is when I am teamed up with a co-worker who may not be as committed as I am to getting the job done right, the first time. I know I should be more tolerant of people like this, but I'll readily admit that it does bother me.

"What I like most about my job . . . hmm . . . actually there are quite a few things I like about my current job, but let me just mention a couple. First, I am almost always included on the teams that get involved in the most exciting, cutting-edge projects. That makes me proud and happy. And, second, for the most part, I have the privilege of working with some really great, very creative, very dedicated people."

What the hiring manager may be thinking: I like this candidate's attitude. He or she seems to always take the high road. Obviously, the candidate is not happy about *everything* in his or her current job or he or she wouldn't be looking in the first place. I also like how the candidate turned one of his or her "dislikes," i.e., having to work with people who may not be as committed to the job as the candidate seems to be, into what is essentially a positive. We don't tolerate slackers very well on our team, either.

Question: "Tell me about your biggest failure during your career and how you handled it?"

How you may be *tempted* to respond: "Actually, I really haven't had any failures in my career, or at least no major failures."

YET ANOTHER SHADOW ON THE WALL! Liar, liar, pants on fire! Sure you have had failures! We all have had failures during our careers, and some of them have indeed been MAJOR!

LEARN TO TELL STORIES!

A very effective way of answering questions such as the **"strengths and weaknesses"** and **"greatest career achievement/failure"** questions is to tell stories. That way, the hiring manager not only is *hearing* what you are saying, he or she is also *seeing* what you are saying!

How you *should* respond:

"Well, like most people, unfortunately, I have experienced some failures during my career. Let me relate one of them to you.

"The team I led a couple of years ago was involved in bringing a new production system online. We were expected to have the system fully operational within six months, but it became obvious after the first three months that, at the pace we were going, we simply were not going to be able to meet the deadline, for a whole lot of various reasons. None of us, of course, were ready to accept defeat, so we began meeting at breakfast Monday, Wednesday and Friday, before work, to come up with a plan that would result in our meeting the deadline—if we really applied ourselves. Thank goodness, we were able to ultimately meet the deadline.

"I blame myself and my leadership for putting the team in this position. I should have recognized the problem much sooner and taken corrective action. The whole thing could have turned out to be disastrous for the team and our company, which was depending heavily on us to get the new system up and running, on time.

"Believe me, I learned a valuable leadership lesson then—that, as a team leader, I need to constantly be on top of things and head off problems before they can mushroom."

What the hiring manager may be thinking: This candidate seems to have his or her head on right. He or she readily accepts responsibility and appears to be the type of leader to take charge and FIX problems before they can get totally out of hand, rather than to try to place blame on others.

As just indicated, all of these types of "gotcha!" questions are designed to see if you can be caught off guard. They are also intended to reveal how well you can think on your feet. While you may think that most candidates wouldn't fall into such obvious traps set by a hiring manager, you may want to think again. Un-coached and inadequately prepared candidates fall into them day in and day out. They are also the candidates who are routinely *excluded* first from further consideration!

Face-to-Face Interview
'Barbara Walters' Questions—They're Back!

During her heyday on TV, interviewer Barbara Walters invariably asked her guests some (apparently) frivolous question such as this:

"If you were a tree, what kind of a tree would you be?"

Of course most people thought these kinds of questions were humorous, but in truth, they also tended to suggest quite revealing traits of a guest's "hidden" personality. Perhaps predictably, some job interviewers—maybe out of sheer boredom from asking all the same routine questions, interview after interview after interview—soon started asking job candidates these same types of questions. Then, just as suddenly as their use appeared, they then disappeared for some years. I have been noticing, however, that these "Barbara Walter" questions seem to be making somewhat of a comeback in certain hiring circles.

So, with that in mind, you also ought to be at least *generally* prepared to answer such questions, if they are posed to you during a job interview. Favorite phraseologies include animal and automobile analogies. For example, you might be asked,

"If you were a car, what kind and color would you be?"

Laugh if you must, but nonetheless assume that the question is being asked in earnest and that you should therefore *answer* the question in earnest. For example, if you were applying for, say, an accounting position, here is the type of answer that would probably serve you best:

> **"I would be a Toyota Prius because it is fuel efficient, economical to own, yet quite practical as a means of transportation. I think the color it would be is black. Black *is* very important in the accounting business, right?** (Laugh)"

On the other hand, if the position you are applying for is a sales position, this probably wouldn't be the type of answer you would want to give. Maybe a better answer would be something like this:

> **"I definitely would be a red Corvette! It's sporty, high performance and would get me where I wanted to go—to see as many customers and prospects as possible in the fastest time—without speeding of course!"**

Sure I'm using exaggeration here, but I use it to make a point. If—and I will readily admit that, for the time being at least, that it's a BIG if—

you actually are asked a "Barbara Walters" question, you will be able to answer it quickly and appropriately, while at the same time, have some fun with it, which will show more of your human side during an interview.

MOST QUESTIONS WILL BE *PERFORMANCE*-BASED

Certainly I'm not suggesting that the entire interview will be taken up by the "gotcha!" type questions or off-the-wall questions such as the "Barbara Walters" type. To be sure, clearly you should anticipate that the *bulk* of the questions you'll be asked during the interview will focus on questions that will adequately address the FOUR key issues the hiring manager *actually* wants to learn about a candidate—whether or not the hiring manager himself/herself is even aware of it. Remember these key issues from a previous chapter? To refresh your memory, here they are again:

- Can you *do* the job?
- Do you actually *want* to do the specific job under consideration?
- *Will* you do the actual job under consideration?
- Are you a good *cultural fit* for the unit AND the hiring company?

And to further reiterate, be sure to **"lead the witness,"** i.e., the hiring manager, when you are asked performance-based questions by specifically addressing these concerns. For example, if the hiring manager asks you a question such as this:

"Where do you see yourself being, say, five years down the line, if you are the candidate I select for this position?"

The question that the hiring manager is *actually* asking—whether or not he or she is even consciously aware of it—is related to TWO of these issues/concerns, isn't it?

- Do you actually *want* to do the specific job under consideration?
- *Will* you do the actual job under consideration?

Make sure that your answer therefore *addresses* BOTH of these key concerns. An appropriate answer might be something like this:

"I am very excited about the opportunity to do this job. I think it will provide me very valuable experience that I must first have if I want to advance in my career, which I do of course. At the same time, this job will give me the opportunity to make a significant contribution to your unit and the company.

"If I do become your candidate of choice, and if you are still my boss five years down the road, and I am performing at a level that suggests I am ready for additional responsibilities, then I am sure you will help me advance in my career."

AS THE INTERVIEW COMES TO AN END

Once the hiring manager feels that he or she has exhausted all the pertinent questions (and perhaps *you*!), the interview will quickly start to wind down, after having lasted about an hour, if your interview is at all typical. This is the time that you should be on full alert because the *most* important question of the interview is about to be asked. Remember from previous sections what the question is? Here it is again:

"Now, do you have any questions for me?"

As I've said previously, regarding *all* interviews and other contacts made during the job search, how you answer this question can oftentimes spell the difference between *staying in the game* and being automatically and summarily *excluded* from further consideration.

Once again, the unprepared or ill-prepared candidate will almost inevitably answer this key closing question with a response like this:

"No, I think you've pretty well covered everything and answered all of my questions."

The *well-prepared*, *well-rehearsed*, savvy professional answers it this way:

"Well, you've certainly been quite thorough, but I do still have just a couple of questions . . ."

And then you ask questions that you have prepared *beforehand*, questions that you can reasonably expect will *not* be asked during the face-to-face interview, such as,

> "If I were to become your candidate of choice for this position, what would I have to do, say, in the first 12 months, for you to be able to say, 'I made a good hiring decision'"?

Or, perhaps you could word the question this way:

> "What would the successful candidate for this position have had to accomplish, say, during the first year on the job, for you to say, 'I made a good hiring decision.'"?

Closing questions such as these show at least TWO things:

- You actually **paid attention** during the interview.
- You have a *genuine* interest in the position.

After the hiring manager responds to questions such as these, what's the last (or very nearly the last) question you should ask? Yes, it's the **NEXT STEPS** question! Here is how you can effectively phrase this question:

> "Thank you very much for taking the time to interview me today. I sincerely appreciate it.
>
> "After learning more about the position today, I am even more excited about the career opportunity, and I can assure you that, if given the chance, I will prove to be a great addition to your team and to your company.
>
> "What are the NEXT STEPS in the hiring process and what can I do to make sure I remain in the process?"

Normally, the hiring manager will say something non-committal (and perhaps largely unresponsive) to your closing, NEXT STEPS question by saying something such as . . .

> "Well, I've got a number of other candidates to interview, and after I've had a chance to do that, my staff and I will put our heads together and make a decision. You will of course be notified one way or the other."

Do NOT be put off or discouraged by such a response because rarely is it reflective of how well the hiring manager feels you did in the interview. It's simply the standard, non-committal close most hiring managers take at this point. Why? Primarily because it's the *safest* response at this point.

> ## AS IT TURNS OUT . . . YOUR PARENTS WERE RIGHT!
>
> Remember when you were a youngster and your parents were continually admonishing you to "Stand up straight!," "Sit up straight!," "Look people in the eye when you're talking to them!," "Always give a firm handshake!"
>
> Well, as it turns out, that was excellent advice, particularly when it comes to how you present yourself at a job interview. Over the years I have had *excellent* candidates be excluded from further consideration because of poor posture and/or because they projected, at least in the hiring manager's opinion, very negative body language, e.g., slouching, having a "fish" handshake, not being able to maintain eye contact, etc., etc., etc.
>
> So, focus, and focus intensely and continuously, on projecting a *positive* attitude and *professional* bearing from the very first time the hiring manager lays eyes on you until you have completely left the company premises after the job interview.
>
> ### OTHER KEY CONSIDERATIONS
>
> During the interview, you should also keep the following key considerations in mind:
>
> - **Match your *energy* level, as well as the *volume* level of your voice, to that of the hiring manager.**
>
> - **Adjust the *cadence* of your speech to that of the hiring manager,** i.e., if he or she is a "slow-talker," while you are a "fast-talker," slow down your speaking pace to match that of the hiring manager.
>
> - **If you tend to be a demonstrative person**, i.e., "talk" with your hands and arms as well as with your voice, **and the hiring manager obviously isn't that demonstrative, keep your urges under control.**

As You Are Leaving . . .

If you have reason to think (or believe) that you ACED the interview, you'll probably be on Cloud Nine as you're leaving the hiring manager's office area and then the company premises. Now is *not* the time to let your guard down, however. Be assured that, while it may not seem like it, you are still under close observation and critical evaluation—and will be until you get in your car (or other transportation) and are completely away from the company premises.

Here are a few things to focus on at this juncture:

- As you are leaving the office continue to **engage in conversation, even if it's nothing more than small talk.** Talk about plans for the upcoming weekend, the rest of day, etc., being sure to ask the hiring manager (or whoever else is walking you out of the office) about his or her plans as well.

- **Continue to project *positive* body language**, e.g., head and chin up, shoulders back, continuing to look people in the eyes, etc., and maintain a positive attitude, one of confidence and self assuredness.

- **Be sure to thank the receptionist and/or administrative assistant** if you made contact with him or her upon your arrival at the interview or engaged them (or anyone else in the near vicinity) in conversation while you were waiting to be interviewed by the hiring manager.

- If you've turned your cell phone off (and you better have before you went into the interview!), resist the temptation to turn it back on as you're leaving. And certainly **don't even *consider* taking (or placing!) any calls (or answering any voice mail messages) as you are leaving the company premises**!

How Well *Did* You Do in the Interview?

Once the interview is over and you are leaving the company premises, you will undoubtedly replay the interview over and over in your head, wondering how well you did, what your chances are at this point of ultimately landing the job. The fact of the matter is, however, the only way you'll ever really know how well—or, for that matter, how poorly—you did in the interview is if you are called back for a *second* face-to-face interview. Conversely, if you receive the dreaded "Thank you for your interest in ABC Company" letter in the mail soon after the interview, how well you did in the interview will become irrelevant because you will know that you were not selected for the position and you can expect no further consideration.

If you have been working with a headhunter during your job search, chances are very good that you will know how well you did almost immediately after the interview. Or, more precisely, the headhunter will know how well you did and will communicate that information to you.

In the final analysis, unless you are in fact called back for a second (or third, or perhaps fourth!) face-to-face interview, you should *not* dwell on the matter. As is the case with any "sales" endeavor—and remember, when you are in a job search, you *are* in sales, and the product you are selling is yourself!—you never look back. You only look *forward*, to the next sales opportunity, i.e., the *next* face-to-face interview—whether it's with the company that just interviewed you or with the next company coming up for consideration.

WHAT ARE *YOUR* NEXT STEPS NOW?

As I just indicated above, if you happen to receive the "thanks but no thanks" letter from the company you just interviewed with, then there are no next steps with this company. It's "Game Over" for this company and on to actively pursuing the next career opportunity awaiting you!

On the other hand, if you have managed to keep from being excluded following the first face-to-face interview, several things can await you:

- You may be called back in for a **second** (or third, or perhaps, even a *fourth!*) **face-to-face interview**.
- You may be called back in for a **"group" interview**, consisting of the hiring manager and select other members of his or her team (usually, after the second or subsequent face-to-face interview).
- You may be called in to **interview with the hiring manager's boss** (usually after the hiring manager and his or her team have all had a shot at you, and the hiring manager is feeling really comfortable with you).

- If the position is in the executive ranks, you usually will be called in to **meet the company president or CEO**.
- **You may hear absolutely NOTHING further after the initial face-to-face interview**! Hey, it sometimes happens, so be prepared for it!

HOW MANY INTERVIEWS TO THE FINISH LINE?

How much of a face-to-face interview gauntlet will you have to run before you either land the position or are eliminated from further consideration?

What I am finding in our executive recruiting firm—and this is quite typical—is that you can expect *at least* **TWO** face-to-face interviews, but some companies are requiring as many as **THREE** to **FIVE**!

If you are ultimately the successful candidate, it usually takes from 45 to as many as 90 days from the first face-to-face interview until you receive the "official" job offer.

Why is it taking so long? Some hiring managers and the companies they represent are still nervous about adding new staff, so they are still taking their sweet time when making a FINAL candidate decision.

TOP 5 REASONS FOR BEING *EXCLUDED* AFTER THE FIRST FACE-TO-FACE JOB INTERVIEW

No matter how well you prepared, or how well you feel you performed during a face-to-face job interview, you still could end up being *excluded* from further consideration after just one interview. Here are the **TOP FIVE reasons** for candidates experiencing this fate:

1. Despite what your résumé indicates, the **hiring manager simply didn't think/believe you have the experience and/or background to perform the job** as he or she expects/desires.

2. You may have the experience and background to suggest that you *are* qualified to do the job, but **other candidates were deemed to be *more* qualified** than you.

3. The **hiring manager may simply not have liked you** or the way you may have presented yourself—for whatever reason(s), valid or not.

4. The **hiring manager may have concluded that you would not be a good "cultural fit"** for the unit and/or the company, e.g., you may have been "too loud," or "too quiet," or "too-something."

5. No matter how well you prepared and practiced before the interview, **you still ended up "blowing it"**—for any number of reasons.

A GENTLE REMINDER

Regardless of how many interviews it may take you either to win the job or to be eliminated, always, always, always be sure to **send a Thank You card or email following the interview**! And make sure you CORRECTLY spell the names of ALL persons who interviewed you! (HINT: Get business cards from *everyone* you meet at the interview.)

THE 'DINNERVIEW'—IT'S NOT ABOUT EATING!

While it is becoming rather rare today, sometimes following a face-to-face interview you may be asked, "Hey, let's go to lunch (or dinner)." If this happens to you, and you're like most people, you will undoubtedly think, Wow! I must have done GREAT in the interview to be asked to lunch (or dinner)! And maybe you did—or maybe you didn't. Only time will tell.

Regardless of how things ultimately turn out for you, however, you can be assured of one thing at this point: The meal is NOT about eating—it is designed as a means to further evaluate YOU as a candidate!

Here are a few key points to bear in mind about the "dinnerview":

Purpose of the meal: To "Seal the Deal." As I said above, the true purpose of the meal is NOT to eat, it is to "seal the deal"—or not! All eyes will be on you, and the hiring manager will be attempting to determine if your meal etiquette is up to snuff, to see how well (or how poorly) you may reflect on the company if your job may include taking clients out to lunch/dinner.

Pasta? Steak? Burger? Or Chicken? What to order? Rule of thumb: Never order *anything* that is messy, such as bar-b-que, spaghetti, or similar dishes. Be wary of ordering steak because it is usually the most expensive item on the menu (you won't want to appear wasteful of the company's money!). Burgers are usually too messy. Best advice: Order something that you can cut into small bites, such as fish or chicken.

"I really want a beer (or cocktail)!" Maybe so, but resist the temptation if it's before evening. If it's an evening meal, and only IF the hiring manager orders a beer (or a cocktail), go ahead and order one for yourself. But make it only ONE beer (or glass of wine). No hard liquor. If the position you're interviewing for requires driving a company car, then no alcohol at all, period.

"What's with all this silverware?!" For most of us common folks, a fork, spoon and knife are usually the only utensils we find necessary to complete a meal—any meal. What do you do, then, if you happen to eat at a "fancy" restaurant and are faced with an *array* of utensils?

While I'm certainly no rival to Emily Post, here, essentially, is what you need to know about handling all that silverware and seeming to know what you're doing (at least a *little* bit):

THE 'DINNERVIEW' *Continued*

- Forks are to the left of the plate, with the salad fork being to the far left. (If salad is the main course for you, it is permissible to use the dinner fork.) When finished with the salad, leave the fork on the salad plate/bowl. Your dinner fork is the one closest to your dinner plate.

- To the right: If there is an appetizer, the small appetizer fork will be to the far right. Working your way inward generally is the soup spoon and closest to the plate is the knife.

- Dessert forks/spoons and stirring spoons are often at the 12 o'clock position.

- When eating, put the knife across the top of the plate with the blade turned toward you. If you used your spoon to stir your beverage, it, too, goes on a plate.

"Do I cut one bite of meat, two or three bites, or all of it?" Cut up to three bites, no more.

"They waited until I took a bite to ask me a question, didn't they?! Maybe! That's why you should take *small* bites! Simply hold up a finger signaling "one moment, please," finish chewing and then answer the question.

"Oh no! I just dropped food on my shirt (or blouse), what now?!" Simply use your napkin the best you can, call over a waiter, apologize for the inconvenience and politely excuse yourself to the restroom, if necessary.

"Whew! I'm finally done, now what?" Place your napkin to the left of your place setting, silverware parallel on your plate with the handles at 3 o'clock.

This "dining etiquette" advice is by no means all inclusive, and I do not pretend to be an expert in this area. What I DO know is how often hiring managers talk about the table manners (or the lack thereof) of candidates they have interviewed. Don't you risk losing out on a GREAT career opportunity because of poor "table manners"!

QUESTIONS TO ANTICIPATE IN SUBSEQUENT FACE-TO-FACE INTERVIEWS

Will you be asked the same questions over and over during each face-to-face interview following the initial one? Usually, no. You may, however, be asked to clarify (or expand on) some of the questions you earlier answered during previous interviews. Normally, the hiring manager's goal during second and subsequent face-to-face (or "team") interviews is to probe further. For example, he or she might be facing a particular challenge in his or her unit and ask you to outline how you would effectively deal with it. Or, you might be asked a series of hypothetical, "what if" questions.

If you have been called back in for an interview (or interviews) after the initial face-to-face interview, you have reason to be somewhat confident that you got beyond the "gotcha!" or "trick" questions hiring managers can sometimes throw at a candidate during the initial face-to-face interview. That is not to say, however, that you are home free, either. As indicated earlier, today the interview process can be a somewhat drawn-out process, so you must constantly be on high alert—whether it is your second, third or even fourth interview!

WHAT SHOULD YOU DO WHILE YOU'RE WAITING . . . WAITING . . . WAITING?

Do NOT make the mistake so many job seekers tend to make and simply curtail all of your job search activities while you relax, sit back and wait . . . and wait . . and wait . . . for one (or more) career opportunity(ies) you've interviewed for to come to fruition. It/they *might* come to fruition, and then again, it/they might not! And that is the case no matter how many face-to-face interviews you may have undergone, and no matter how *sure* you are that you will be the candidate selected for any given position for which you've interviewed. (The only time you can be absolutely *sure* that you are the candidate selected is when you actually have the *written* offer in your hand.)

Best advice: Don't wait for anyone or any particular career opportunity. Keep pursuing *all* career opportunities available to you. Otherwise you risk losing very valuable time during your new job search. As I advised you earlier, just keep on keepin' on.

A REVIEW

A Headhunter's EIGHT Basic Rules for ACING the *Face-to-Face* Interview

Virtually each and every week of the year The HTW Group has candidates going in for face-to-face job interviews. **The candidates we present, versus those who choose to go it alone, end up winning the job offer 70% of the time!** What makes the difference? In short, it's the fact that the candidates we present are *thoroughly* coached on and prepared to adhere to **EIGHT** basic rules that will *significantly* improve their chances of ACING the face-to-face job interview—and then ultimately walking away with the job offer.

How did I come up with these eight basic rules? Essentially, through years of experience presenting candidates. As a result of that experience, I know what works, and equally important, what does *not* work, when it comes to a candidate branding himself/herself as the ultimate—and clear—candidate of choice. Here are the **EIGHT** basic rules:

> **RULE 1**

UNTIL AN OFFER IS ACTUALLY MADE, THE JOB INTERVIEW IS *ALWAYS, ALWAYS, ALWAYS* ABOUT THE *HIRING COMPANY*, NOT ABOUT YOU, THE JOB CANDIDATE.

At the end of the hiring process, of course, you will need to be as sold on the company, your future boss, his or her team and the company's culture as much as they are sold on you. So, before it is over, both parties (you and the company) need to have sold each other 100%. However, **until you actually *become* the candidate of choice, like it or not, it is your responsibility to do 100% of the selling**. It is all about the *company's* needs, problems, challenges and, in particular, how *you* may be a solution to those needs, problems and challenges.

The best advice: Actively listen, ask good, informed questions and learn about the company—*before* you go to the interview. In doing so, the hiring manager (and the company he or she represents) will ultimately want to know more about *you*, i.e., specifically, what will it take to hire you and make *you* happy!

Face-to-Face Interview

> **RULE 2**

THE PRINCIPAL OBJECTIVE OF *EVERY* INTERVIEW IS TO GET THE *NEXT* INTERVIEW.

Until the *final* interview the objective of *every* interview is simply to get to the next one. Only by doing that can your candidacy advance to the finish line. In fact, if a company ever wants to make you an offer after just one interview, proceed with caution. Why is the company so anxious? Is the job for real? In turn, at the end of each interview, don't "close" on the job, either. The *company* will wonder why *you* are so anxious. Instead, at the end of each interview, close on the *next steps*. For example, beginning with the initial telephone interview and continuing through every subsequent interview, always close by asking a question along these lines:

> **"Based upon our conversation today, is there anything that would prevent us from moving ahead together?"**

Also, however, never withdraw from the interview process until you have ALL of the information! Remember, you can't turn down an offer you don't have.

> **RULE 3**

NEVER, NEVER SAY OR DO *ANYTHING* NEGATIVE DURING *ANY* JOB INTERVIEW.

This is what I refer to as casting "shadows on the wall." Here is an example: Suppose the hiring manager asks you why you would consider moving a thousand miles to take a new job, if it was offered, and your response was something like this:

> **"I need to get as far away from my present job as possible because my spouse is cheating on me."**[39]

Ouch! You would be eliminated on the spot, at least in the hiring manager's mind. Remember, when it comes to a job interview, *anything* you say or do during the interview *can* and *will* be used against you!

---

[39] Yes, some candidates actually SAY things like this in interviews!

RULE 4

ADOPT AND CONTINUALLY PRACTICE THE BOY SCOUT MOTTO.

The Boy Scout motto is "Be Prepared," and that is certainly what you had better be when you go in to a job interview today. Here is how most men and women go in to a job interview: They hand over a copy of their résumé[40] and then sit back waiting to be drilled with questions. Then, they answer the questions at "face value," usually with answers that wander all over the place. (Refer back to Zig Ziglar's cautionary remark about making sure you are a "meaningful specific" instead of a "wandering generality.")

Instead of taking this approach, anticipate most questions you can expect to be asked during the interview and then answer those questions very succinctly, powerfully, and in a way that will clearly brand you as being a candidate who at least has *potential* value to the hiring company.

Here is a real life example of what I'm talking about. When recently screening a potential candidate for a position we were working to fill, we asked him this question (one of many we knew he would be asked in an interview with a hiring manager):

"Why would you consider leaving your current job?"

His answer was both genuine and quite typical:

"I have been with my current company three years and I no longer see any growth potential. My boss and his boss are just a few years older than me and they won't be going anywhere anytime soon so, as I see it, I will be doing the same thing five years down the road that I am doing now. So I am looking for a company where that same ceiling isn't there."

On the face of it, you might think that this candidate's answer really isn't all that bad, but you would be wrong! I refer you back to **RULE 1**. At this point in the game the hiring manager doesn't really care about *your* needs, concerns or desires. All he or she really cares about at this point is what, if anything, you can bring to his or her company to address problems, concerns and challenges.

---

[40]Take extra copies of your résumé with you in case others join in the interview.

Since this candidate clearly was a very strong performer, we decided to work with him, and here is how we recommended he revise his answer:

> "I have been at my current company for three years. During that time we have been able to strongly penetrate the food-processing market with our disinfectants, growing our market share from 12% to 27%.
>
> "So it isn't so much that I am looking to leave my current company as it is the opportunity I see with your company.
>
> "In addition to having an effective product line of disinfectants, you also have the equipment available for ease of application. That is a powerful combination and one I am quite excited about.
>
> "With my knowledge of the industry, I believe I could make a relatively quick impact on helping the team achieve its sales objectives for the year."

See the difference? The typical answer *before* coaching was all about the *candidate*, not about what he could possibly offer the hiring company. Conversely, the *coached* answer clearly demonstrated the candidate's potential value to the hiring company.

(He ended up being offered—and accepting—the position.)

RULE 5

EVERYONE—AND I DO MEAN *EVERYONE*—LISTENS TO RADIO STATION WIIFM (WHAT'S IN IT FOR ME).

Yes, the most popular, most-listened to "radio station" on the planet is **WIIFM** (**W**hat's **I**n **I**t **F**or **M**e?). You would be wise to keep that in mind when dealing with other people, especially hiring managers. Show genuine interest in the hiring manager (and the company he or she represents), and the way you can accomplish that is by having done your homework. Did you, for example, Google the hiring manager? Did you research him or her on LinkedIn or ZoomInfo? Did you make sure you researched—and thoroughly read!—the latest press releases from or about the company?

Face-to-Face Interview

The candidate who shows interest, knowledge *and* curiosity during a job interview is the candidate most likely to be perceived as *new, different, better*, and you certainly should know the positive implications of that kind of perception.

Rule 6

AMP UP YOUR ENERGY AND PROJECT ENTHUSIASM!

It's certainly not necessary (or desired) that you appear to be over the top during a job interview, of course, but clearly you should be fully awake, totally engaged and on HIGH alert! After all, you are the *main attraction* here, and no one I've ever met wants to hire a dullard or a bore.

Rule 7

NEVER APPEAR "STAND-OFFISH" OR PLAY "HARD TO GET."

Demonstrate genuine interest in and commitment to getting the job by *immediately* sending a **Thank You email** or **note** to the person(s) who interviewed you. Ideally, you should make the note (or email) both personal *and* professional, by picking two to three points from the conversation and highlighting them in the Thank You email or note.

Also, if time is *not* of the essence, send *both* an email and a note. Your note should be *handwritten* and sent via USPS ("snail mail").

Remember, though, once you send the Thank You note, any immediate, additional follow up designed to nudge the process along, such as leaving a voice mail and saying something like . . .

> **"Just calling to follow up on where things are in the process. . . ."**

actually *weakens* your position. Seven to ten days after the interview, if you still haven't heard anything, an appropriate follow up could be a bit of information in regard to the company, a competitor or the industry, etc. A quick email such as . . .

"Pam, didn't know if you saw the attached article on the new disinfectant XYZ company is coming out with or not. Here's the link in case it is of interest. . . ."

will illustrate that you are still involved *without* being pushy.

RULE 8

PRACTICE, PRACTICE, PRACTICE . . . REHEARSE, REHEARSE, REHEARSE, AND THEN PRACTICE AND REHEARSE SOME MORE.

Look at a job interview the same way an actor or actress looks at a play or movie audition because, after all, that is precisely what a job interview is—an *audition* to see if you can "get the part"!

Record your answers to anticipated interview questions and then play them back. Video yourself and then watch how you will appear to others. If you're like most people, you won't believe how you *sound* and *look* before practicing and honing your skills.

I'm sure you are familiar with the saying that goes, "You only get ONE chance to make a good first impression." Certainly that definitely is true when it comes to a job interview.

Incorporate the principles, tactics and strategies featured in this chapter into your own repertoire and you will be perceived as being an "A" team member. And believe me, those are the only team members being seriously considered for the really GREAT jobs in today's job market!

WILL 'PROJECTS' BECOME THE NEW JOB INTERVIEW?

Some business commentators think they might! Writing for the online edition of Harvard Business Review (www.hbr.org), Michael Schrage, a research fellow at MIT Sloan School's Center for Digital Business, put it this way, in his "Projects are the next interviews" article: "Résumés are dead. Interviews are largely ineffectual. LinkedIn is good. Portfolios are useful."

"Projects are the real future of hiring," he says, "especially knowledge working hiring."

No matter how good one's references may be, or how much of a dynamite professional brand one may have created and maintained, s*erious* firms will increasingly ask *serious* candidates to do *serious* work in order to get a *serious* job offer, Schrage contends.

Some job seekers are already being asked to put their money where their mouths are *before* being seriously considered for certain jobs, and Schrage says many more will be asked to do so in the future, by successfully completing projects for potential employers.

"The real question will be how well candidates can rise to the 'appliject' [a contraction of "application" and "project"] challenge," he says.

Why the move toward project-based candidate screening?

"Most organizations have learned the hard way that no amount of interviewing, reference checking and/or psychological testing is a substitute for actually working with a candidate on a real project," says Schrage.

Schrage adds that, just as many organizations have grown more skillful at conducting Skype interviews and using web-based quizzes and questionnaires to more effectively screen candidates, he is betting that we'll soon see new genres of *project-based* enterprise hiring practices.

Something to think about!

Part IV
When EVERYTHING Comes Together!

The time it can take in today's job market to get from Point A (when you actually begin your new job search) to Point B (when you begin getting actual job offers) can, of course, span several months or longer. The *actual* time it will take *you* to make the journey depends, essentially, on **THREE** primary factors, one of which you have *absolute* control over, while the other two remain largely beyond your personal control:

1. **How much *quality* time and concentrated focus and genuine effort you actually devote to your new job search.** That means that you must be doing things *right* as well as doing the *right* things, and if you have been following the recommended tactics and strategies outlined thus far in this book, you will be in good shape on this factor! (This is the factor over which you have *absolute* control in today's—or any other—job market.)

2. **Your specific professional specialty.** Obviously, if the demand for top candidates in your particular area of expertise exceeds the supply, then it normally takes far less time to land a new job than if the supply of top candidates exceeds the demand.

3. **General business and economic climate/outlook**. No matter how badly companies may want to add new people to the payroll, in order to stay competitive in the global marketplace, if the general business and economic climate/outlook is bleak or even cloudy, chances are, they will continue to take a wait and see attitude. And if they do decide to hire new people, they will continue to take their sweet time in doing so. Conversely, if companies have a high degree of confidence in both the present and the future, they are much more likely to move ahead with hiring plans, sometimes even *rapidly* move ahead!

Assuming that all three of these factors are in reasonably good alignment, you should therefore start getting bona fide job offers sooner rather than later, as the result of your diligent job-search efforts. Certainly you will start getting job offers far sooner than those job hunters who continue to play by the *old* set of rules in the hiring "game"!

Part IV addresses the **FOUR remaining general elements** of **your new job search**:

1. **Getting** and then **evaluating** a **job offer.**
2. If currently employed, **how** and **when** to **resign your current job.**
3. If currently employed, **anticipating,** and then **effectively** *deflecting* any **counter-offer** from a current employer.
4. **Clearing ALL contingencies** for your new job.

In virtually every aspect of life—and this is particularly true when it comes to one's *professional* life!—there are basically FOUR types of people:

1. Those who *make* things happen;
2. Those who *wait* for things to happen;
3. Those who *watch* things happen; and
4. Those who *wonder* what happened!

In these final stages of your new job search you need to make sure the first statement best describes the type of person you are—as someone who clearly and consistently *makes* things happen! Remember, if *you* don't take *complete* charge of your own career, someone else (such as your current employer!) will certainly be glad to do it for you.

As I hope you have learned thus far in this book, during all stages of the hiring "game" leading up to these final steps in your new job search, unless *you* drive things forward, by being thoroughly prepared, persistent and assertive at the appropriate times, nothing good and positive is likely ever to happen.

Chapter Sixteen

THE JOB OFFER

You've Got an Offer! Whoopi! Now, the *Really* Hard Decisions Come into Play:

Salary
Benefits
Relocation
(To name but a few!)

You've spent the time and made the effort to target the career opportunities that looked the most promising for delivering on your quest for a new job, your *ideal* job. You've diligently followed, and then consistently applied, the advice and recommendations throughout this book. You've made the necessary contacts with key hiring professionals, utilizing an intelligent, well-thought-out, well-orchestrated combination of telephone, email and direct mail. You've weathered the initial telephone screens and the telephone interview(s) with the hiring manager. You've survived the gauntlet of face-to-face interviews.

Is there light at the end of the tunnel? Is there an actual *payoff* for you? Yes, there definitely is, and it's a payoff that the vast majority of your competition, i.e., others seeking the same positions as you, will not likely see, or at least not as soon as you will. It's called a JOB OFFER! If you have been *extra* diligent in your job search efforts, by simultaneously exploring *numerous* career opportunities, you might even be able to make that *plural*, as in JOB OFFERS!

INITIAL JOB OFFER LIKELY TO BE A TELEPHONE CALL

Typically, when you are the candidate of choice, the hiring manager himself/herself will personally call you up and "officially" offer you the job. Why "officially" in quotation marks? Because, even after being notified that you have been selected as the winning candidate for a new job, there still remains a whole lot of additional paperwork and other "i's" to dot and "t's" to cross before you can finally—and actually—call the job yours.

Why isn't all the paperwork completed *before* the hiring manager calls and offers you the job? The *most* important reason is because the hiring manager wants to make sure that, after he or she generally explains the offer to you, i.e., proposed salary, specific job title, anticipated start date, etc., that you will actually *accept* the offer, or at least *initially* accept it over the telephone.

Obviously, if you have—and then actually *express*—some major problems with or reservations about anything the hiring manager says regarding the position during this telephone offer, as far as the hiring manager is concerned, the job stays open until any and all of these problems and/or reservations can be satisfactorily addressed by both you and the hiring manager. That's why it is *crucial* that you don't show your hand in any way shape, form or fashion during this telephone call! Act excited and enthusiastic—even if you don't particularly feel that way at the time. The time to begin negotiations on salary, vacation time, or any other factors of the job offer is NOT during this telephone call! Wait until you get the actual *written* offer from the company and have had adequate time to evaluate the *entire* job offer.

The Written Job Offer

In most companies—and this is definitely the case with the larger companies—the *written* job offer, which is actually the *official* offer, will usually come from the Human Resources Department. This offer almost always covers virtually all of the key elements comprising the job offer:

- Proposed **salary** for the position.
- Employee **benefits**, e.g., health insurance, life insurance, 401(k) plan, vacation days, company car, company retirement plan, etc.
- Proposed **start date**.
- **Relocation** benefits (if any and if applicable).

The written job offer will normally arrive in the mail a few days after the hiring manager has called offering you the position. Obviously, you do not want to tarry in your evaluation of the written offer. As a matter of fact, it is a good idea to call the hiring manager upon receiving the written offer, thanking him or her and saying that you will thoroughly evaluate it and get back to him or her within a day or two—and then make sure you do that! Now is *not* the time to start playing hard to get. Continue to act positive and enthusiastic too.

Salary Offered ... Surprise?! Disappointment?!

In a perfect world, the salary component of a job offer would elicit few surprises and disappointments. After all, weeks if not months quite probably have elapsed from the time you, the candidate, first applied for the job until you were ultimately selected as the candidate of choice and offered the position. So certainly, by this time, the hiring manager ought to have a pretty good handle on the amount of salary it will take to get you to accept the position. Similarly, you should have an equally good handle on what to expect in return from the hiring manager and his/her company—if and when you are offered the position.

Unfortunately, however, the world we live in is nowhere near perfect, and as a result, sometimes there is considerable surprise and disappointment associated with a job offer, and by far, the element of the offer that is usually most in contention is—you guessed it!—salary, or more precisely, the *amount* of salary offered.

THE JOB OFFER

Remember back in **Chapter Fourteen** when I advised you how to handle the salary issue, which I said would come up early and often during the entire job search process? (And it did, too, didn't it?!) Here is where *how* you ultimately chose to deal with the salary issue can either pay dividends or come back to haunt you! If, for example, you acquiesced early on (I could have said, "caved in," but chose not to) and told the hiring manager both what your current (or most recent) salary is/was and what your *specific* salary expectations are, well, you just removed virtually any wiggle room you may have had in negotiating salary, if that becomes necessary. In other words, you painted yourself in a corner early on in the process.

If you totally showed your hand on the salary issue early on in the hiring process, unless the hiring manager is a total fool (and I assure you that most are *not* fools), guess what *maximum* salary you can reasonably expect to be offered? That's right, the amount you specified as your *expected* salary for the new position—even if the company anticipated being required to pay a higher salary to attract the right candidate. More realistically, however, it quite probably will be less than that amount because, just like you, the hiring manager and the company he/she represents also want to make the very best deal possible.

NOW COMES THE L$_o$W BALL SALARY OFFER

But let's take a more positive approach and assume that you did virtually everything right, everything I have recommended throughout this book, during your entire job search. That, of course, would mean that you literally breezed through all the preliminary screening steps, and you ACED several face-to-face interviews and clearly positioned yourself as the candidate of choice. You left the final face-to-face interview confident that you would be offered the position.

Several days later you learned your feelings were justified. The hiring manager called you and offered you the position! There was (and is), however, just one tiny little "problem" with the offer—the annual salary being offered is nearly $5,000 less than what you earn at your current employer!

Welcome to the wonderful world of the low-ball salary offer. While somewhat of a rare occurrence, it does indeed happen in today's job market, particularly among the larger companies that are leaders in their industries. Why do some of these leading companies engage in this practice? The quick, easy answer is because they can! Or at least they can until there is a greater equilibrium between the supply of candidates and the number of available career opportunities.

To say that you are totally flabbergasted by the salary offer is of course a gross understatement. What happened?! How could you and the hiring manager be so far out of sync on salary?! Certainly, by the time an offer is made, both you, the candidate, and the hiring manager should reasonably be on the same page, right? Right!

When you express your "disappointment" with the salary offer to the hiring manager (later, i.e., *not* during the call in which he/she makes you the job offer), here is how he/she may explain his/her (and by implication, the company's) rationale:

> **"As I am sure you are aware, since we are a leader in our industry, we have a constant influx of top-notch candidates seeking positions with us. And, while our salaries for new employees are not necessarily the highest in the industry, they still are very competitive. Once these new hires prove themselves with our company, the sky literally can be the limit, though. That's the kind of opportunity we're offering you.**
>
> **"We understand that you are going to have to take a slight step backward in order to ultimately move ahead with our company, but once you do prove yourself to us, we offer unparalleled career opportunities with great salaries to match."**

Your initial reaction (silent, I hope) to the hiring manager's explanation about the salary offer is likely to be something along these lines: "Bull feathers" (or words to that effect). My professional advice? No matter how tempting it may be, no matter how insulted you may feel, ***do NOT automatically dismiss the offer out of hand***. Thank the hiring manager for the offer and tell him/her that you will need a day or two to seriously consider it. Then, after you hang up the phone, take a deep, deep breath and ask yourself these key questions:

- Is this career opportunity really so tremendous that you should seriously consider taking two steps (or more) backward in order to (possibly) later make a quantum leap forward in your career?

The Job Offer

- What effect, if any, will taking a salary cut have on your professional brand, particularly at your new company, if you decide to take the position? ("We were able to hire him/her 'on the cheap.'")

- Is your level of dissatisfaction with your current job (if currently employed) so high that you will consider *any* new position with a company you perceive as better, even if it involves a salary reduction?

- What other career opportunities have you developed (or are you developing) during your new job search that also have potential for coming to fruition? How do these other opportunities stack up with the one you're currently considering?

- Do you think (or believe) that there might be at least *some* room for salary negotiation with the hiring manager? If not, here is another suggestion: Try negotiating a "signing bonus" of, say, $10,000. That would make up for the salary reduction for two years and give you breathing room until you can prove yourself on the job.

Once you have asked, and then satisfactorily answered, all of these (and similar) questions *honestly* and *thoroughly*, you should be able to make an *informed* decision about the job offer. Remember, this is your *career*, your *life*, we're talking about here. So make sure your final decision is indeed an *informed* one, not one where you're merely flying by the seat of your pants or one based on over reaction or hurt feelings.

Let's suppose that you conclude that, yes, this is a GREAT career opportunity, money aside. And yes, even though you don't like the idea of taking a salary cut, you are so thoroughly dissatisfied with your current job that you believe, in the long run, you will actually be money ahead if you take the offer. Plus, even though you have other career opportunities in various stages of development, clearly your company of choice would still be the one that just made you the job offer. And, although you don't think there is a *lot* of room for possible negotiation on salary, you believe that there may be at least *some* room for negotiation. (See the next chapter for tips on negotiating a job offer.)

In this case your decision would be to try to negotiate a somewhat better salary offer (or a "signing" bonus), and if that proves to be impossible, then accept the position anyway.

On the other hand, what if your current job (assuming you are currently employed, of course) certainly is not your *ideal* job, but is nonetheless still an *acceptable* job? Does the new company you're considering really offer so much more potential, so much more job prestige, that it's worth taking a reduced salary? Do you believe (or at least strongly suspect) that, if you are unable to negotiate a better salary and still end up accepting the offer, that you will begin your employment with the new company under a cloud, with feelings of resentment and of being deceived?

If these are your feelings, your conclusions, then my advice is to politely thank the hiring manager and move on to other career opportunities that you have developed (or are developing) during your new job search. In other words, you should move on to greener pastures.

Continue to brand yourself as being among the very top candidates available for key positions with GREAT companies and it's extremely likely that other GREAT job offers will certainly be forthcoming, again, sooner rather than later.

Consider TOTAL 'Compensation' Package, Not Just Amount of Salary Offered

If you are like most people, the element of a job offer that you are likely to spend the most time on is the salary being offered for the position. (That is assuming, of course, that salary is in fact an issue with the offer.) That's entirely human and very understandable. Face it, the only thing the grocery store, or the mortgage company, or the utility companies will accept as payment is *money*! So, the amount of salary—money—you will actually be taking home each payday is somewhat more than just an idle consideration when evaluating a job offer.

But the *strict*, nearly *exclusive* focus on salary, at the expense (you should pardon the pun) of the *entire* compensation package, which consists not only of actual salary paid but also of benefits paid by the company on your behalf, can also prove to be extremely short sighted and ill advised. As shown in the boxed item on the next page, employee benefits have become a far bigger, far more important element of total employee compensation than ever before—and the trend is growing!

BENEFITS ACCOUNTING FOR FAR BIGGER CHUNK OF OVERALL EMPLOYEE COMPENSATION

Even though salary increases over the last decade have consistently been rather paltry, employee benefits have steadily increased, going from 10% in the 1960s to nearly 17% by 2000, to nearly 20% (or more) today.

Benefits increases amounted to $1,302 per fulltime employee from 2007 to 2011, for example, or an inflation-adjusted increase of 10.8%. Wages registered a miniscule 1.4% increase over that same period.

The THREE most valuable benefits are the following:

- Company contribution toward health insurance.
- Company contribution toward Social Security and Medicare.
- Company 401(k) matching, profit sharing, bonuses, etc.

Because benefits are largely "invisible," when salaries grow at such an anemic pace, as they certainly have in recent years, employees feel they are either losing ground or at least not gaining any, once the cost of living is factored into the equation.

"(Employees) prize good benefits but often don't understand their financial cost (to the company)," says economist Kevin Hallock, director of the Institute for Compensation Studies at Cornell University.

A pay raise is something that is clearly visible to an employee, Hallock added, but increased benefits? Not nearly so much.

"When health premiums go up $100 a month," he said, "the (employee) may pay $25 more and suffer a drop in take-home pay. (But) the $75-a-month benefit increase (if the company pays 75% of the premium for employees) is invisible."

The Job Offer

Before medical costs began to head toward the stratosphere, around the 1970s, company contributions toward health insurance premiums, for example, were somewhat of a ho-hum benefit because premiums were still relatively low. Nowadays, health insurance premiums for a family can—and quite often do—easily top $1,000 or more a month! So, if the company whose job offer you are considering pays, say, 75% of the total premium, while your current (or most recent) employer is paying, say, just 60% (or less) of the total premium, you need to look at that as *increased* total compensation—because it is! And it's usually tax-free!

If you are currently employed, does your employer offer a 401(k) plan for its employees? And if so, what is the company match, if any? If your current employer does indeed offer a 401(k), and the company match is, say, 10%, but the company you are considering also offers a 401(k) and its match is the maximum allowed by current law, you need to consider the difference between the two plans as "hidden" (and *tax-deferred*) compensation.

Certainly, it's not my intention in this section to provide a comprehensive primer on employee compensation. The point is, do your homework—and the "math" involved—as you are considering a new job offer. If you need assistance from an appropriate professional, e.g., a tax attorney, financial planner, et al., then by all means seek that assistance. Any fee involved in such assistance could certainly be well worth it in the long run.

Other Elements of the Job Offer

Other important elements that *may* be included in the *written* job offer from the company can include such things as the following:

- Number of annual vacation and/or sick days, paid holidays and other time off the company will allow you.

- Eligibility requirements for such company employee benefits as group health/life insurance, retirement plan (if any), 401(k) participation, etc.

- Company job description and assigned position/pay grade, if applicable.

If you have any lingering, specific questions regarding overall company benefits, you should not hesitate to ask the hiring manager to contact Human Resources and have them provide you a current Employee Benefits booklet/publication. Although some hiring managers *may* interpret this request as hesitation or uncertainty on your part, a greater percentage will simply perceive your request as you doing your due diligence. Best advice? Don't just frivolously make such a request, but if you genuinely feel you have important, unanswered questions about company benefits that haven't been satisfactorily answered for you, then go ahead and request more information from the company.

DON'T TARRY IN RESPONDING TO JOB OFFER!

Regardless of how long (Weeks?! Months?!) it took the hiring manager and the company he or she represents to make the ultimate decision to offer you the position under consideration, *you* do *not* enjoy the same luxury of taking your sweet time in responding to the offer—one way or the other. (Yet another example of how life oftentimes is *not* fair!)

As I said earlier in this chapter, you should be upbeat and enthusiastic when you receive the offer over the telephone from the hiring manager, and you should adopt this attitude regardless of what your initial reaction may in fact be to the offer. During that telephone conversation, you should thank the hiring manager for the offer and then tell him or her that you would like a day or two (never longer!) to *seriously* consider the offer in its entirety, and that you will get back to them within that time frame. This is certainly an acceptable response *and* time frame for the overwhelming majority of hiring managers.

After you have taken this day or two to indeed *seriously* consider the offer, then it is crucial that you contact the hiring manager at that time and either accept the offer unconditionally, or accept it provisionally. Or, if you honestly believe it isn't the offer you've been looking for, reject it with your thanks for his or her consideration of your candidacy. Your response should be via telephone to the hiring manager and you can then follow up with an email, if necessary.

If your acceptance is a *provisional* one, then briefly specify your concerns to the hiring manager over the telephone, telling him or her that you still are very excited about the offer, very interested in pursuing the position and then request a face-to-face meeting to further discuss your concerns, in an attempt to come to a mutually satisfactory agreement.

THE JOB OFFER

Do NOT attempt to negotiate your concerns over the telephone or via email—unless the position is located out of your current locale and the company will not pay for you to travel to its offices. (See the next chapter on how to *effectively* negotiate any elements of a job offer that may be of legitimate concern to you.)

THE 'EXPLODING!' JOB OFFER

If you are in one of the professions that are perennially in very high demand, e.g., certain healthcare specialties, key engineering fields, accounting, etc., you may encounter what's known as an "exploding" job offer. This type of offer typically has a relatively short acceptance deadline and usually includes elements that are either non-negotiable or *largely* non-negotiable, e.g., salary range, position grade and/or title, etc.

The idea, of course, is for hiring companies to reduce both recruiting costs *and* the time it takes to bring high-demand candidates onboard to fill key *critical* positions. That can mean both good *and* bad things for candidates. The wise job-seeker should approach such offers with pleasure and pride, but also with a healthy dose of skepticism and careful consideration/evaluation.

Historically, exploding job offers have largely been used to recruit recent (or soon-to-be) graduates with degrees in high-demand specialties from top colleges and universities, but with literally millions of high-demand, *critical* positions going unfilled month after month in today's job market, we are now seeing a broader application of the approach.

While there is no one-size-fits-all type of exploding job offer, here is how the offer usually works:

- The hiring company stipulates a largely non-negotiable, though *usually* competitive, starting salary or salary range.
- The benefits, e.g., number of annual vacation days, performance review periods, etc., are pretty much set in stone and generally applicable to *all* high-demand candidates targeted by the hiring company.

The candidate is usually given a very short deadline to either accept or reject the offer, essentially "as is." This deadline can be as short as just a few days or perhaps as long as a couple of weeks, but usually never longer than that.

Best advice? If you qualify for an exploding job offer, carefully consider it, of course, but also be sure to look before you leap!

Chapter Seventeen

NEGOTIATING A JOB OFFER
The Fine (and *Delicate*) Art of *Effective* Negotiation

If you're the type of person who enters into *any* negotiation with the sole intent and purpose of being the "winner," while the other party (or parties) is/are *ipso facto* the "loser(s)," then chances are, *you* will end up being the real loser. Certainly, that's particularly true when it comes to negotiating the elements of a job offer. Unless the job offer negotiation results in a WIN-WIN situation for both you *and* the hiring manager and the company he or she represents there simply will end up being no winners.

To *effectively* negotiate virtually any aspect of a job offer which may be preventing you from accepting it as initially presented, you, the candidate, must therefore absolutely, positively, unerringly and continually strive for a win-win result! Likewise, of course, the other party to the negotiation, i.e., the hiring manager, must also be willing to adopt this same attitude and this same approach. If either you or the hiring manager start out negotiations by digging in your heels and/or by refusing to compromise on even the smallest of details, unfortunately, it is quite unlikely that you will ever be able to reach a satisfactory agreement.

NEGOTIATING TIPS FROM AN EXPERT

Since most of us are not regularly engaged in negotiations of *any* kind, it can definitely be to your advantage to take some pointers about how to *successfully* and *effectively* negotiate anything, including, of course, a job offer, from expert **Stuart Diamond**, a Harvard Law School graduate who teaches negotiation tactics and strategies to students and Fortune 500 executives at The Wharton School of Business at the University of Pennsylvania.

Professor Diamond's negotiation research spans over two decades and is informed by data generated from over 30,000 people in 45 countries.

He offers **FOUR basic tips** for what he calls **"never-fail" negotiation**:

1. Don't think about "winning."

Diamond says that if you think about negotiation strictly from the standpoint of "winning," you'll probably just end up losing.

"Negotiation is not a competition," he points out, "it's a collaboration."

Instead of winning, you should focus on meeting your goals.

"If you think of it as 'winning,' you will think about beating them," he says. "And if you do that, you will not collaborate as much."

Diamond's advice: Define what your *true, principal* goal is in the negotiations and then make sure that your actions *and* reactions are helping you meet/attain that goal, not largely undermining your efforts in that direction.

Example: If your true, principal goal is to land the particular job you are being offered, but not every aspect of the offer is necessarily to your liking, first concentrate on doing that which will help you realize your goal, i.e., landing the job. Then, to the extent possible, *honestly* attempt to negotiate those parts of the offer which are causing you genuine concern.

2. Ask what *you* can do for the other person.

Negotiation is very much a give-and-take proposition, Diamond stresses, and when you ask the other person what you can do for him or her, it can go a long way toward successful negotiation.

Example: When discussing your job offer concerns with the hiring manager, ask if you are perhaps overlooking some key concern(s) of his or hers. Then ask what, if anything, you might be able to do, or how you might be able to give ground on something, that would perhaps bring the two of you closer to a mutually satisfactory agreement. Maybe there actually is nothing you could do, but the mere fact that you indicate that you are at least *trying* to see things from his or her perspective can go a long way toward establishing additional rapport and common ground.

3. Uncover and then *clarify* any misconceptions that may exist.

Whenever there is a conflict/disagreement between what *you* think is the root cause of any sticking points during negotiation and what the other person thinks the root cause may be, don't automatically assume that you know what the other person is thinking or what, specifically, may be motivating him/her to take any particular position. *Ask the other person what his or her perceptions of the situation are, and then seek further clarification, if necessary.*

"Anytime you have a conflict with someone, ask what (they) are perceiving," Diamond advises.

Knowing what the other person's *true* perceptions are—and not what you *think* or *suppose* they are—no matter how discordant these perceptions may be with your own, gives you a better starting point for persuading the other person to see things the way you see them, he adds.

Why?

"Because you (will then) understand the pictures in *their* heads," he says. (*Emphasis mine.*)

Example: Suppose the hiring manager is adamant that he/she simply cannot (or *will* not) go any higher on the salary offer on the table. Rather than merely *assume* that he/she is just being contrary or hard-headed, if possible, seek to learn *why* the hiring manager is taking that position. It may be something as simple as restrictions built in to the company salary administration system, restrictions that the hiring manager may be *unable* to override.

4. Never threaten, issue ultimatums or "walk out" on negotiations.

When faced with an apparent impasse during negotiations of any kind, some people respond in a somewhat less than professional manner. Don't you take this approach! They may make threats and/or issue ultimatums ("If that's the way things are going to be, I am no longer interested in even discussing the issue . . ."), or, they simply walk out on negotiations, either figuratively or literally, and any potential deal under consideration can quickly and easily be doomed from that point on.

Here is what Diamond has to say about acting in such an ill-advised fashion:

"Keep your emotions in check or you'll be checking out of your negotiation."

Example: As a headhunter, unfortunately, I experience hard-line reactions/responses from time to time—from both candidates *and* hiring managers.

"There is no way I am even going to consider such a ridiculous (salary, benefits packages, etc.) offer," a candidate might say, when I present a hiring company's offer to him or her.

"This is all we are going to offer for the position and the candidate can either take it or leave it," a hiring manager may say, when I come back with a counter-offer from the candidate.

Obviously, when either (or both) parties to job offer negotiations take such apparently hard-line, *irrevocable* positions, there can be no winners, only losers.

FACE-TO-FACE BEST NEGOTIATION METHOD

Unless there are unavoidable geographic considerations, it is *strongly* recommended that you conduct ALL job offer negotiations face-to-face with the hiring manager. Next best is the telephone, but never, never, never use email to negotiate a job offer.

ROLE OF PROFESSIONAL *BRAND*, EMPLOYMENT STATUS IN SUCCESSFUL JOB NEGOTIATIONS

All four general negotiation tips Professor Diamond offers are certainly right on the money, as far as I'm concerned and based on years of being professionally involved in job offer negotiations of one kind or another. However, it is significant to note that, in the case of job candidates, successfully negotiating *any* aspect of a job offer *presupposes* that the candidate has *branded* himself/herself in such a fashion as to be in a *position* to negotiate![41]

---

[41] Also, I'm sure that it will come as no surprise to you that, if you are currently employed, your bargaining position is generally stronger than if you are not.

If the candidate has in fact branded himself/herself as clearly and unmistakably being among the very TOP candidates available for the position under consideration, then he or she certainly is in a position to be taken seriously and genuine negotiation is possible. If that is not the case, however, then there is a far greater risk of the hiring manager issuing a take-it-or-leave-it ultimatum and moving on to the next candidate.

To learn more about what Professor Diamond has to say about successful, "win-win" negotiating, check out his book on Amazon.com:

Getting More: How You Can Negotiate to Succeed in Work and Life

REMEMBER: NOT EVERYTHING NEGOTIABLE IN JOB OFFER

Don't make the mistake that some job candidates make by attempting to negotiate elements of the offer that simply *cannot* be negotiated. Not only will you be wasting your time—as well as the hiring manager's time—you also risk looking very naïve and very unprofessional.

Below are some of the more common elements of a job offer that usually *are* open to further negotiation:

- **Salary**, of course. (It's significant to note that most hiring managers and the companies they represent actually *expect* candidates to negotiate salary—at least somewhat.)

- **Starting date**. Although there is usually at least *some* flexibility here, normal expectations are for the successful candidate to give two weeks' notice to his or her current employer and begin the new position soon thereafter. Unless there is a *genuine* emergency, or an important event that has been planned for some time, such as *your* wedding (but not a lengthy honeymoon!), it's a good idea to keep within this expected time frame.

- **Vacation days**. This can be a tricky one to negotiate because there is always the risk that the hiring manager will get the impression that you're more concerned with taking time *off* from the job than in diving right in and *doing* the job.

Still, handled correctly and professionally, you can successfully negotiate additional vacation days. Say, for example, that, at your current employer (if you are in fact still employed), you have three weeks of vacation, while the offer you are considering allows for only two weeks. Provided you have *thoroughly* sold the hiring manager on the *significant* value you will be bringing to the new position, and if you have significant tenure in your current position and/or profession, most hiring managers will go the extra mile to get you the additional week of vacation.

- **Relocation expenses**. It used to be rather routine for companies to provide reasonable relocation expenses for professional positions, i.e., the so-called exempt positions. In recent years, though, with more and more companies keeping a more focused eye on the bottom line, this benefit has become far less liberal.

    Typically, today, the larger companies can be expected to pay for movement of the successful candidate's household possessions and perhaps temporary living expenses for up to 90 days.

    Unless the position is in the top executive ranks, however, rare indeed is it today that a company will purchase the candidate's home so that he or she doesn't have to be bothered selling it himself/herself before making the move to the new company.

    Best advice: Request a copy of the company's relocation policy and make sure it meets your specific needs and desires *before* accepting the position.

With the exception of *executive compensation plans* (for those companies having such plans), the **following elements,** which *may* be included in a job offer, **usually are *not* negotiable—at all!**[42]

- **Insurance benefits**. Typical of these benefits are **group health** (sometimes including dental, vision, etc.) and **group life insurance** (the total amount of coverage

---

[42]The primary reason is that making exceptions in these areas can be a violation of the Equal Employment Opportunity Commission (EEOC) rules and regulations.

usually calculated by using a multiple of your annual salary, e.g., two times your annual salary, etc.). Also included might be **disability insurance** (either long-term or short-term, depending on position grade and type, i.e., exempt or non-exempt).

- **Company retirement plan** (if offered). When it comes to company retirement plans, "one size" does indeed "fit all"! Every employee in a company plan is required by law to be treated the same, so no changes can be negotiated in this aspect of the offer. Same goes for a **401(k) plan**, if offered.

- **Paid holidays, sick leave and similar "time off."** These benefits are also set in stone for all employees and are therefore *not* negotiable.

SOME SALARY NEGOTIATION TIPS

Since salary is by far the issue most often in contention in a job offer, here are some tips to keep in mind if and when *you* must negotiate salary.

- **Make sure you know your true "worth" in terms of salary expectations in the *current* job market.** (If you've followed my advice and recommendations up to this point, you should already have a good, solid handle on this matter because you did your salary homework *before* you began your job search in earnest. What?! You mean you didn't?! Then get thee to www.salary.com and/or www.glassdoor.com!)

- **Enter salary negotiations with a pretty good idea of the absolute *minimum* salary you will be willing to accept.** You know what you need and desire to maintain your current lifestyle. If you accept less than this amount, chances are, you will *never* be satisfied in *any* new job, no matter how great the career opportunity. If you are able to get to that minimum acceptable amount, great. If you are not, then you probably ought to keep looking.

- **If the salary being offered is, say, $70,000, but your minimally acceptable salary is $75,000, open with a statement such as this:** "Thank you for the salary offer, which is a good one. However, I really can't even consider an offer for less than $75,000 and be able to maintain my current lifestyle and meet my obligations."

  What's the worst thing the hiring manager can say? "Sorry, I can't go any higher than $70,000 (because of company restrictions, etc.)." What if, however, the hiring manager were to come back with this: "I think we might be able to get pretty close to that amount, if we put a pencil to it."

- **Approach salary negotiation the same way you should approach any and all negotiation—with a commitment toward working together with the hiring manager.** You already know the hiring manager *wants* to hire you or you wouldn't have been offered the position! Work honestly with him or her.

When a GREAT Offer Comes, Don't Choose 'Stable Misery' Over *Career Opportunity*!

During the entire search for your new job, your *ideal* job, everything was more or less still in the realm of the surreal, the theoretical. Now that you actually have an offer of a new job (or maybe, even *more than one* offer!), obviously, your job search moves very much into the realm of REALITY!

If you're ever going to get cold feet and be sorely tempted to settle for what I refer to as "stable misery"—that state of being where a *known* employment situation, no matter how miserable, is perceived to be preferable to an *unknown* employment situation—over a genuine career opportunity, now is when that is most likely to occur.

Why do many job seekers hesitate at this point? There are several key reasons, and all of them are quite common among men and women seriously considering a job/career change. Chief among the reasons are that they . . .

- Believe that **work is not meant to be "fun"** and that following one's passions will simply make one poor.
- Believe they **can't afford to make a change**.
- **Don't know how to change** their situation.
- Believe they're **"too old" to make a change**.
- Are not entirely sure **what else** they could be doing.
- **Lack self-confidence** and really **don't believe they're good enough** to do what they really want to do.
- Are simply **terrified of making a change**.
- Keep telling themselves that, **one day, they'll do something to change their situation**, just not now.

If *you* harbor any (or all!) of these feelings, **STOP**! There was a reason (or reasons) why you began looking in the first place. Has anything changed to improve your current situation? Do you have any genuine reason(s) to believe change is imminent in your current position, if still employed? Or, are you simply settling for "stable misery"?

Remember, only *you* can change your current situation! NOW is the time to take FULL and COMPLETE control of your own career, your own life. If you don't, it is likely someone else will.

Chapter Eighteen

RESIGNING YOUR CURRENT JOB
When It's Time to Resign . . .
'Take This Job and Shove It!'?
Perish the Thought!

All of your efforts, careful planning and thorough preparation for a new, recharged career have finally paid off—you've landed your IDEAL job! Now comes the time that you have probably both been excitedly anticipating and, truth be told, also somewhat dreading. It's time to submit your resignation to your current employer. But a note of caution is in order here as you prepare to resign.

No matter how angry you might now be with your current employer, if you're employed, no matter how bitter you may have become in recent years, or how very dissatisfied overall you may be with the way you've been treated, when it finally comes time to resign, you must avoid—*at all costs!*—the temptation, however strong and attractive, to adopt the attitude so brazenly and foolishly expressed by the late Country singer Johnny Paycheck in his 1970s hit song, "Take this job and shove it!"

Professionals, *true* professionals, do NOT burn bridges on the way out the door from a current job. Remember, you never know when you may need to cross one of those bridges in the future. Always take the high road. Or, as yet another sage, baseball great Yogi Berra, said, "It ain't over till it's over."

Adopting *any* position other than a strictly *professional* one when you submit your resignation can—and very often will!—come back to bite you BIG time. What if, for example, down the road in your career you should ever need a recommendation from one of the current bosses whom you may have insulted/angered when you resigned? Happens all the time. Any short-term satisfaction you may receive from telling off or otherwise alienating a boss or supervisor at your current employer simply will not be worth the potential cost to you professionally.

You should also be aware that more and more companies today are using what's known as a 360° system to check references. Rather than calling a candidate's references, companies using this system send an *anonymous* survey online regarding the candidate under consideration. Do you really want to risk such a survey going to a former boss you may have maligned or otherwise alienated? Of course not!

A Note of Caution
Before submitting your letter of resignation to a current employer, make **100% certain** that ALL contingencies, e.g., drug screen, background check, credit check, if applicable, etc., have been cleared, and get it *in writing* from the hiring company (email OK).

THE BEST, *PROFESSIONAL* WAY TO RESIGN

When *you* submit *your* resignation to take your new position, simply arrange a meeting with your current boss and say something like this:

"I am tendering my resignation. Here is my letter of resignation and I am more than happy to give you two weeks' notice, in order to ensure a smooth transition."[43]

Then, hand him or her your letter of resignation and don't say *anything* further at this point! Remember, a resignation is *not* the same thing as an exit interview, and it shouldn't be treated as such. Don't, for example, get emotional and say such things as, "It's been great working here," or "It's so hard for me to do this," "I've learned so much here and I'm really going to miss all you guys," etc., etc. Similarly, neither is this the time to vent about all the things you feel are wrong with the boss, the unit or the company.

By the time you reach the resignation stage, you will have made—or at least you *should* have made—the *irrevocable* decision to leave your current job for a better career opportunity, and you certainly should *not* waiver in any way, shape, form or fashion at this point. Otherwise, you could easily create the situation where the boss, in order to buy himself/herself more time (in order to get rid of you later, at his or her discretion, because of your obvious "disloyalty"), can make you a counter-offer, either on the spot or sometime during your remaining two weeks on the job. (Accepting a counter-offer is almost always a *very* bad idea for a whole variety of reasons, many of which are addressed in the next chapter.)

On the next page is an example of a resignation letter that The HTW Group recommends to our candidates who are leaving their current companies and taking a new position. While there certainly is nothing magic about the specific words used in this example, you should take the same basic, very concise, very focused approach.

It's also significant to note that a resignation letter is a *legal* document that is subject to inspection by the Department of Labor, so it's always a

---

[43]If a current employer asks that you stay on the job for *more than* two weeks, politely decline. Otherwise you risk jeopardizing your new job offer! Why? Because, quite likely, the new hiring manager is expecting you to *start* two weeks after you resign your current job!

good idea all the way around not to include *anything* more than what is in this sample letter.

Sample Resignation Letter
The HTW Group
Recommends Our Candidates Use

[Date]

Dear [your boss's name]**:**

Please accept this letter as my formal notice of resignation from [Company name]**, effective** [date, two weeks from date above]**.**

My decision is final and irrevocable.

I will help ensure that there is a smooth transition during this process. If I can help train my replacement, or tie up any loose ends, please let me know.

Sincerely,

[Your signature]

One last, *very important* consideration: Remember: Never, never, never submit your resignation until *all* contingencies from your *new* employer are lifted and/or satisfied! (See previous Yogi Berra quote.)

I am going to assume that you have worked long and hard to build your career up to this point and that you have always taken the high road, that you've consistently demonstrated that you are a true professional in every sense of the term. Otherwise, it's unlikely that you would have been selected for your great new job! Don't risk tarnishing your hard-earned reputation, your professional brand, by doing something rash and foolish when it comes time to resign.

While venting your spleen on leaving a job may make you feel better, at least temporarily, experience has shown that the long-lasting effects are almost always negative and will likely prove extremely counterproductive to your overall professional career development.

My professional advice: Continue to take the high road, and leave the "Take this job and shove it!" resignations for those who are far less professionally astute than you!

Chapter Nineteen

THE COUNTER-OFFER

If Your Current Employer Tells You How Much They Value You and Say They'll Do *Anything* to Keep You . . . They're Probably Lying!

Once you have officially turned in your resignation, and if you are indeed among the very top candidates in the job market today, it's almost a certainty that you can expect to have your current employer (if currently employed, of course) present you with a counter-offer to entice you to stay with the company.

No matter how tempted you may be to seriously consider such an offer, if you end up accepting it, you quite possibly could be making a BIG career mistake. Why? Consider this: **Over 80% of those people who accept a counter-offer are GONE . . . GONE . . . GONE within 12 months!** That's why!

Usually, once your current employer learns of your intention to leave the company, and provided you have indeed been a good (or even an *excellent*) employee, they will *immediately* begin mounting a counter-offensive to prevent you from leaving. The purpose of this counter-offense, though, actually has little, if anything, to do with you and what you need and desire. Actually, the company and your immediate boss are more concerned about how your leaving may affect the *company* and the boss!

Let's put your resignation into proper perspective here. Why, honestly, should the company—any company, really—even be concerned that you (or any other employee, for that matter) have chosen to leave and take a new position? Here is the *principal* reason:

- By your leaving **you may well have caused possible embarrassment and considerable inconvenience to both your current boss and the company**. Your boss may even be called in to his or her boss's office and be asked very pointedly, "Why didn't you see this coming?!" "What are *you* going to do about it?!" "Won't this risk meeting the deadline for the 'XYZ' project?!"

So, in order to make the problem, i.e., you and your decision to leave the company, go away, at least temporarily, management quickly puts their collective heads together to come up with a plan. And that plan is a counter-offer to you, in order to persuade you to stay with the company—until the *company* is ready to get rid of you (which, you can almost be assured, won't be all that far down the trail!).

Here are the kinds of provisions that typically will be included in the counter-offer:

- An *increase* in your current salary, perhaps even a *significant* increase!

- Either an **immediate** or ***promised*** **promotion** in the very near future.

- The *promise* of **increased authority** and perhaps greater **responsibility**, if the company can determine that this issue may, in part at least, have driven your decision to leave the company.

Hey, what's not to like about this offer, right? Wrong! Very wrong! If this is the kind of counter-offer you are presented with, ask yourself these questions:

- Why now, all of a sudden, does the company believe I am worth a salary increase, and possibly, even a *significant* salary increase? And why did I have to resign in order to get it?

- I also had to resign to get a promotion? Or even to be *considered* for one?

- Why, all of a sudden, am I now being offered increased authority and greater responsibility? My boss and the company obviously didn't even consider these things for the last "x" number of years!

- If I really am such a highly valued employee, why has my boss largely ignored me and my contributions for the last several years? What am I missing here?

More to the point, however, is this: Just because promises are made in the counter-offer doesn't necessarily mean that they will ultimately be honored! If you end up accepting the counter-offer, what is to prevent your boss from coming back to you in a couple of months and telling you that, "because of recent budget cuts in the department," etc., your anticipated (and promised!) raise has been "temporarily put on hold"? Your promised promotion? Unfortunately, it, too, had to be put "temporarily on hold."

Don't think such things happen? Think again because they happen all the time! And they happen in virtually all companies and in all professions and in all industries. Every single business day of the year.

Your Likely 'New Image' if You Accept a Counter-offer

It's only human, of course, to feel "special," "needed" and "important" when you are courted and/or wined and dined by a current employer and presented with (usually) what amounts to a quite attractive, very tempting counter-offer. Expect your positive feelings to be short lived, however.

There is considerable risk that, after you have accepted your company's counter-offer and rejected the great new career opportunity you were considering when you went in to resign, this will be how you will subsequently be viewed by your boss and company. This quite likely will become your "new image":

- You will be largely viewed as an **"ingrate,"** a **"traitor,"** someone who really can't be trusted or be perceived as a part of the team. (Never mind the fact that, if the company had ever decided it no longer needed *your* services, you would have, perhaps, 20 minutes to clean out your desk and leave company premises.)

- If you do in fact receive the promised salary increase and/or promotion (and increased authority and greater responsibility), **your boss probably will harbor ill feelings about you** because he or she will feel they were blackmailed into giving them to you.

- Your **future job security** at the company will very likely become—and remain!—**very, very shaky** and quite tenuous.

- Whereas before you may have been rated "excellent" on job performance, expect that rating to gradually (or, perhaps not so gradually at all) start heading south.

- Because of your new image, as well as your boss's obvious displeasure with you, which won't take long at all to be apparent to all, fellow employees may well begin avoiding you, so that nothing rubs off on them!

Are you *still* going to consider a counter-offer from your current employer?

IS IT TIME TO GO BACK TO THE 'DRAWING BOARD'?

If, after seriously considering and carefully evaluating all the admonitions *against* accepting a counter-offer from a current employer, you still aren't convinced (and I don't see how you could *not* be *thoroughly* convinced at this point!) that such a move would be very, very unwise and pose great potential jeopardy to your career, then I ask you to consider (or *reconsider*) TWO key, additional factors that should influence your ultimate decision regarding accepting a counter-offer:

- **Think about the issues/concerns/problems that prompted you to begin your search for a new, more fulfilling, better career opportunity in the first place**. Were you having problems with your boss? Did you feel that you were, in fact, in a dead-end job, or that your career had indeed *stalled* and the only way to get it headed back in the right direction was to seek other, new career opportunities?

  Will the **new salary** and/or **increased authority and expanded opportunity** you've been promised (but yet to receive) **make all of these issues, problems and concerns simply go away?** Remember a job that causes you constant grief, anxiety and stress will *not*, and *cannot*, be made better simply by being paid a higher salary.

- Are you really willing to risk **tarnishing your professional image, your professional *brand*, by accepting a counter-offer** and staying with your current employer? Do you honestly believe that you will be one of the **two** in **ten** who won't be on the street within 12 months if you accept the counter-offer? What are your plans if you are *wrong* in this expectation?

During an entire career most men and women are presented with good options, bad options and quite a few other options falling somewhere between these two extremes. When it comes to accepting a counter-offer, however, the option is nearly always a BAD one, and one that can suddenly and quite unexpectedly derail an otherwise promising career!

A TRUE STORY ABOUT THE PERILS OF ACCEPTING A COUNTER-OFFER

Here is a true, although quite sad, story about the *tremendous* risks involved in turning down a GREAT new job offer to accept a counter-offer from your current employer.

Recently our executive recruiting firm, The HTW Group, presented a "headhunted" candidate, a 32-year-old mechanical engineer, to one of our Fortune 500 client companies. At the time he was earning an annual salary of $65,000 with his current company. Because he had positioned himself among the Top 20% of available candidates, our client company agreed to offer him a salary of $72,000, even though the company's salary band for the position topped out at $70,000. That's how badly the company wanted to hire the young, talented engineer.

The candidate gladly accepted the offer and tendered his resignation to his current company. Then began the full court press! His boss wined and dined him and his wife, telling him how very valuable he was to the company, how foolish it would be for him to throw away the great career he had, etc., etc., etc.

Soon thereafter came the counter-offer. And it was a very, very sweet counter-offer—an annual salary of $100,000! The candidate and his wife needed no further convincing. He was staying with his current employer.

A mere four months later the HAMMER fell, and it fell HARD! The division the candidate was part of was sold and the young engineer was laid off. Suddenly, his very promising career lay in shambles. Whereas before he had been competing for career opportunities from a position of *strength,* i.e., being *currently employed*, now he joined the ranks of other *unemployed* men and women, making getting a new job exponentially much more difficult.

"How could my company do such a thing to me and my family?" he bitterly said later. "I feel deceived and cheated."

Think this kind of thing couldn't happen to *you*? Think *your* company would never do such a thing? Think again!

Chapter Twenty

THE WINNER'S CIRCLE
Where YOU can Expect to Find Yourself . . . Sooner Rather Than Later!

If you have read, absorbed, and put into practice (or at least *started* and/or are *committed* to putting into practice) all of the tactics and strategies presented in this book, you should congratulate yourself because you have accomplished a great deal more than the "average" job seeker would even think about accomplishing! And, unlike many other job seekers, you will soon find yourself (if you're not already there) in the place you want—no, make that, *deserve!*—to be: the **WINNER'S CIRCLE**!

The job search knowledge you have acquired definitely makes you far more qualified than the overwhelming majority of your competition in today's job market, or in any other job market, for that matter. Most job seekers won't even come close to being as qualified or as thoroughly prepared as you are to *successfully* compete in today's job market.

As I've shown you throughout this book, the typical job hunter today is, for the most part, merely spinning his/her wheels, by continuing to play by the *old* rules of the hiring game, hoping that "the good old days" will soon return. By now, you should certainly know what I'm talking about here . . . when you could go online, find a job (or jobs) that looked "interesting" or "promising," fire off a résumé and an application, and then sit back and wait for at least *some* ACTION! In today's job market that simply is no longer happening, and I don't expect to see it happen again any time soon. (Neither should you.)

By stark contrast, you, however, now know the *new* rules of the *new* hiring game and the key role these rules play in it. You are now equipped with tactics and strategies that will allow you to play *effectively* in the all-new job market.

To strongly reiterate, absolutely *none* of the tactics and strategies featured in this book are based on theory, or what I *think* might work. The HTW Group coaches each of the candidates we present on how to effectively implement these tactics and strategies. And, as I've noted several times already, when our candidates go up against the competition for the same open positions, our candidates walk away with the job offer **seven out of ten** times! So, not only do I *know* the tactics and strategies presented in this book actually work, I also can *prove* it!

What all of this means, of course, is that you now have a *significant* advantage when it comes to landing one of the really great jobs that *are* available in today's job market, with more really great jobs coming online as the economy and the job market continue to bounce back from the devastating effects of the Great Recession. Most other job hunters will remain doomed to continue being "also ran's," or they really never will actually get in the game at all, in any real sense.

IMPORTANT NEXT STEPS FOR YOU AT THIS POINT

But *knowing* what to do—and equally important, knowing what *not* to do—to be in the winner's circle of today's job market is merely the first step in the entire process of landing your *ideal* new job. If you haven't yet taken that all-important first step, NOW is the time for you to begin *applying* and *implementing* what you've learned in this book in your new job search.

You literally have to change your whole way of thinking about what it takes to get a great new job in today's still competitive job market. A pretty tall order? Yes, it certainly is, but the ultimate pay off for you can be tremendous!

There is an old saying that I think says a lot about the whole concept of success: **If you act like something long enough, before long, it's really not acting at all, anymore.** Start acting like a *winner* and soon you will *become* a winner! Continue acting like a *loser* . . . well, I'm sure you get the idea.

While most other job seekers will still be playing by the *old* rules of the hiring game, and therefore making little if any progress toward a new job, you will be making meaningful and significant strides, day in and day out, toward landing your new job, your *ideal* job!

As indicated at the beginning of the last part of this book, remember, in virtually any endeavor—including a job search, of course— you will find essentially FOUR types of people:

1. Those who **make** things happen;
2. Those who **wait** for things to happen;
3. Those who **watch** things happen; and
4. Those who **wonder** what happened!

Sadly, the overwhelming majority of job seekers today fall into categories 2 through 4. Obviously, the best position to be in is in category 1, and that's precisely the position you'll be in—if you diligently and consistently apply what you have learned in this book during your entire new job search, starting TODAY!

Remember: *You* now hold the key to your own career future. Your current employer (if still employed) doesn't, nor does any prospective future employer. *You* do. Insert that key into the ignition that is today's job market, FIRE! up your career, get it back in HIGH gear and headed for the stratosphere!

APPENDIX A

THE TOP TEN NEW RULES OF THE 'HIRING GAME'

These Top Ten NEW rules of the "hiring game" were first introduced in the inaugural book in the **Headhunter Hiring Secrets** series of career development & management publications, **Headhunter Hiring Secrets: The Rules of the Hiring Game Have Changed . . . Forever**! That was over six years ago, in 2010. I wish that by now, as we enter 2016, when these words are being written, that I could say that a.) I was at least somewhat off the mark in my disturbing assessment of the job market at that time, as well as my projections for the job market in the years ahead; and b.) That today, as we enter a new year, everything in the job market has *finally* gotten back to "normal," but I can't.

Unfortunately, from a substantive standpoint, not really all that much has changed in the current job market. There *have* been improvements, but overall, the job market today still remains mighty challenging for millions of men and women, not only in the U.S., but also worldwide. Despite the fact that unemployment across the board has indeed declined, many millions of men and women remain either *un*employed or *under*employed.

Here, then, are the (*slightly*) revised) Top Ten NEW rules of the "hiring game" TODAY:

NEW RULE 1

Today's unemployment/underemployment situation is *not* merely part of a "normal" job cycle. Many if not most lost jobs simply are NOT going to return—ever.

NEW RULE 2

Recent worker productivity *increases* necessitated by *decreasing* numbers of employees is *not* a temporary phenomenon.

New Rule 3

The economic landscape has already changed *significantly*, and that change can only be expected to continue, with substantial, long-term implications for future job seekers.

New Rule 4

Job seekers who continue to rely *exclusively*, or nearly exclusively, on the Internet for job leads will no longer be effective and will only be seeing a very small part of the whole picture.

New Rule 5

It is *substantially* more difficult today to get one's résumé in front of a hiring manager/company, and it can only be expected to become even more difficult to do so in the future.

New Rule 6

The interview process is still taking longer today than ever before.

New Rule 7

Hiring managers today still remain at least somewhat under the gun and are still quite leery of making hiring "mistakes."

New Rule 8

Due to economic business pressures and downsizing in some markets, many hiring managers and Human Resources professionals remain at least somewhat "frazzled" and over worked.

New Rule 9

Get used to the frequent economic and job market upheavals because it appears that they are here to stay, at least for the foreseeable future.

New Rule 10

In order to be effective in the current (and future) "hiring game," job seekers must STOP playing by the *old* set of rules and START learning and then begin playing by the NEW set of rules.

APPENDIX B

RECOMMENDED ADDITIONAL REFERENCE SOURCES[44]

RÉSUMÉS & TACTICAL JOB SEARCH/CAREER COACHING

<u>Mary Elizabeth Bradford</u> - I *strongly* recommend that job seekers at least have a professional *proofread* and *edit* their résumés. One of the professionals I recommend to assist you in this is Mary Elizabeth Bradford, also known as **"The Career Artisan."** You may also want to consider the superior job coaching services Mary Elizabeth offers.

<u>Hallie Crawford</u> - Hallie is another career coach I highly recommend to job seekers. Since 2002, she and her team of job coaches and career counselors have helped thousands of professionals nationwide identify their ideal career, navigate their transition and nurture their career.

****

EDITING, PROOFREADING & RÉSUMÉ SERVICES

<u>Shelly Rosenberg</u> - Another professional I *strongly* recommend for providing résumé editing and proofreading services. It can actually *pay* you to contact Shelly for a quote! Remember, you are quite likely only going to get *one* shot with your résumé, so make sure it's the very best it can be!

****

'CUTTING-EDGE' JOB-HUNTING, PROFESSIONAL DEVELOPMENT BOOKS

<u>*Guerrilla Marketing for Job-Hunters 3.0: How to Stand Out from the Crowd and Tap Into the Hidden Job Market using Social Media and 999 other Tactics Today*</u> by **Jay Conrad Levinson** and **David Perry**. The authors deliver precisely what is promised in the subtitle: About 1,000 *unique* ways to stand out from the job-hunting crowd in today's still highly competitive job market and position yourself among the very top candidates.

---

[44] No, these are *not* paid advertisements! I have used the services of each of the sources cited here in one way or the other during recent years (or have read their books), and I *know* that it is worth *your* time and effort to learn more about each of these top-notch professionals.

RECOMMENDED BOOKS *Continued*

SNAP Selling by **Jill Konrath.** While not written specifically for today's job hunters, in her book, prolific international bestselling business author and sales strategist Jill Konrath shows jobs seekers how they can sharply hone their sales skills—to more effectively reach today's busy, frazzled hiring managers and other decision-makers.

The Essential Guide for Hiring and Getting Hired by **Lou Adler**, president of the Lou Adler Group, an international training and consulting firm assisting companies with its performance-based hiring concepts.

This book is written for *everyone* involved in the hiring process: Hiring managers, recruiters, and job hunters themselves. Definitely a *must* read!

Purple Squirrel: Stand Out, Land Interviews, and Master the Modern Job Market by **Michael B. Junge**, a career coach, author and entrepreneur who formerly served on the leadership recruiting team at Google, Inc. and is currently Director of Talent Acquisition at TGS Management.

He has helped hundreds of clients land positions with such high profile companies as Nestle, AT&T, Warner Brothers, Disney, Boeing, Humana, GMAC, et al.

Definitely, another *must* read reference book for job hunters!

What Color is Your Parachute? by **Richard N. Bolles,** the recognized "godfather" of job-hunting and career development books.

His books have sold more than 10 Million copies over the years and are rewritten/updated every year. They have been translated into 20 different languages and are available in 26 countries worldwide.

Without question, his books definitely are *must* reads for ALL job seekers!

Promote Yourself: The New Rules For Career Success and *Me 2.0: 4 Steps to Building Your Future* by international bestselling author **Dan Schawbel.** Dan shows job seekers, as well as established professionals, how to effectively leverage the power of online media for personal empowerment and career development/success. Both *must* reads!

Dan is the Managing Partner of Millennial Branding, a Gen-Y research and consulting firm. He is a *New York Times* bestselling author and a columnist at *Time* and *Forbes*. He has been featured in over 1,000 media

Recommended Books Continued

outlets, such as *Wired Magazine*, "The Today Show" on NBC, "Street Signs" on CNBC, "The Nightly Business Report" on PBS, "The Willis Report" on Fox Business and *Elle Magazine*.

LinkedIn Secrets Revealed: 10 Secrets to Unlocking Your Complete Profile by **Patrick X. Gallagher**. Confused and slightly dazzled about where to begin unleashing the unparalleled professional networking power of LinkedIn? If you want to learn how to begin making *maximum* use of LinkedIn, Patrick can help!

Harper's Rules: A Recruiter's Guide to Finding a Dream Job and the Right Relationship by **Danny Cahill**, "headhunting" guru and owner of one of the nation's largest recruiting firms. Danny delivers clear-cut strategies for getting a job and building a solid career, all offered in an intimate and funny, parable style.

A GREAT (and humorous) read!

Any Publication by Zig Ziglar, world-renowned motivational teacher and trainer. He has taken his unparalleled and inspirational messages for success throughout the world. He is recognized as THE quintessential motivational genius of our times.

Ten of his 28 books have been on the bestseller lists, and his titles have been translated into more than 38 languages and dialects. Check them ALL out!

INDEX

A **Adler, Lou**, 302

B **Benefits (employee)**
  As part of total compensation package, 267-270
  Trends, 268
Bolles, Richard N., 302
Bradford, Mary Elizabeth, 301

C **Cahill, Danny**, 303
Counter-offer
  Your "new image" after accepting counter-offer, 291
  Necessity for considering why you resigned in the first place, 292
  Primary reason for company to make counter-offer, 289
  Provisions typically included in a counter-offer, 289-290
  The perils of accepting counter-offer, 293
Cover Letter
  As "preamble" to your candidacy, 73
  Nine cover letter "secrets," 76-79
  Recommended length, 80
  Recommended sample cover letter, 75
  Sample of "typical" cover letter, 72
Crawford, Hallie, 301

D **Data.com**, 94, 117
Diamond, Stuart, 274
Direct Mail
  Five critical components of a successful direct mail letter, 171-175
  Follow-up email to use in direct mail campaign, 178
  Follow-up phone call used with direct mail campaign, 175-177
  Follow-up voice mail to use in direct mail campaign, 177

D   **Direct Mail** *Contin.*
Contin.
    Sample direct mail letter used in successful direct mail campaign, 173

    Sample email used as follow up in direct mail campaign, 179

E   **Email**

    Basic considerations for effective prospecting emails, 162

    Body of the email, important considerations, 164

    Business email, other important considerations, 167

    How to find email addresses, 160-161

    How to get your email opened and read, 162

    Importance of the subject line, how to write an effective one, 163

    Incorporating email into your prospecting activities, 160

    Making emails part of overall "touch" plan, overall marketing package, 166-167

    Recommended body copy length, other considerations, 164

    Sample prospecting emails (before and after), 165

    Testing email addresses, 161

F   **Face-to-Face (FTF) Interview**

  Pre-planning for the FTF interview, 221-223

    Doing homework prior to interview, 223-225

    Overall dress, appearance & grooming, 221-223

    Preparing your 90-second elevator speech, 225-227

  Day of interview

    Getting the ball rolling, 230-232

    Importance of being on time, 227-228

    Lights, camera, ACTION, 229-230

    While you're waiting to be interviewed, 229

  Questions to anticipate being asked

    Most important asked by candidate, 242-243

    Performance-based questions, 241-242

    The "Barbara Walters" Questions, what they are, how to answer them, 240-241

F
Contin.

Questions to anticipate being asked *Contin.*
    The "Gotcha!" questions and how to answer them to avoid being excluded, 236-239
    The "Tell me about yourself" question and how to effectively answer it in THREE parts, 232-236

Questions to be asked in subsequent FTF interviews, 251

Headhunter's eight basic rules for ACING FTF interviews, 252-257

Gauging how well you did in the interview, 245-246

NEXT STEPS after FTF interview, 246-247

Top five reasons for being excluded after FTF interview, 248

G

Gallagher, Patrick X., 303
Glassdoor.com, 200, 281
Google Plus, 94, 117
Google Search, 126
Google.com, 94, 117, 126, 131, 160, 184
    How to use to find *most* open jobs, 126-127

H

Headhunters
    Becoming part of a headhunter's inner circle, 120-123
        Be findable, 116-118
        Be desirable, 118
        Be contactable, 118-119
        Be selectable, 119-120
    Conducting "due diligence" on a headhunter, 123
    Getting on, staying on a headhunter's radar, 115
    How to locate a headhunter, 124
    Myths, misconceptions about headhunters, 113-114
    Services offered by a headhunter, 115-116

"Hot" jobs
    Weigh opportunities, challenges, 47

I   **Ideal Job**
     Creating own job description, 31
     Factors to consider, 25-31

   Inbound Marketing Plan
     Advantages of Inbound Marketing Plan, 185
     Sites that can get jobs, career information/news coming to you, 183-184

   Indeed.com, 130-131, 183
     Use with SimplyHired to TURBO-CHARGE job search, 128

   Internet
     How job hunters *use* the Internet real problem, not the Internet itself, 111
     Necessity to get off Internet and "See the People," 111
     Online job applications, 141
     Playing the "online lottery," 142
     Online "job boards," with a twist, 142-146
     Typical experience when posting for jobs on the Internet, 169-170

   Internal job sponsor
     Five-step approach, 142-146

J   **Job Market**
     Definition of "full employment," 44
     JOLTS report, 42
     Monthly "Jobs Report," 40
     Official unemployment rate, 39
     Some bright spots, 44
     The "hidden" job market, 41-42
     U.S. unemployment rate trend table, 39

J
Contin.

Job-hunting
  Scheduling job-hunting time each day, 103
  Make sure all activities *on your time, your dime,* 103
  Stealth job search, 135-138

Job Offer
  Employee benefits to consider in offer, 267-269
  Negotiating a job offer, tips from an expert, 274-277
  Responding to a job offer in a timely manner, 270
  Salary component of offer, 263-266
  Telephone offer, 262
  The "exploding" job offer, 272
  Written offer, 263

Junge, Michael B., 302

K   **Konrath, Jill**, 302

L   **Levinson, Jay Conrad**, 301
  Leading the witness, 207
  LinkedIn
    Additional vital information to include in profile, 89
    Creating company profile, 90
    Creating strong, specific profile masthead, 85-86
    Enhancing your LinkedIn presence, 92
    Getting started, 83
    How to network on LinkedIn, 92-93
    Importance of key words, 85
    LinkedIn "hack," 131-133
    LinkedIn-assigned URL vs. user-friendly URL, 85
    Making connections, soliciting recommendations, 91
    Professional Summary, 89
    Profile, 84
    Staying actively, continually involved in LinkedIn, 92
    Your LinkedIn profile picture, 87-89

M   **Mayer, Marissa**, 138

N   Networking
    Enhance image, enrich network through professional associations, 107
    Importance of NOT asking for a job, 105
    Staying under boss's, company's radar if networking while still employed, 104
    Sample networking script, 104

Negotiation tactics, 274-277
    Role of professional brand, employment status in job negotiations, 277-278
    Salary negotiation tips, 281
    What is NOT negotiable in job offer, 278-280

O   Other important elements of a job offer, 269-270

P   Perry, David, 110, 111, 301

Prospecting
    Key methods/approaches, 140
    Telephone prospecting, 146-148
        Finding time to telephone prospect if currently employed, 149
        Getting around gatekeepers, 152-155
        Getting around resistant hiring managers, headhunters, et al., 155
        Types of resistance to expect, 146
        Typical voice mail message left, 150
        Voice mail message left by true professionals, 151

PUTT (**P**ick **U**p **T**he **T**elephone), 146

Q   Questions typically asked during FTF interviews
    Performance-based questions, 241-242
    The "Barbara Walters" Questions, 240-241
    The "Gotcha!" questions and how to answer them to avoid being excluded, 236-239
    The "Tell me about yourself" question, 232-236
    What questions do you have for me?, 242-243

R **Résumé**
    Before and *after* sample résumés, 64-68
    "Blasting," 69
    Choosing an email address, 59
    Eleven "Résumé Truths," 52-58
    Importance in winning job, 51
    Naming, 59
    Phrases to avoid using, 60
    Use of professional designations, 61-62
    Visual résumé, 70
    What hiring managers look for in a résumé, 49-50

Resigning a current job
    Best, professional way to resign, 285-287
    Make sure ALL contingencies cleared before resigning, 284
    Sample resignation letter, 286

Rosenberg, Shelly, 301

S **Salary.com**, 28, 200, 281

Salary issue/question
    Critically evaluating salary as part of the job offer, 263-267
    Employee benefits as part of total compensation package, 267-269
    Establishing reasonable salary expectations early in job search, 200
    How to respond when brought up during an interview, 198-202, 212
    Salary as just part of total "compensation" package, 267-269
    Salary negotiation tips, 281
    The low-ball salary offer, 264-267

Schrage, Michael, 258
Schawbel, Dan, 302
Shadows on the wall, 206
SlideShare, 94
Social media
    Use for candidate screening, 95

S **SimplyHired**
Contin.
    How to TURBO-CHARGE your job hunt, 128
    How to use to find jobs, 128-129
    Integrating with LinkedIn, 129-131
  Stealth job search
    How to keep it stealthy, 135-137
    Should you ever tell your boss you're looking?, 137

T **Telephone Interview**
    Following up after telephone interview, 219
    How typical initial screening call conducted, 195-199
    Initial screening call from Human Resources, 192, 201-203
    NEXT STEPS after telephone interview, 218-219
    Primary purpose of initial screening call, 194-195
    Preparing for the telephone interview, 209-210
    Most important interview question asked by you, 203
    Screener call from headhunter, hiring manager, corporate recruiter, 204-205
  "Touch" Plan, 166
  Thank You note/email, importance of sending after each interview, 248
  Top Ten Rules of "Hiring Game," 298-300

U **U.S. Postal Service**, 168
    Six steps to using U.S. Mail to reach hiring managers, 170-175

V **Voice mail**
    Follow-up voice mail to use in direct mail campaign, 177
    Typical voice mail message left, 150
    Voice mail message left by true professionals, 151

W **Winner's circle**, 294-297

X **X-ray function (Google)**, 132

Y **Your current job**
    Determining how "safe" it really is, 108

Z **Ziglar, Zig**, 60, 303
ZoomInfo.com, 94, 117

Made in the USA
Lexington, KY
16 October 2016